Praise for *The Yes Code*™

"*The Yes Code* is a must read for anyone interested in peak performance, living with purpose, and breaking through to the next level of abundance and success. I'm so grateful EFT Master Carol Look has made these easy to implement practices available to us all. Life changing!"

—**Sara Connell,** 5 X Bestselling author, National Book Award Nominee and Founder of Thought Leader Academy

"Self-sabotage means that your actions produce a "No" when your intention was a "Yes." Carol Look has for decades been helping people find their way into "Yeses" that support their highest callings and bring them into more productive, fulfilling, and happier lives. In *The Yes Code*, she guides you in the ways she guides her enormously enriched clients. You have much to gain by giving this empowering years-in-the-making program a whirl."

—**David Feinstein,** Ph.D., co-Author of *Tapping: Self-Healing with the Transformative Power of Energy Psychology*

"*The Yes Code* is a game-changer for anyone feeling stuck and frustrated. Carol Look's insightful guidance helps you understand and end self-sabotage, offering powerful solutions to unlock your potential. This book is essential for anyone ready to break through barriers!"

—**Jessica Ortner,** New York Times Best Selling author and co-creator of The Tapping Solution app.

"Carol Look's *The Yes Code* is a transformative guide for anyone feeling stuck or held back by self-sabotage. As a fellow professional in emotional healing, I've witnessed firsthand the power of her unique emotional technology. Carol combines deep experience with practical tools to help people release hidden fears and limiting beliefs. Her warmth and relatability make this book an inviting and essential read, empowering you to express your authentic gifts and thrive."

—**Rick Wilkes,** Thrivingnow.com

"*The Yes Code* is a beautifully written book that provides a blue-print for anyone looking for a breakthrough in their life. Carol is one of the most inspiring trauma experts of our time, and offers a transformational method of healing to allow for a more joyful life, full of purpose and fulfillment."

—**Roos van der Blom,** Functional Medicine Practitioner and Founder of DNA Care

"This book is the answer for those looking for an easy-to-follow, clear guide to personal healing and transformation. Carol shares her own compelling, and sometimes heartbreaking story, and then leads you through her brilliant healing process, The Yes Code. Inspiring, transformative, and completely do-able, *The Yes Code* is a much needed game changer for those seeking pro-found changes in their lives."

—**Alissa Smith,** Intuitive Counselor and Spiritual Mentor, alissasmithintuitive.com

"In *The Yes Code*, Carol Look provides a practical and transfor-mative approach to overcoming self-sabotage. Drawing on her expertise as an EFT Master and her personal journey, Carol iden-tifies deep-seated fears and beliefs that hinder personal growth. Through clear guidance and her skillful use of EFT, she equips readers with effective tools to break free from procrastination, perfectionism, and other obstacles. The Yes Code is a beacon of empowerment, offering a path to silence self-doubt, transcend limitations, and embrace a life of fulfillment and success."

—**David Riklan,** founder of SelfGrowth.com

"Anyone who reads this book will be deeply changed forever. Carol eloquently calls out the patterns underlying our greatest challenges and shows how to resolve them at the root. *The Yes Code* puts the power in your hands and makes it easy to release the faulty beliefs that sabotage your success."

—**Kim D'Eramo,** D.O., Bestselling Author of *The MindBody Toolkit* and Founder of the American Institute of Mind Body Medicine

"I have admired Carol Look and her work for close to two decades. She is a clear and concise teacher who helps people get to the heart of the matter as to why they are stuck and self-sabotaging. *The Yes Code* is a culmination of this work. Like everything that Carol has created, it is easy to understand and most importantly, easy to use. The step-by-step approach makes transformation accessible to everyone who engages with it."

—Gene Monterastelli, TappingQandA.com

"Why do we struggle to shine our light and reflect our true unlimited selves? The Yes Code answers these questions and provides a pathway to help you break through and break free of the procrastination and self-destructive behaviors that hinder you from showing up with all of your glory, talent and unlimited possibility. The world needs you to shine, and within these pages are the practices that will set you free and help you to soar!"

—Mark Romero, Renowned Sound and Energy Healer, MarkRomeroMusic.com

THE
YES
CODE

THE
YES
CODE

Transforming Sabotage
Into Success

CAROL LOOK

LCSW, DCH, Founding EFT Master

The Yes Code: Transforming Sabotage Into Success
© 2024 Carol Look

Published by Thought Leader Academy Publishing
Thought Leader Academy Publishing
3901 N Kildare Ave
Chicago, Il 60641

Cover design by Claudine Mansour Design
Interior design by Liz Schreiter

Library of Congress Control Number: 2024918895
Hardcover ISBN: 979-8-9913592-0-7
Paperback ISBN: 979-8-9913592-1-4
Ebook ISBN: 979-8-9913592-2-1

Dedicated to my "favorite 5" of
the next generation:

Zoey

Stellan

Conor

Esben

Rowan

CONTENTS

Author's Note xiii

Foreword: The Yes Code™ 1

Introduction 4

How to Use This Book 26

PART ONE: THE BEGINNING

Chapter 1: My Story 13

PART TWO: THE PROBLEM

Chapter 2: Self-Sabotaging Behavior Defined 65

Chapter 3: The Cost of Self-Sabotaging Behavior 69

Chapter 4: The Key to Getting Better Results 75

Chapter 5: The Root Cause of Self-Sabotaging Behavior 81

Chapter 6: Self-Sabotaging Behaviors Unpacked 87

PART THREE: THE SOLUTION

Chapter 7: The Yes Code™ 107

Chapter 8: All About EFT ("Tapping") 118

Chapter 9: Procrastination 133

Chapter 10: Perfectionism 153

Chapter 11: People Pleasing 170

Chapter 12: Addictions 187

Chapter 13: Clutter 203

Chapter 14: Relationship Drama 217

Chapter 15: Self-Care Neglect 231

Chapter 16: Bonus Tapping Scripts 248

Chapter 17: Additional Tools for Support 257

Resources 267

End Notes 268

Acknowledgments 269

About the Author 271

AUTHOR'S NOTE

Emotional Freedom Techniques (EFT) and "tapping" are gaining scientific support, but please note that they are still considered experimental in nature. All readers are required to take full responsibility for their physical and mental health, and their use of EFT or tapping for any psychological, emotional, or physical challenges.

The material in this book is educational in nature and is not intended to be a substitute for traditional medical care, assessment, diagnosis, therapy, or advice and treatment from a health care professional.

Neither EFT nor any of the information in this book is intended to be used to diagnose, treat, cure, or prevent any disease or disorder. If after using the tapping exercises in this book you feel overwhelmed with emotion or you remember past events or previously forgotten memories that are disturbing, it is your responsibility to seek professional help from your medical doctor, your therapist, mental health counselor, or a trained and experienced EFT practitioner.

All names and identifying details of clients have been changed to protect their privacy. *Unless I received express permission from a client to share the details of their journey, the stories you will read in* The Yes Code™ *are amalgams of clients, friends, family members, and colleagues I have had the honor of working with using EFT and* The Yes Code *process.*

THE YES CODE™

Have you ever felt like you were your own worst enemy? Like there was an invisible force holding you back from achieving your dreams and living the life you truly desire? If so, you're not alone. We all have self-sabotaging behaviors that stem from deep-rooted fears and limiting beliefs, and they can be incredibly difficult to overcome.

In *The Yes Code*, founding EFT Master Carol Look takes us on a transformative journey, providing a powerful roadmap to break free from self-sabotage and unlock your full potential. Through her own personal experiences and profound insights, she unveils the seven most common self-sabotaging behaviors – procrastination, perfectionism, people pleasing, addiction, clutter, relationship drama, and self-care neglect – and reveals the underlying fears and beliefs that drive them.

What sets this book apart is its unique approach to addressing the root causes of our self-sabotaging patterns. Carol masterfully guides us through the process of understanding how our past traumas and experiences have shaped our beliefs and behaviors, and how prolonged stress can perpetuate these destructive cycles.

However, *The Yes Code* is more than just an exploration of what contributes to our problems; it's a practical guide to overcoming them. By introducing the revolutionary coaching method, *The Yes Code*™

process, using EFT (Emotional Freedom Techniques,) Carol provides a proven tool to release the fears and limiting beliefs that have been holding us back. Through a step-by-step process, she teaches us how to clarify our vision, ask the right questions, clear the blocks to our success, and make empowered decisions that align with our true desires.

What makes this book truly remarkable is Carol's ability to weave her personal story of overcoming the trauma and challenges of being raised by alcoholic parents and other traumas into a powerful narrative that resonates with readers from all walks of life. Her vulnerability and authenticity create a safe space for us to confront our own struggles and embrace the journey of self-discovery and transformation.

The Yes Code is not just a book; it's a call to action. It's an invitation to break free from the chains of self-sabotage and embrace a life of abundance, fulfillment, and success. By following the principles and practices outlined in these pages, you'll learn to silence the inner critic, overcome your fears, and step into your true power.

Having known Carol now for some years, I know she truly walks the talk, and practices everything herself that she offers others. She has her own EFT daily routines, and this is the first time she has shared her own story and how EFT truly transformed her life.

Whether you're struggling with procrastination, perfectionism, or any other form of self-sabotage, *The Yes Code* offers a path forward. It's a must-read for anyone who has ever felt stuck, unfulfilled, or held back by their own limiting beliefs and behaviors. Prepare to be inspired, empowered, and transformed as you embark on this life-changing journey.

Peta Stapleton, PhD
Professor, Clinical Psychologist
Author of *The Science Behind Tapping*

Between *stimulus and response there is a space.*

In that space there is the power to choose our response.

In our response lies our growth and our freedom.

Viktor Frankl, *Man's Search for Meaning*[1]

INTRODUCTION

After Kate returned from a three-day success workshop on The Gold Coast in Australia, her husband Mat called his best friend and asked, "What the hell happened to my wife?" He was shocked about the changes he noticed in Kate.

Kate had been in the audience for my keynote speech and attended my breakout workshop entitled: *"The Yes Code with EFT for Personal and Professional Success."* In the first exercise, I asked the audience members, "What is the upside of staying stuck and sabotaging yourself?"

When I asked the audience members to clarify their vision of what they wanted in their life, I noticed Kate crying in the audience near the front, so I approached her and handed her the microphone.

"I'm sabotaging myself in business and at home with procrastination, perfectionism, and constantly fearing what others will think of me," she told the group. "I can't say no, and I take care of everyone other than me."

Audience members nodded and clapped. She spent the rest of the day actively participating in my workshop, reducing her fears, and releasing her limiting beliefs.

I lost touch with Kate until a few years later when I was invited back to teach in Melbourne, Australia. "Do you remember me?" she asked during a break in my workshop. Of course, I did. But she looked very different. There was a brightness about her. "I was the one who couldn't get clear," she said. "I was procrastinating, playing small, taking care of others. I was so afraid to shine." She told me the story about how surprised her husband was with her transformation, and what he had said to his best friend. "Everything in my life changed after your workshop," she said. "I used the tools you taught to dissolve the fears and beliefs that kept me playing small and I have been more connected and vibrant, with high energy in all my relationships."

When I interviewed Kate for this book, I asked her what she remembered about the workshop experience. "I will never forget your workshop," she said. "I knew I couldn't shine. We worked on the advantages of playing small and not standing out, and I realized I was addicted to suffering, working hard, and not asking for help."

Kate recounted how she had always been there for others but neglected her own needs. Her family was loving and close growing up, but they were poor and worked extremely hard. They believed in creating a good life, but they wanted to avoid the "tall poppy syndrome." They didn't want to stand out or be perceived as being better than anyone else. Within one month of clearing her fears and beliefs during the workshop, Kate had launched her website, created new products, offered a new seminar, cleared her cluttered calendar, and added much more fun and freedom into her schedule and her life. She also started asking for help and receiving it.

That's how quickly you can change when given the right directions, the right questions, and the best cutting-edge tools available in the mental health field.

You don't have to be stuck anymore.

This book is about hope, making impactful choices, and finally getting the results you want. If you have been getting in your own way with self-sabotaging behaviors that block your true potential, I am passionate about this opportunity to help you change these patterns.

Does it ever feel as if you have one foot on the gas pedal and one foot on the brake? Maybe it feels as if someone else has their foot on *your* brake? It's not someone else, it's you – **the part of you that is afraid to move forward.**

A workshop participant recently asked: "How would I know if I am getting in my own way with self-sabotaging behavior?" I told her that all she needed to do was to look at the results in her life. Did she like what results were showing up in her friendships, at work, in her bank account, in her health and at home? If not, she likely had a problem with one or more of the top seven self-sabotaging behaviors:

- **Procrastination**
- **Perfectionism**
- **People Pleasing**
- **Addictions**
- **Clutter**
- **Relationship Drama**
- **Self-Care Neglect**

An article in Zippia.com reported that 42.6% - nearly one-half of adults – admitted they procrastinate "often" or "daily." You have likely tried to stop this behavior and are also likely suffering from expensive professional and personal fallout. While the same article estimated that procrastination costs the US economy $70 billion a year, procrastination is costly in many other ways, not just financially.[2]

Procrastination is a common self-sabotaging behavior that prevents you from achieving the results you want. We all know what procrastination looks like – we put off a task that requires attention and are easily distracted by something else.

The truth is, you ARE getting results – but you're getting the results you need, not the ones you want.

Take Jenny for example, who couldn't get herself to finish her website to launch her coaching business. While she was deeply frustrated and baffled by her own behavior, she kept avoiding the final steps she needed to take. When she came to me for coaching, I asked her what the possible *downside* could be of reaching the goal that she had been working towards for so long. "There is always a good reason behind procrastination, even if you hate it," I said.

Jenny teared up and admitted that if she reached this goal, she was afraid she might become too visible. "And what's wrong with being visible?" I asked.

"Oh, I would definitely get hurt."

"And when were you hurt in the past from being visible?" I asked. When there's a fear of standing out and being visible, there is always a previous experience of being hurt, shamed, or humiliated.

Jenny recounted how she had taken the risk to try out for the school play in 6th grade, and her voice cracked in the middle of her solo. Her face turned beet red, and her classmates roared with laughter, especially the boys. She felt humiliated by what happened and felt completely rejected by their reactions. She admitted she never overcame feeling exposed and ridiculed, and has kept herself "hidden under the radar" ever since.

Procrastination solved a problem for Jenny. No website, no ridicule, no rejection.

The result Jenny wanted was to finish her website so she could attract new clients. The result she was getting instead was staying invisible to avoid criticism and rejection.

Jenny's experience could be considered a trauma – an event that gives you long-lasting emotional effects. Just because it wasn't a horrendous car accident or childhood abuse doesn't mean it wasn't traumatic. An event can be considered traumatic if you end up feeling threatened or helpless about what's happening. Traumatic events are stored in our bodies, and until we use the right tools to get to the core shocks and fears that are recorded in our nervous system, these old traumatic events will operate like a computer program running in the background – draining your battery and directing your behavior from behind the scenes. Many clinicians categorize traumas as "small t" trauma or "big T" trauma.

When I was growing up in New Jersey, I was an athlete, and in junior high school, I played field hockey. The girls in the older classes were upset that I was given the "glory position" of goal maker on the field hockey team by our coach. It didn't occur to me that they would be jealous and, even more upsetting, mean to me about it. I got the same message Jenny did – don't stand out and be visible or you'll get in trouble. It was the first but not the last time I would hear "Who does she think she is?" Unpacking my own sabotaging behavior around my fear of success led me to realize that this was one of the memories I needed to release so as not to block my success by avoiding standing out and shining.

Do you want to move forward, but your behavior keeps holding you back?

Maybe you are a perfectionist and sabotage yourself by trying to live up to the impossibly high standards you have set. You will recognize a perfectionist by their excessive self-criticism and the unrealistic hurdles they've set for themselves. They work harder yet achieve less and stress more. They fret over every little detail and nothing they do is ever good enough.

Ally never thought her work was good enough. She would write emails, revise them, and then re-write her revisions. She cleaned her kitchen and then re-cleaned what she had just cleaned. Nothing ever seemed perfect enough. When I asked her "What is the upside of trying to be perfect?" She quickly said, "If I get it right, they can't criticize me anymore. I'll finally be good enough."

No matter what she did when she was growing up, Ally's parents criticized her and belittled her achievements. Household chores, homework, walking the dog – none of it met her parents' standards. She was told that her B+ should have been an A and her neat and tidy bedroom should have been spotless. *Yet she kept trying.* She believed she was inadequate and deeply flawed, and this belief fueled her quest for perfection. Even though she never got the results she wanted – getting approval from her parents – she was convinced that if she kept trying, she'd get there one day. Where? To a place where her parents would approve of her.

Perfectionism is counter-productive: You achieve less but stress more.

Perfectionism served a purpose for Ally – it gave her a plan for how to try to be better and get her parents' approval. Trying to be perfect was, sadly, a repeatedly failed attempt to have a temporary fix from the outside to make her feel good enough on the inside. She was convinced if she kept striving to do more, and do it flawlessly, she'd eventually get her parents' approval and then finally feel good enough about herself. Instead, she was exhausted, burned out, confused, and on the verge of giving up.

Are you like Ally – achieving less but stressing more? Chasing an impossible dream of approval because you still don't feel good enough?

Procrastination and perfectionism are two of the most common forms of self-sabotage.

> *Self-sabotaging behavior refers to intentional action (or inaction) that undermines people's progress and prevents them from accomplishing their goals. Self-sabotage occurs when people hinder their own success.*
>
> **www.Cambridgedictionary.org**

Your action or inaction blocks you from achieving your desired goals. If self-sabotage slows down your progress, why would you do it? The reasons are inside you, not outside of you.

These outside behaviors are protecting your emotional insides.

Success is no accident. The results that show up in our lives come from our emotions (fear, guilt, resentment), our beliefs (success is dangerous; I'm not good enough; being visible is unsafe) and our behaviors (procrastination, perfectionism, people pleasing). If you let go of your fear of being visible, you'll stop procrastinating and your results will speak for themselves. If you exchange a limiting belief such as "it's unsafe to shine" for a more positive one, such as "I deserve success," your behavior will change, and you'll see your desired results. And if you change your behavior from people pleasing to setting adequate boundaries and asking for help, your results will be dramatically different and much more in line with what you want.

Our culture is hyper-focused on our behavior, and so are the personal growth books trying to help us change. But the truth is, self-sabotaging behavior is the result of our fears and beliefs, so the only way to change your behavior is to neutralize your fears and reduce your limiting beliefs. The only way to neutralize your fears and your limiting beliefs is to do some serious emotional digging, ask the right questions, and remove these blocks to getting what you want in your life.

How you feel and what you believe govern your behavior.

The reason self-sabotaging behavior is so common is because above all other priorities, **human beings need to feel safe**. And if being visible, shining or being successful makes you feel unsafe, you won't take the necessary steps to achieve your goals. You might try to convince yourself and others that you want to reach your goals, but **your need for emotional safety will win every time**. If you have experiences from your past where standing out made you a target of envy or ridicule, your nervous system will remember these incidents and store them as traumas (either "small t" or "big T",) and you will work tirelessly to stay under the radar and play small as an adult. Remember, a trauma can be any incident that makes you feel terrified or helpless. It doesn't have to be childhood abuse, an attack, or a life-threatening accident.

Everyone who has ever taken a beginner's psychology class has learned about Abraham Maslow's theory of human motivation, *The Hierarchy of Needs*. The theory suggests that human beings will predictably choose safety over every other need except our basic physiological needs of food and shelter. You won't care about your self-esteem, relationships, or professional goals when your safety is at stake. If we extend this theory to cover emotional safety, you'll understand how emotional safety is the foundation for all your behavior.

Preserving your emotional safety comes before almost anything else you might need in your life.

One of the most common self-sabotaging behaviors is self-care neglect. This will prevent you from being as successful as you want to be in every area of your life and will inevitably lead to serious health challenges. I spent years draining my energy and taxing my body. I spent too much time overworking and spent just as much time socializing late into the night during my corporate job in New York City. What I didn't know at the time was that several past traumas had built up in my nervous system, and I would eventually hit a tipping point with health challenges in my 20's. The old traumas that had been stored in my nervous system were not dormant; they were siphoning off my energy in the background. This meant that I wasn't as resilient as I or my peers presumed I was.

I thought I was just being a typical 20 something. My body thought otherwise and started whispering in my ear that I needed to slow down. When I wouldn't listen, it started yelling in my ear. After my body started pushing back with insomnia, a breast tumor, 25 extra pounds and years of battling a chronic low-grade fever, I got the message: *start taking care of yourself.*

Maybe your chronic people pleasing has gotten in the way of your success. People pleasers make the needs of others their priority. They try to rescue others in order to feel safe and get the appreciation they are deeply hungry for, all under the guise of "being helpful." They don't ask for help and they feel too guilty to say no.

Kari thought the solution to being burned out was to leave her corporate job and start a private business consulting firm. However, since she hadn't resolved her need to please others, she still didn't ask for help, avoided setting reasonable boundaries, and couldn't say no when she needed to. She was under-charging her clients and spending much more than the scheduled amount of time with each one. When I asked her what the upside was of not charging what she was worth, she said she didn't feel her work was worth that much, and that she felt guilty charging people for helping them. Just the thought of saying no triggered too much guilt, so Kari got easily overwhelmed by the favors and extras she promised others. It felt emotionally safer for her to avoid disappointing anyone. Helping at any cost – the hallmark of a people pleaser who hasn't resolved their underlying needs or feelings – is very expensive to your health and self-esteem. When I was being overly "helpful" in one of my first jobs as a counselor, my supervisor taught me, "Never be the most motivated person in the room." Not only does it take the responsibility away from the client, but it will also burn you out. Everyone loses.

In addition to being very expensive financially and physically, self-sabotaging behavior can be frustrating, embarrassing and waste much of our precious time. These behaviors also degrade our self-esteem and integrity. And what about the emotional cost? The same 2023 Zippia article I mentioned earlier reported that 94% of the respondents indicated that procrastination had a negative effect on their happiness.[3]

Despite all these tremendous costs of self-sabotaging behavior, they don't act as a deterrent *if your emotional safety is at stake.* If missing important deadlines, arguing with your boss, or regaining the weight you just lost *protects you from feeling visible or exposed*, then that's what you'll do.

Maybe your favorite self-sabotaging behavior is creating some kind of relationship drama. Maybe you rebel against authority, maybe you pick a fight, maybe you choose unavailable partners in an attempt to keep your emotional distance, and ultimately, your safety. Creating relationship drama will help you avoid real intimacy, which ensures that when the relationship ends, you won't be emotionally attached enough to suffer from feeling abandoned. That's the point of the drama – keep yourself safe no matter what.

Connie told me she had found her soulmate. Again. "This one may be the one…" Connie's last two "soulmates" were also possibly "the one" but were inappropriate at best. In her attempt to seek the adrenaline high of new love to distract her from emotional pain, she forgot to check whether these men were married, emotionally stable, or even employed. The distraction of a new relationship always prevented her from feeling her deeper fear of abandonment that had kept her unhappy for so long. No sooner would she get dumped by one of these supposed soulmates than she would find another equally unavailable one. "Unavailable" meant they lived in foreign countries, were married, were addicted to alcohol or cocaine, couldn't recognize an emotion if it came up and bit them, or all of the above. In spite of the cost of this chronic drama, staying in this cycle helped protect her from true intimacy which terrified her. Her tendency to choose unavailable men served a purpose – it kept her from ever being emotionally close to another human being.

We wouldn't need to use these behaviors if they weren't useful to us on one or more levels.

**Even though you don't like them
and repeatedly try to change them,
self-sabotaging behaviors solve a
problem for you.**

You might be afraid of rocking the boat, so you sabotage your success by playing small at work. You might be afraid of failure, so you never share your new ideas with friends or colleagues. Playing small will feel safer. *You'll be stuck and upset, but at least you'll be "safe."*

At first glance, these sabotaging behaviors seem irrational. How could it be true that you *want* to be more successful at home, at work, or in your relationships if you keep getting in your own way?

**If you keep doing what you've always done,
you'll always get what you've always gotten.**

Self-sabotage serves a purpose for you, or you wouldn't do it. The trick is to find that purpose – the real reason that you're slowing down your progress. You will find the reason in your feelings and your beliefs. Once I discovered that my self-sabotaging behaviors were trying to protect me from a consequence I feared, I could address those fears, discard the behaviors, and start living the life I wanted to live.

Identifying the Root Cause of Sabotage

After years of working with myself and my clients to change the most common self-sabotaging behaviors, I changed direction from focusing on the behavior and started asking simple but effective questions to get to the root cause. *I wish I had been asked these questions when I first sought help.* It would have saved me a lot of time, money, and protected my self-esteem. I started asking my clients, *"What is the upside of staying stuck?"* and *"What is the downside of reaching your goal?"* While these questions weren't new, they were new to how I approached treating self-sabotage. This changed my practice, my life, and the results in my clients' lives.

Maybe you would include yourself in the 54% of Americans who are overwhelmed by their clutter, a statistic uncovered by the National Association of Professional Organizers.

Elise wouldn't let anyone near her home; she was too embarrassed about her clutter. While she wanted to invite friends over to socialize, she couldn't stop buying and collecting unnecessary items. This definitely cost her money, but it also cost her friendships, a place for community, and her peace of mind. With so much "downside" to this behavior, what could possibly be the "upside?" Elise admitted, "I don't feel safe without my clutter." Growing up in an emotionally unsafe and chaotic environment meant people weren't safe for her to be around, but her "stuff provided comfort." The benefits of feeling safe outweighed the downside of keeping her clutter, so as much as she hated and felt ashamed of it, keeping it served a useful purpose. Identifying this root cause helped Elise release her need to surround herself with things.

Addictions are the turbocharged way to sabotage your dreams and your goals. My client John was referred to me by a colleague. I asked him what he wanted to accomplish in our work together. He said, "I woke up one day and found out that I was married with two children. I'm not sure how that happened, but I know my drinking had a lot to do with it." While this story may sound overly dramatic, working for nearly a decade at an outpatient facility for alcoholics and their family members taught me to never be surprised by the stories I heard or by the chaos and trouble addictions caused.

When you drink, abuse drugs, smoke, or eat to excess, it creates conflicts in your relationships, erodes your health, and diminishes your reliability at work. Yet these behaviors are also serving a purpose, or you wouldn't keep doing them. Your friends and family might be hounding you to stop, but you can't give up the "benefit." In the beginning, abusing substances such as alcohol, drugs, or food is very useful because it keeps you from feeling the emotional pain you want to avoid and from looking at the changes you might need to make in your life. But soon the substances betray you – you get a DWI, constantly fight with your spouse, gain an unhealthy amount of weight, or you don't follow through with your commitments. But feeling protected by numbing yourself from feeling emotional conflicts or old traumas seems worth the risks – in the beginning.

Why are the Surgeon General's health warnings on the back of a pack of cigarettes so useless? Because the negative consequences of smoking are no match for the positive benefits of keeping your feelings shut down and numbed.

The desire to stay safe
from feeling painful emotions
will outweigh any medical warning.

My client Hannah had successfully quit smoking and was proud of her accomplishment. Then two years later, she arrived in London for a much-needed vacation. She was in Heathrow airport and was told that the airlines had lost her luggage. Then, they announced over the loudspeaker that Princess Diana had been killed in a car crash. She walked into a shop, bought a pack of cigarettes, and started smoking again on the spot. She couldn't handle her overwhelming emotions and returned to smoking.

With addictions, eventually, the initial "solution" – using substances to numb your feelings – turns into the problem, and you start suffering from the serious consequences of alcohol dependence, emotional overeating, or smoking.

I am the granddaughter of, the step granddaughter of, the great-niece of, the niece of, the daughter of, the sister of, the cousin of, the 1st cousin once removed of, and the 2nd cousin of an alcoholic. And that's not a complete list. You might be thinking *wow, Carol, your family members sure drink a lot!* And it's true, they do… but the real problem is the fear of feeling all the emotional pain and unresolved trauma. No fears or traumas? No need to drink, use drugs or eat excessively.

So does this mean we get in our own way on purpose?
Yes.

Why would we slow ourselves down?

Remember, while your self-sabotaging behavior is creating a block for you, it is also solving a problem. Identify what problem your self-sabotaging behavior is solving for you and then you can use the most efficient tools available to heal and release these blocks. The self-sabotaging behavior then becomes unnecessary. In fact, it stops on its own.

Overload and Overwhelm

In today's world many of us feel overloaded by information and over-whelmed by responsibilities and conflicts over which we feel helpless. The stress from a 24-hour news cycle, too much incoming information, and constant conflict in the world has taken our capacity to function in a balanced way and stretched it to its limit. The American Institute of Stress estimates that stress has cost the global economy $1 trillion in lost productivity, not to mention sending millions of people to hospitals with panic attacks, anxiety disorders, depression, and health challenges. Mentalhealth.org.uk reported that 74% of adults were so stressed that they described themselves as feeling overwhelmed and unable to cope. This is called an epidemic.

What does stress have to do with self-sabotage? When we feel overwhelmed by our environment and our inadequate responses to stress, our nervous systems become overloaded and unable to process or handle daily life. This sets us up to resort to our familiar self-sabotaging behaviors.

Have you ever felt yourself "freeze" as a reaction to a sudden shock or frightening event? While it was useful for our ancestors to have our brain's fight, flight or freeze response turn on when danger was lurking behind every tree, this system wasn't meant to be on high alert 24/7. It's true that all humans need to have this alert system in good working order, but only when we need a warning sign, not all day and night. However, now we are triggered not only by dangers right in front of us, but also by posts on social media and by daily breaking news stories that feel threatening to our survival.

The brain and nervous system don't differentiate between a real threat and a threat we imagine in our minds.

Our bodies respond with the same cascade of stress hormones that get released when your boss is yelling at you, or when you see a car veering into your lane, as when you *simply imagine* a catastrophe at work or at home.

The result is that we are spending way too much time entangled in our sympathetic nervous system response. While it's a biological imperative to keep your fight or flight response alive and well, it is also a biological imperative to be able to enter the parasympathetic phase so that we can "rest and digest." It's understandable to have our fight or flight response triggered when someone cuts us off in traffic, but we have lost our ability to bounce back, and have stretched the rubber band to its snapping point. Since we are constantly operating from our sympathetic nervous system, our heart rate and respiration increases to handle danger, *even when we're not in real danger*. We spend less and less time in the rest and digest phase, or the parasympathetic part of our nervous system. We become dysregulated, and so do our kids and our colleagues. As a result, our bodies and relationships are fraying around the edges. Our nervous system is on high alert all the time and never gets to take a vacation.

The problem isn't stress. The problem is unpredictable, uncontrollable, prolonged, and extreme stress.

Dr. Bruce Perry addressed this in his book co-written with Oprah Winfrey, *What Happened to You,* repeatedly emphasizing that it's not just stress that is causing our problems. Stress can be productive and useful, but when stress is prolonged and extreme, our nervous systems get overwhelmed and flooded. We develop a hyperactive stress response and become less resilient to everything life throws us.[4]

When I'm cold, I am dysregulated, so I put on a sweater and regulate myself. But when we are overwhelmed or threatened by something outside of ourselves over which we feel helpless, we don't know how to return to our baseline of stability and safety. This causes a chain reaction in our bodies, with our relationships, and out in the world.

I live in NYC, and after the shock of 9/11, I got into the shower with my socks, shoes, and glasses on. Then I threw my dirty socks into the toilet bowl instead of the hamper. I was on overload and couldn't think straight. Embarrassing, yes, but totally understandable because I couldn't process all the information; my brain was flooded. Many of us couldn't regulate ourselves after 9/11. Our nervous systems had been put into overdrive and we didn't know how to calm down. We were being flooded with horror stories of the attack. Many new clients who were referred to me at the time announced that they were quitting their jobs, initiating a divorce, moving across the country, having a baby, anything to feel back in control again. They were desperate to try something to regulate their nervous systems. Their impulse was to flee by making a dramatic change. And today, I see the same thing – clients who consistently report their stress levels have spiked because their nervous systems have been hijacked by the constant barrage of world horrors, wars, and interpersonal strife. We all need to find ways to regulate our nervous systems and find peace and quiet in the middle of the unrelenting chaos.

I wrote this book because I wish I had this roadmap when I was struggling with my self-sabotaging behaviors. I'm hoping it will help you stop the cycle of putting your foot on the brake when you want to put it on the gas. If you follow the steps, you have a great chance of turning your self-sabotaging behaviors around and enjoying exceptional results, happiness, and satisfaction in your life.

What I didn't know at the beginning of my career as a talk therapist was that conflicts and traumas get trapped in our physical bodies, so you can talk all you want, but the remnants of the car accident, the public humiliation, or the abuse will stay in the memory of your nervous system and cause background interference to your happiness and your success. Post-traumatic stress disorder (PTSD) symptoms can show up years later when one more event – even a small one – becomes the straw that breaks the camel's back. Thankfully, trauma research has come a long way in the last 30 years.

Your nervous system will remember anything that looks like, sounds like, or feels like an old trauma, and will go into overdrive to protect you from the perceived danger. And if you feel unsafe because you sense danger, you will start to resort to your self-sabotaging behaviors. You can get away with this for only so long before your body or your relationships start to fall apart. This is why our culture's obsessive focus on changing behavior never delivers the results we have set out to achieve. Have you ever made a commitment to go to the gym and get in shape, only to find yourself falling off the wagon within a few weeks? Focusing solely on the behavioral change isn't enough and never will be.

I developed my simple coaching method called *The Yes Code*™ to help clients move from fear-based behavior to being able to make thoughtful, impactful decisions about how to live balanced lives and still contribute to others. The Yes Code provides a systematic, three-step plan to clarify the vision of what you want, to release the blocks that are keeping you from realizing your vision, and to choose the next inspired steps, one yes at a time.

Whether you procrastinate, try to be perfect, people please, are addicted to substances, collect clutter, create relationship drama, or neglect your self-care as a way to slow down your success, The Yes Code offers you the steps to get to the source of self-sabotaging behavior, heal it, and make new and inspired choices in your life.

In this book, I will walk you through the three-step process of The Yes Code to get the results you want.

Step One of The Yes Code will help you clarify your desired vision for your life and put you on the right track towards what you want, not what someone else wants for you. And by asking the right questions, I will help you explore why you don't have what you want yet by identifying what emotional conflicts, limiting beliefs, or memories of past events have caused you to be afraid to stand out or rock the boat.

Step Two of The Yes Code will guide you to heal and release the fears and beliefs that were uncovered by the questions in Step One. After breaking through these emotional blocks and limiting beliefs you will no longer need to put your foot on the brake.

Step Three of The Yes Code will help you reevaluate your choices, come from a place of alignment and gratitude, and take inspired actions. You will start to move forward with ease and grace as you *find your next yes*.

I wrote this book because I wish I had The Yes Code roadmap when I was struggling with my self-sabotaging behaviors. I know from my personal and professional experience that it will help you stop the pattern of putting your foot on the brake when you want to put it on the gas. If you follow the three steps of The Yes Code, you have a great chance of *transforming sabotage into success* and enjoying exceptional results in your life. But it's not magic; you're going to have to do the work to get there.

The good news is that you get to define success by your own standards, not by measuring the dollar amount in your bank account. Success is how you feel, not how you compare yourself to anyone else.

Success is feeling satisfied in your relationships and getting off the treadmill of trying to beat your last achievement. It's not based on the price of your car or the size of your house, but on the size of your heart, the quality of your relationships, and your sense of satisfaction.

I don't want to just give you more information, I want to save you time, money, and heartache by giving you the roadmap, the routes, and the tools you need so you can heal the source of your sabotaging behavior – your fears and your beliefs.

The primary tool I have used to get the best results in letting go of self-sabotaging behaviors is EFT (Emotional Freedom Techniques), or what is commonly referred to now as "tapping." I will teach you how to use this tool to heal the emotional conflicts, limiting beliefs, and memories of past events you have stored in your body and nervous system that are causing your self-sabotaging behaviors.

While EFT and forms of tapping have been around for 40 years, you may be new to the process. Buckle up. Tapping turns off the stress response in your brain, and as a result, will allow you to neutralize the fears and beliefs that have been blocking you from moving forward. You will feel free from past events and emotional conflicts that have been operating behind the scenes and interfering with your success and fulfillment in your life. Research studies from Dr. Peta Stapleton, the leading EFT researcher using Clinical EFT, have highlighted phenomenal changes from using EFT including a 40% decrease in anxiety, a 37% reduction in cortisol (the stress hormone), a 74% reduction in food cravings, and a 32% reduction in PTSD symptoms. After the treatment protocols were followed, the study showed a 31% increase in reported happiness, and a 113% improvement in immune system markers.[5]

EFT, or what is simply referred to as tapping, is a revolutionary clearing method from the new and cutting-edge class of energy techniques that has been developed over the past few decades as a way to move us from being in a chronic state of fight or flight – the sympathetic part of our nervous system – into the parasympathetic state of rest and digest. Too much stress equals too much time spent with your sympathetic nervous system on high alert. This causes exhaustion, crossed wires, and a breakdown of communication between your organs and your systems. In this chronic state of stress, there's no room for recovery time, and you will drain your immune system and deplete your ability to be resilient. This is why you keep aiming for one set of results in your life, yet continue to get other results that you don't want.

I have ample stories of people reversing their self-sabotaging behavior because I have been in the helping profession for over 30 years, supporting people to get to where they want to go. I also have my own personal wins of reversing self-sabotaging behavior.

I was trained as a traditional psychotherapist at one of the best graduate schools in the country, and I have a doctoral degree in Clinical Hypnosis. But when I was introduced to the method called EFT, the results I witnessed in others and experienced in my own life set me on a new and life-changing path. I sought advanced training by the method's founder, Gary Craig, and in 2006, I became one of the first designated EFT Masters worldwide. I have been combining my background as a psychotherapist, clinical hypnotist, and EFT Tapping Master for decades and have been invited to teach workshops in England, The Netherlands, Belgium, France, Canada, Australia, and all over the United States. Using EFT on myself helped me heal from chronic insomnia and put a stop to yo-yo dieting so I could finally drop the 25 extra pounds I had been carrying around, putting down, and picking back up again. Tapping helped me break through financial ceilings so that I could double, triple, and more than quadruple my income. And it gave me peace of mind amidst grief I didn't think I would survive.

If you're new to EFT or tapping, please keep an open mind. The research and results of using this "emotional technology" will astound and delight you.

Practitioners tell newcomers it's like psychological acupuncture that will rewire your brain.

Once you've rewired your brain, your behavior will support the goals and achievements you are working towards, and you'll experience emotional freedom, work-life balance, and a deep level of satisfaction. After clearing the fears and beliefs that have been blocking you, you will enjoy the space and energy you need to find and follow your next yes in each area of your life.

If you're like Kate, and you can't get out of your own way, I'll teach you how to use tapping to clear the fears of letting go of suffering and heal the belief that staying small is necessary so you can step into a fulfilling life.

If you're like Jenny, and the thought of being visible triggers your fear, I'll teach you how to use EFT to clear the fears and built-up traumas wreaking havoc in your nervous system so you can get back on track to achieve your desired results.

If you're like Ally, and you're constantly looking for approval, I will teach you how to use EFT to release the belief that you're not good enough so you can enjoy a sense of emotional balance in your life.

If you're like Elise and the idea of giving up your clutter makes you feel insecure and threatened, I'll teach you how to release your fear of being without your clutter so you can enjoy being calm and peaceful in your space around you.

If you're like Connie and true emotional intimacy scares you, I'll teach you how to reduce the fear of being abandoned so you can learn to enjoy closeness and healthy intimacy in your relationships.

There's no getting around it – humans want and need to be safe above all else. It's part of our survival mechanism. And just talking or gaining insight about self-sabotage won't deliver the changes you want.

Remember you may not be getting the results you want, but you are getting the results you need – protection and safety.

If you want to envision a life full of satisfaction and joy without taking wasteful detours that spend your precious time, energy, and money, then stop focusing on the behavior and start uncovering and healing the fears and beliefs that fuel the behavior you keep trying to stop. Imagine how satisfied you'll be when you finally get the results you truly want. You'll be able to align your feelings, beliefs, and behaviors with your values and see positive results in your health, your finances, and your relationships.

You don't have to stay stuck anymore. This book offers you the solution to releasing your self-sabotaging behavior. My mission is to help you use The Yes Code process to clarify your vision, ask the right questions, identify the real reasons you sabotage yourself, and use the best evidence-based energy tools available to create the life you were meant to live, *one yes at a time.*

Let me be your Exhibit A. I stopped using procrastination and perfectionism to protect me from standing out and shining. I healed the hurts, fears, and traumas that convinced me I should stay small. I stopped neglecting my self-care and started prioritizing the needs of my body and nervous system. This in turn allowed me to conquer my insomnia, weight, and grief in my body. I also dumped several truckloads of clutter. Finishing this book in record time is proof that procrastination is in my past. I no longer suffer from the fear of failure or the fear of success; I allowed my intuition to come back online, and I now feel deserving of the incredibly fulfilling life I am living.

You are welcome to borrow my optimism. **You don't have to be stuck any more.**

HOW TO USE THIS BOOK

This book is divided into three sections. In Part One, I tell you my story – my upbringing and how the experiences of my childhood taught me to use self-sabotaging behaviors as a way to stay safe from feeling painful emotions. Part Two outlines the steep cost of the seven primary self-sabotaging behaviors outlined in this book – the emotional, financial, spiritual, and physical costs. You may see yourself in numerous client stories and recognize some of the fears and beliefs that have been keeping you putting your foot on the brake.

In Part Three, I offer you the specific solution – The Yes Code™ process. With detailed steps, client stories, and actual EFT tapping scripts, I'll lead you through multiple exercises to help you release the fears, beliefs, and memories of past events that have kept you stuck in the cycle of self-sabotage.

Even if you only see yourself as having one or two of the self-sabotaging behaviors, I highly recommend you complete each chapter and practice the tapping on yourself. Even if you don't see yourself as a people pleaser, you will benefit from the tapping sequences related to guilt about saying no and the fear of asking for help. Even if you don't collect clutter, you will benefit from the tapping exercises on being clear and releasing the blocks that make you feel safe.

After providing a detailed map for how to use The Yes Code process for all seven of the self-sabotaging behaviors, I offer Bonus Tapping

Scripts on the topics of comfort zones, identity issues, healing your nervous system, and Gratitude Tapping.

And finally, I invite you to engage in several other self-care practices from meditation to music, and from emotional connection to physical movement, to help support you to release stress and detangle yourself from self-sabotaging patterns.

Let's get started building the life you want, *one yes at a time.*
Carol Look

Scan this QR code or visit www.TheYesCode.com for supporting materials for The Yes Code™.

PART ONE
THE BEGINNING

CHAPTER 1

MY STORY

Nobody's story ever unfolds in a straight line, and I don't know anyone who has experienced a particularly easy or smooth life. I wanted to share the journey I have been on so you know that with the right tools for healing, the same results I've enjoyed are available to you as well.

Let's start at the beginning. Not the very beginning because that would bore you with too many details. All you need to know about the very beginning is that I'm a Taurus, 3rd in birth order out of four sisters, and I grew up on the East Coast of the United States.

The beginning I really want to tell you about comes 24 years later. That's when I knew what I was going to do with the rest of my life.

A group of about 60 people were in a small lecture hall. We were gathered with one thing in common – we had a close family member who had been admitted for in-patient treatment to a famous midwestern alcohol and drug rehabilitation facility. I knew that all the family members in this lecture hall were angry, hurt, hopeless, and frustrated because I had been in the morning session with many of them as we started to confront our family members about the damage their substance abuse was causing. I knew the tension was thick because I could hear voice tones that were serious, heavy, and slightly irritable. And no one was laughing. I could also feel the tension in my own body, something I would later learn to rely on as valuable information instead of something to avoid. Our "patients" were in the lecture hall with us too, and based on their body language and voice tones, many of them were also resentful, angry, hurt, and frustrated.

Earlier that day, I had been interviewed by our family liaison counselor so I could help share any details about my mother's drinking history. I reluctantly told her that over the past 10+ years, my mother would have short bursts of being sober, and then flip into days, weeks, or months of drinking. Whether her drinking was on and off or full on, she would deny that she had been drinking at all, 100% of the time. This would plant the seed of me being trained to ignore my intuition until I learned how to listen deeply enough to get it back online years later. I would say "you've been drinking," and she would say "of course I haven't." Back and forth; rinse and repeat. But I always knew. I knew by the awkward way she held her hands, the glassy look in her eyes, and how she spoke too carefully. I knew by how she leaned on the counter. I felt disloyal revealing these details, but I was promised this was part of the healing process.

Then the counselor said, "Let's talk about your drug and alcohol history." I momentarily stopped breathing and nodded.

"How many times a week do you drink?" she asked.

"About 4x a week..."

"How many times a week do you smoke marijuana?"

I cleared my throat and smoothed my jeans. "I smoked lots of pot in high school and some in college, rarely now."

"And what about other drugs?" She leaned forward as if she had just caught me in a trap. Wait, was I being examined now too?

"Yes, I used harder drugs several times in high school. I think I took a science test while on speed..."

"We have a policy, or an invitation. As long as we're asking our patients to stop drinking, we invite their family members to do the same while they're here. Do you think this will be a problem to stop using substances during family week?"

"Absolutely not." It wouldn't be a problem because I had seen cupcakes and cookies in the cafeteria. I just needed something to quiet the anxiety, the hurt, and the helplessness. Watching my mother continue to drink when we begged her to stop was confusing and frustrating. It was obvious she had lost control, but I just couldn't understand why, or what to do.

The counselor stared at me, and her voice sounded stern. "Based on your answers and the information on the form you filled out earlier, you too could have a substance abuse problem down the line if you're not more careful. Addictions run in families you know…"

That was part of the education process: addictions run in families. And it's not just about inheriting the predisposition to the chemical addiction; it's about inheriting the habit of avoiding emotions, dodging fears, and being stuck with the limiting beliefs and patterns of behavior that would lead to using drugs or alcohol.

Later on in my life, I would be able to count how many alcoholics were in my immediate and extended family without even trying. I counted 17 alcoholics in four generations, including spouses and adult children, and I'm sure I've missed a few. In contrast, my husband can count two. While many are dead now, some are sober, and some are still struggling. They all were, or are, trying to dampen anxiety and emotional distress.

This counselor would have saved me a lot of time and trouble if she had stopped focusing so much on my drug and alcohol history and told me what everyone else seemed to know:

If you love an alcoholic, you will always feel inadequate and think you haven't done enough. You will always try to do better or be better.

If you love an alcoholic, you will have your heart broken millions of times and the grief will often feel unbearable.

What she didn't know was that I couldn't care less what substance I used. I wasn't attached to drugs and alcohol; I had just always felt anxious. While my mother's alcoholism didn't really hit a tipping point until I was in my early teens, I think I knew something was brewing before then and I was often on high alert. I was told I was "too sensitive" which, while true, didn't help me combat the anxiety.

Rather than being a curse, being too sensitive turned out to be a gift I learned to appreciate over time. It was a gift wrapped in crappy wrapping paper and caused me a lot of emotional pain before I knew what it was, but I wouldn't give it up for anything. It has helped me enormously in my work and my relationships. As a teen, though, I was highly functioning and channeled my anxiety in adaptive ways. Instead of failing out of school or becoming an addict early on, I was an athlete, landed parts in school plays, sang in the church choir, and maintained high grades – so my anxiety often flew under the radar. If you're a high achiever and engage in sports and enough after-school activities, no one notices your internal unrest. It was no secret to me that being calm and peaceful did not come naturally. Then came the family alcoholism, which included the denial, fears, grief, guilt, and shame on top of the anxiety, and I was a sitting duck to reach for something, anything to suppress the chaos, confusion, and fear.

Not only did many close and distant family members have an alcohol problem, but many also struggled with their weight, smoked, or *all of the above*. Yes, my family was riddled with substance abuse, but what I didn't know at the time was that the real problem was untreated worry, hurt, and anxiety. There was plenty of numbing going on in my life, too. I was just lucky that I hadn't turned the corner into becoming dependent on drugs and alcohol. The truth was that cigarettes and food were my drugs of choice, and I was never asked about either of those.

The counselor kept pressing. "And would you consider stopping drinking for the duration of your family member's treatment here after you return home?" This would be a minimum of four weeks, possibly six.

"No problem at all," I said. I didn't think it would be difficult to stop drinking when I went back and spent time with my colleagues in my corporate job. I believed that at the time anyway. What I know now is that I always needed something to quiet the unrest inside – cigarettes, food, a chemical distraction – so that I didn't feel the depth of the pain from watching my mother lose control of her life and disappear from mine, breaking my heart over and over again. When she wasn't drinking, she was loving, supportive, joyful, and affectionate. People flocked to her and told her all their secrets. She was extremely sensitive, listened deeply, was sweet, funny, intelligent and a great storyteller. I could feel so close to her. And then poof, she'd disappear, and I'd feel hurt, helpless, and terrified. I constantly missed her. I often fluctuated between anger, frustration, and confusion, but the truth that would define my life was that I felt repeatedly heartbroken, helpless, and always on edge. Nobody ever defined this as traumatic, but constantly waiting for a disaster to happen was traumatic to my nervous system and set me up for classic self-sabotaging behaviors and health challenges.

Back to the lecture hall: everyone was taking their seats. I was feeling hopeless and tense and my father was uptight and angry. He thought the exercise about emotions we had been instructed to complete was ridiculous and he refused to participate. My mother desperately wanted to be forgiven, and was trying to sound upbeat, reassuring us that her drinking had stopped for good this time. The knot in my stomach was starting to interfere with my already shallow breathing. By the way, my father was an alcoholic too, but nobody had said that out loud. Yet. He was definitely a different species of alcoholic, and at the time was what they considered "high functioning" at work and at home.

We had spent the previous day and a half of that family week in family counseling with three other families and their addicts or alcoholics. Although finding out we weren't alone was somewhat comforting, the process of hearing and revealing upsetting stories, confronting my mother, feeling sometimes hopeful, but usually hopeless was excruciating. This was the third rehab for my mother – the third attempt at getting long-term sobriety under her belt. Other families were threatening that they'd walk away if this time didn't work. I felt my pain, I felt their pain, and I felt my mother's pain. I would later learn that I was what they call an "empath" and had difficulty creating boundaries between my feelings, yours, and others'. This came with the package of being "overly sensitive." I could feel all of it. Combine this with my need to protect myself by wanting to know who was upset, what was about to happen, who was about to explode, and you'll understand the fragile state of my nervous system.

Then the crowd hushed, and this perky, sassy, upbeat woman in her forties walked onto the stage in front of us and proceeded to tell her horrendous story, which included constant blackouts, drunk driving, leaving her baby crying for hours in the crib, neglecting dirty diapers, insane relationships, the list went on and on. Anxiety, depression, suicidal thoughts, a miserable marriage; you name it, she claimed it. Yet here she was, sounding pretty happy. Fulfilled even.

She clearly had a mission and a purpose. She told us every dark detail about how crazy her life had been when she drank. And yet, she was smiling. She made us laugh. She said it wasn't our fault if our family member continued to drink. Before she got sober, she had been confronted about endangering her child and yet she still refused to give up drinking at the time. She assured us that there was a way out of this mess. She encouraged us to get support and help *whether our family member stopped drinking or not*. Before that moment, it had never occurred to me that I could be happy without my mother getting sober.

I was riveted, on the edge of my seat. Had she really left her baby wailing in the crib for hours with dirty diapers and no food? Why did she seem genuinely happy? What was the way out? How could I be happy if my mother continued to drink?

I felt hopeful for the first time in a long time. Maybe I didn't have to stay chained to a desk in my unbelievably dissatisfying corporate job. Maybe I could envision a career that was fulfilling and satisfying.

She divulged all her dirty secrets and was still happy. She talked about shame, guilt, anger, and betrayal, and encouraged us to do the same.

She was inspiring, and I was inspired. That's when I knew. I made the decision then that I was going to help other people feel better. Period. I didn't know how or when or what I'd do about my current corporate job, but I had decided. To fulfill this vision, I would have to do the hard work to identify my own emotional conflicts, feel them without guilt, express them without blame, and feel free enough to find and follow my own yes. That of course has been a lifelong process, with many ups and downs, and twists and turns. It has been a process that has led to a deeply satisfying and fulfilling life.

House Rules in a Dysfunctional Family

A week later, we all left with a referral to attend Al-Anon meetings and aftercare therapy. These both reinforced what I had started to learn during family week about the effect of my childhood experiences. I learned about "house rules" that were unspoken, yet still extremely clear. These rules aren't just for alcoholic families; you also might learn them in a family where there is a narcissistic parent, a workaholic parent, an accident or trauma involving a sibling, a shameful secret, or a home where one family member is always on the verge of exploding in anger.

I'm telling you these rules, because to stop sabotaging yourself and be fulfilled and successful, you'll need to break them.

1. Don't ask for help or show any weakness; do it by yourself.
2. Don't tell anyone what's really going on; keep a smile on your face.
3. Don't say no; be a good people pleaser.

In other words, don't rock the boat.

To hide any sign of dysfunction, these rules were mandatory. It was understood that I shouldn't show my upset feelings or tell anyone outside the family about the internal chaos. Things had to look calm at any cost. And the cost to me was an intense burden on my nervous system. People assume that trauma comes from a single devastating event, such as a car accident, a sudden death, or an incident of abuse. Numerous trauma experts and researchers agree that the primary emotional features for an event to be categorized as *traumatic* are feeling unsafe and feeling helpless. I felt repeatedly unsafe and helpless, and the effects of being hypervigilant and constantly waiting for the other shoe to drop built up in my nervous system, diminishing my resilience and my ability to bounce back.

Despite my mother's long-term recovery after this rehab experience, the mixed messages and confusion I had grown up with still haunted me and fed my self-sabotaging behaviors. From the ages of 12-24, I couldn't understand why she would say she loved me but not stop drinking. What I "heard" was, I love you, but…not enough to stop drinking: I love you, but…I'm going to drink anyway. I had to be taught and convinced that I didn't cause it, and that nothing I did would make her stop.

Not only did my mother's drinking create this atmosphere of impending doom, but my father also drank heavily and refused to discuss it – or no one ever dared bring it up to him. I developed people pleasing tactics to lower the stress levels and try not to rock the boat, or at least not make any waves. Of course, people pleasing didn't curb anyone's drinking, but it was the only thing I thought might have a positive impact.

The helplessness I felt around the drinking in my family also led to another self-sabotaging behavior – perfectionism – trying to be perfect, to be better, do more, help more. The upside? Maybe I could finally get it right, or at least know that I hadn't done anything wrong. While I eventually learned that nothing I did caused or contributed to my parents' drinking, it took a long time to really believe that. *And believing it didn't stop the heartache.* As I explain to my workshop audiences, if you grow up in France, you'll speak French. You're going to have to learn a new language.

Ignoring my needs and feelings didn't stop their drinking. I would eventually unpack the unspoken rules and crossed wires as the years progressed. I felt chronically inadequate, always searching for what I missed or what I could still do to make a difference. The belief that I was responsible for holding the family together made me continue to search for a solution.

My Corporate Life

Before the family week experience, I had made the decision to work in the corporate world after college. My father had been a banker for years and felt trapped by the paycheck, and yet I thought it was a good idea to follow in his footsteps. The truth is, when you don't have a clear vision, you end up somewhere you didn't intend.

I was accepted into a training program of a prestigious bank, was offered a great salary, and moved to New York City. I couldn't believe how much I was going to get paid to be in their training program, but now I could stop worrying so much about finances. I met a fabulous group of fellow trainees, fell in love with New York City, and enjoyed being young and carefree. Our group of trainees worked tirelessly during the day and then went out to the bars for drinks every night. I don't know how we did it night after night. As the famous trauma therapist Bessel van der Kolk details in his book, *The Body Keeps the Score*, my body was adding up the points, and my immune system was losing.

The effects of my primary sabotaging behavior – self-care neglect – were becoming glaringly obvious. The late nights took a toll on my health. Insomnia was always lurking, and I suffered from swollen glands and a chronic low-grade fever. If I stayed up too late, I would come down with flu-like symptoms. My father said I was burning the candle at both ends, and it was bound to happen. He was right; there was no doubt that after working 10-hour days and partying until 2 am, I was running on empty.

You couldn't consult Dr. Google back then, so I was at a loss for theories about my symptoms until I got desperate enough to ask for a day off to go to the doctor. Not asking for help had also been high on the list of self-sabotaging behaviors, so this was a big deal for me.

I went to the famous eye, ear, nose, and throat hospital in Manhattan for an appointment to check on "all of the above." After I described my symptoms and their frequency, an elderly nurse asked me, "Do you like your job?" I was taken aback. Was it that obvious? "Not at all, why do you ask?"

"Well, you've been chronically sick, and it might be related." Her response got my attention. The doctor examined me and found a large raindrop shaped polyp dangling down from my uvula, connected by a thin string of skin. One doctor said, "Let's just snip it off." An intern stopped him saying, "Don't, she'll bleed out, don't you see there's a blood vessel inside of it?" This conversation – out loud and in front of me – did not inspire confidence in my medical care. I left with a recommendation to get the polyp removed in a hospital. Their theory was that the polyp was a constant irritant, and might be the cause of my chronic throat infections and fevers.

I was struck by the theory that the nurse offered – I was unhappy in my job, and I was getting sick as a message or as a way out. Maybe she planted the seed of The Yes Code™ process all those years ago – *was there an upside to being sick and being distracted by these illnesses?* If I had been asking my upside/downside questions back then, I would have understood that not taking care of myself was not just because I was young and thought I could get away with it. More importantly, I hadn't learned to value myself enough to make self-care a priority. If you're raised by alcoholic parents, you get the sneaky impression that something is always more important than your needs. I knew my parents loved us: they cared for us, and we had food, shelter, love, attention, and emotional closeness. We played card games on Sunday nights after dinner, had picnics down by the lake, played flashlight tag with the neighbors until the barbecue had been packed up. We had a community network and were surrounded by good people.

And then they would drink, fight, or invalidate my fears.

An obvious upside of my illnesses that I later uncovered was that the physical symptoms kept me from examining the emotional conflicts – the pain and hurt from "losing" my mother over and over again and being frustrated by my father's distance and temper. The safety I got was avoiding looking at my grief. The mixed messages were also hard to digest. My mother was kind, loving, attentive and warm. And then she drank. My father was intelligent, funny, worldly, and charming. And then he drank and started yelling. While germs are germs, something else was obviously going on in my body.

The nurse planted a seed for me that my body and mind were connected and communicating with each other. It was a subject that interested me, but I had never pursued it. I was a left-brained banker, loaning money to the big movie companies. I wore a suit, blouse, and high heels every day to work. What did my emotions have to do with my health? Of course, her message eventually caught fire. Fast forward to the fact that the last 30+ years of my life have been dedicated to helping people reduce their stress, unpack their life's traumas and institute self-care practices that are both effective and sustainable. But I had a lot of work to do to unravel the childhood fears and beliefs before I could fully step into this new life.

Around the same time, in a routine annual checkup, my doctor found a concerning tumor in my left breast. Consultations, second opinions, debilitating fear – it was a long few weeks. I was scared out of my mind. They hadn't been able to determine whether it was benign or not before the surgery. After I stopped vomiting from the anesthesia, my mother and I were invited to the surgeon's office where he pronounced, "Good news, it turned out to be benign."

My mother coming to be with me for the operation and recovery was what I needed. I'd told her that she didn't have to make the trip, but she insisted, and she was caring, helpful, focused, and loving. She was the version of my mother I loved being around. We could laugh at seeing the large metal staples holding the incision in my breast together. She could bring me tea, take care of me, comfort me. She would eventually relapse again, breaking my heart and trust, and teaching me not to let my guard down.

I didn't know it back then, but the tumor was another sign that my body was producing symptoms from all the unhealed emotional stress and strain. Unlike people who suffered a specific event, my body had been managing chronic anxiety. I know now that the chronic overwhelm and worry was draining valuable resources away from my immune system. While I wasn't afraid of something specific like flying, heights, or snakes, I was always afraid that something terrible could happen at any moment.

I eventually had the polyp on the end of my uvula removed, which was extremely traumatic as a specific event – the more typical definition of a trauma. My doctor looked and sounded like New York City's Mayor Bloomberg, and it was disconcerting at best when he narrated the procedure into his small tape recorder as he performed the surgery. *"Patient was anesthetized in the back of the throat... used laser to separate polyp from bottom of uvula... cauterized... patient said there was too much pain... needed more local anesthesia."*

This surgery was supposed to eliminate my postnasal drip, reduce my chronic fevers, get rid of my chronic swollen glands, and prevent me from waking up in the night choking on all the phlegm dripping down the back of my throat. Instead, I couldn't swallow for days without excruciating pain, my voice sounded weak and unlike me, and it was much more painful than "Mayor Bloomberg" had warned. I'd had a panic attack in the cold, empty office after the nurse anesthetized the back of my throat with gigantic needles that she'd assured me "wouldn't hurt." When your throat is anesthetized, you can't tell if you're swallowing or breathing. I was not prepared for the panic this triggered. Since I had been assured it would be no big deal, I told my husband he didn't need to come and pick me up. I was curled up in a ball crying on the floor of the taxi on the way home. While the polyp was successfully removed, the surgery didn't address my chronic anxiety or feelings of helplessness. So cutting it out, much like cutting out my breast tumor, was a sound medical move, but didn't help me do the real healing I needed to do. My nervous system wasn't relieved of any burden.

Years later, after many more ups and downs with my swollen glands and fevers, and too many rounds of antibiotics to count, I consulted an acupuncturist. One session and poof, the swelling and infection disappeared, the fevers never returned, and I was well on my way to getting my mind-body balance back online.

Addictions Work

In addition to neglecting my self-care, my other top self-sabotaging behavior centered around addictive habits. The years of smoking (starting at age 14) were catching up with me and adding to my health challenges. I don't know how much of my overall fatigue and feeling run down was from which behavior – staying out late, struggling with insomnia, staying in an unfulfilling job, a decade of smoking – but my health was suffering. My self-care was in desperate need of an overhaul.

I always tell my workshop audiences that my first true love in high school was smoking cigarettes. This habit bloomed into a pack-a-day habit for the next decade. The distraction of my smoking addiction and my emotional overeating were definite forms of self-sabotage that kept me playing small. Before you get too mad at yourself for your vices (or if they're bad enough, your addictions), just remember that *addictions work*. You wouldn't be using substances unless you needed to numb your emotions. You wouldn't need to numb your emotions if you had taken the time and space to give your traumas airtime and support.

Whether you overindulge in food, alcohol, cigarettes, drugs, people, or drama, you need to remember that using substances serves a purpose. Yes, addictions will absolutely sabotage your success, your health, and your whole life, but using substances is protecting you from feeling unsafe, or you wouldn't need to use them. Unfortunately, people often turn the corner from just trying to numb their feelings to full-fledged addiction that causes chaos, damage, and ruins most relationships. While using substances works initially to numb your feelings, if you want to stop inflicting emotional damage and recover your relationships, you're going to need to admit you've lost control and stop using.

The primary upside of smoking and overeating for me was that it interfered with my ability to connect to and address my anxiety and my grief. It's hard to feel terrified when you're inhaling a Marlboro, and hard to feel inadequate when you're halfway through a row of Oreos.

Inhale smoke; forget the panic.

Eat another cookie; ignore the fear.

A very wise supervisor told me, "Remember that the problem someone brings to your office was once their solution." She was right. My smoking addiction had solved, or at least covered up, my severe anxiety problem and grief as a teenager. It soothed me, gave me something to do with my hands, calmed me down (even though nicotine is a stimulant), but eventually led to a serious addiction.

My smoking addiction was no different than an alcoholic's vicious drinking cycle – the drinking soothes and calms the nerves, the insecurity, and any other emotional conflicts. But eventually, after DWIs, family arguments, and days missed at work, this "solution" presents an enormous problem. Using food, drugs, cigarettes – whatever your drug of choice is – serves a purpose before seducing the user down the dark alley of addiction and catastrophe.

I would later quit smoking after a bout with typhoid fever. I had been on a trip to visit my older sister who was living in East Africa with her husband and two kids. I took all the necessary inoculations for the trip, still got sick, and was vomiting in the tiny bathroom as the plane home was landing at Kennedy airport. The flight attendant was banging on the door insisting I return to my seat for landing. Since I didn't want to projectile vomit all over her, I stayed in the bathroom with the door locked.

At the end of that week, I was still sick and almost fainted on my way to a friend's wedding. I realized I was in no shape to travel, went back to my apartment, slept for four days, and unintentionally quit smoking. I hadn't planned to quit, but the high fever made me repulsed by the thought of smoking, so I couldn't differentiate between the terrible withdrawal symptoms and the typhoid symptoms.

I gained 20 pounds in record time. Not because quitting smoking slowed down my metabolism – the general theory at the time – but because I replaced smoking with eating carbs and sweets. Gaining weight was a snap, and I continued to struggle with my weight for years, which was more evidence that I hadn't healed and cleared enough of what was driving my addictive behavior – my anxiety, hurt, and grief.

After this final rehab experience, my mother had the longest period of sobriety in her life, 17 years, and those years were a pleasure. She bounced back to her loving, kind, warm and funny self. It was obvious how much she loved me. We were able to repair the damage, hurt, and mistrust that her repeated relapses had caused, and we enjoyed an exceptionally close and loving relationship.

This was all before everyone started dying.

Time for a Career Change

It wasn't long after the trip to Africa and quitting smoking that I decided to quit my job too. We had been to the family week at rehab the year before, and I felt empty and unhappy in my corporate job. Besides, I had decided back in the rehab that I wanted to help people feel better. I applied to graduate school, and couldn't wait to start my Master's Degree in Social Work so I could become a traditional psychotherapist.

Much to my corporate boss's horror, I announced I had been accepted to graduate school and was leaving in a few weeks to start a new career as a psychotherapist.

"A what?"

"A therapist. A counselor."

"Why?"

She couldn't make sense of the switch from working in corporate to "helping the downtrodden," as she put it. I'm not sure if her getting in trouble for being drunk at the annual Christmas party had anything to do with her discomfort with my becoming a therapist or not. Clearly, she wasn't dealing with her feelings either.

Graduate school was very stressful. Non-stop term papers, and an internship in the South Bronx working with schizophrenics who refused to take their medications. I often felt threatened and frightened, and as usual, my nervous system recorded everything.

I stood out – young, pale, naïve, dressed like a preppy. And I had never met a schizophrenic before. I had certainly never met any schizophrenics who repeatedly ignored taking their hallucination-blocking medication. It was a rough year. But I learned a lot about psychiatric illnesses, and the fine line between staff and patients. The more stable patients taught me how to shoot pool during their recreation time when I was on duty and there were lighter moments. It was still a hard year.

My second internship was with kids in Harlem at a family center offering after-school programs. Crack had hit the drug scene back then, and many of the kids had crack-addicted parents who repeatedly beat them up, or simply forgot to pick them up after school. I often felt like a glorified babysitter when the kids were sent to our agency for treatment. Another tough year.

After graduating, I started working for Freedom Institute in Manhattan as a staff counselor for alcoholics, addicts, and their family members. It felt like an obvious choice, and I was still looking for answers. Many of my clients had been sent to in-patient treatment for a month and were coming home for what was called aftercare. The family members were also sent for therapy after they attended the dreaded "family week" as I had a few years earlier. While I was an addictions "specialist" from my childhood experiences, I became an official addictions specialist on this job.

At least 95% of the clients who came for an intake session at the Institute claimed their drinking problem *wasn't that bad*: "You should see the other people I drink with at the bar, they're much worse." Businessmen, mothers, therapists, nurses, actors, lawyers, bankers, students – they all said the same thing. This excuse started to seem absurd to me. One time, I burst out laughing (not endearing me to this particular patient), but it gave me a wedge into his denial. "Your boss sent you here; you're in danger of being fired; your wife left you, and your doctor said your liver is shot, so you're right, I'd hate to see those other people drinking side by side with you at the bar." Sometimes being a quiet, calm listener isn't the best way to connect to someone, especially when that person is in deep denial.

Watching the sabotaging behavior of alcoholics was painful, yet eye-opening at the same time. Years of sobriety would go up in smoke with one brief wobble of commitment. They'd head into a bar "just to meet friends" for a diet Coke, and voila: full-fledged relapse, danger, health issues, and family chaos. They often didn't return to treatment. I watched them procrastinate, avoid their responsibilities, deny the severity of their illness, pick a fight with their spouse or counselor or both – all to provide drama as cover for their emotional pain, untreated trauma, and deep worthiness conflicts that made failing feel comfortable and familiar. If they weren't emotionally ready to face the feelings that had made them start using drugs and alcohol in the first place or the truth of the damage their substance abuse was causing, it didn't matter what the counselor said. They couldn't get and stay sober. And, of course, I continued to see that pattern in my family as well. What I didn't want to tell you, but I can't leave out of this book, is that 30 years later, my eldest sister is still drinking and has lost control of every part of her life. It is deeply painful to witness my three nieces struggle with their frustration, grief, and heartbreak as their mother continues to drink. Watching this unfold has been beyond painful, but I am comforted by the depth of connection my nieces and I have.

There were also amazing success stories at the Institute. Families reunited, adult children and ex-spouses moving on to healthy lives even though their addicted family member never put down the drugs and alcohol. But it was a tough decade working at the Institute. There was some kind of crisis every day, and the stress felt relentless.

Still Searching

During this time as a staff psychotherapist, I became interested in clinical hypnosis. I loved the descriptions of how the brain worked, how we could override our conscious decisions, how habits could melt away, how we could affect the brain through different doorways of persuasion, influence, or alignment with the patient's desires. I eventually got my doctoral degree in clinical hypnotherapy and started using hypnosis in my private practice. I enjoyed it, but I was maybe a B+ hypnotist. Good, but not great.

All through this time, I continued to work on myself through therapy and Al-Anon, learned to set better boundaries, and leave work at the office. I also devoured the literature on the interaction between emotional distress and physical illness.

The cliché about becoming a therapist is that you want to try to fix everyone because you couldn't fix the alcoholics, addicts, or the toxic narcissists in your own family. Every therapist I know has their family story. The truth is that those of us who want to become therapists crave emotional depth, meaning, directness, truth, and progress… often with a little side helping of drama.

Graduate school and this first job taught me how to treat different emotional disorders, how to work with a multidisciplinary staff, how to chart notes for clients, and how to be supportive during a therapeutic session. But it didn't teach me how to treat trauma, stop my own sabotaging behavior or how to prioritize my self-care.

All along I had planned to start my own private practice, hoping that it wouldn't be centered around alcoholics who still didn't think their problem was "all that bad." I wanted to help people who were already sober and ready to put their lives back together. After eight years, I went out on my own fulltime. It wasn't without its challenges, but I loved it and felt deeply satisfied. The variety of clients referred to me was refreshing, and every year my boundaries got stronger. I took things that happened in life less personally, and I took better care of myself.

There was no doubt that at this time in my life I was making significant progress. I was learning to release my anxiety and face the fact that I couldn't stop my parents' drinking, no matter how many times I begged, argued, or threatened. I was steadily maturing in my work and enjoying my relationships. But I still wasn't aware of how some earlier traumas were depleting me. In addition to constant worry and anticipation that something bad was always on the horizon, I also experienced specific traumatic events, including being a passenger in three car accidents, several other "close calls" in a car, a dangerous fall from a high ledge of rocks, and other events that would lodge in my nervous system. My response was always to pick myself up, exclaim "I'm fine" and just move on. I also suffered from the typical relationship break-ups, and almost died on a sailboat trip, which I'll tell you about later. All these events continued to strain my immune system and drain my energy. This was on top of an already weakened nervous system from the chronic worry as I waited for disaster to strike at any moment.

Then came more traumatic events. Three months before 9/11, my father-in-law died. The family was heartbroken but close, so they were able to grieve in a healthy way – together, and up front about it all.

Then came 9/11, and it shook us to the core. I lived and worked about 2 miles north of ground zero, close enough to smell the smoke damage for months, far enough away to not have been threatened during the actual attacks. A slew of new clients contacted me for PTSD and trauma work – they had escaped the falling towers, but couldn't get back on their feet emotionally after being so close to an international tragedy. Every single one of them questioned where they were living, the work they were doing, whether they were married to the right spouse, and what to do with the rest of their lives. Tragedies often force people to reevaluate their choices. The only phone call that got through on September 11th was from my 39-year-old sister who was sitting at a Boston hospital getting chemotherapy for metastatic breast cancer. She was watching the news, heard the silence because the planes were blocked from flying overhead to and from Logan airport, and her voicemail came through. Three months after 9/11, she died from the cancer that had spread to her liver and brain.

In the aftermath of all this trauma and grief, some of my physical vulnerabilities started to resurface. My insomnia flared up, and I gained that stubborn 20 pounds back again. I developed another tumor that needed surgical removal – this time in my hand (a globular hemangioma) and I felt lost and depressed for the first time in my life. While I still felt anxious, the dark, low feelings were hard to shake after these three events. I knew I had to keep addressing my deep grief and stress. My self-sabotaging behavior kept showing up as running myself into the ground and overworking, with a healthy dose of perfectionism on the side. I still didn't take enough time to recharge my battery. And I was really good at focusing on helping other people – a sneaky way to sabotage yourself. I was trying to keep two steps ahead of the grief. I couldn't, but I tried.

Most of my family members gained weight after my sister's death as well, and at least two family members relapsed with alcohol. I dug deep, cried endless tears, tried to be perfect and make my parents happy which was not only exhausting, but also impossible. I was never a genuine workaholic, but my work numbed the grief when I needed it to. The simple upside to my self-sabotaging behaviors of overworking and overeating was that it distracted me from my deep grief about losing my sister. We were born only 17 months apart and were very close emotionally. While my own grief was excruciating, watching her kids, husband, and my parents suffer was even more unbearable.

Finding What I Needed

While I had great insight into my family system from therapy, I still felt anxious. I wanted more tools and more solutions. While I was much more comfortable with my discomfort – something we all need to learn if we're going to be present enough to heal – I also needed something more to quiet the anxiety. I was no longer drinking or smoking, but the yo-yo dieting was exasperating. Therapy helped me recognize that all the alcoholics in my family were making their own choices. It wasn't my fault, or from any deficiencies, or anything I had done or not done. But I was still struggling with insomnia, and I was still sabotaging myself by neglecting my self-care and working too hard.

Insomnia had been with me for a long time, mostly driven by anxious thoughts about my family and challenges on the job. My racing thoughts had a life of their own and it was impossible to turn them off. Remember the schizophrenics in the South Bronx? The kids being beaten up or abandoned by their crack-addicted mothers? The enraged alcoholics at Freedom Institute who insisted their problem wasn't "that bad" in spite of car accidents, divorces and pink slips? These challenges were front and center in the anxious movies I replayed at night. And mistakes…I would always chew on the mistakes I thought I had made.

Looking back, I think my insomnia first became a pattern when I would hear my parents fighting – about money, about drinking, about anything. From my bedroom upstairs I couldn't hear the specific words, but I could recognize the tones. I developed a kind of bionic hearing – a keen sense of alertness around "noise" and the tiniest of sounds. It helped me be alert to subtle changes in people's voices, tones, moods, and behavior, and helped me anticipate what might be coming next with my bosses and clients. Unfortunately, it also heightened my hypervigilance.

Around this time, a colleague in my hypnosis class suggested I try EFT, this weird tapping technique for anxiety, phobias, and cravings. While the research hadn't accumulated yet to corroborate all the anecdotal successes practitioners were having, the success stories were impossible to ignore. Massive family traumas healed, doctors shocked by the disappearance of symptoms of life-threatening illnesses, PTSD symptoms neutralized, rifts in relationships repaired as people became calmer, more regulated, and able to tolerate conflict. Addicts were transformed as their cravings and underlying traumas and anxiety dissolved through the tapping technique. EFT is a form of *emotional technology*, and its mechanism of healing – tapping on acupuncture points while tuning into emotional challenges – calms down the fight or flight mechanism in the brain, which in turn creates psychological space for people to process old emotional pain and be less reactive. Tapping "rewires the brain" and allows traumatic memories, stress, fears, and PTSD symptoms to resolve. I was able to help clients reduce their emotional suffering dramatically.

I received my initial training in 1997 from one of the top trainers in the world, followed by in-depth training from the EFT creator, Gary Craig. I eventually became one of the first practitioners to become a designated EFT Master. I knew I had found "my tool" and the decision to pursue the training has defined the rest of my career until today. It was what I had been looking for – a tool to help myself feel better faster with lasting results. Back then, EFT was considered on the fringe by many colleagues. Now, it is used in veterans' organizations, schools, hospitals, clinics, and homes all over the world. Countless people have taken courses, certifications, and studied the application of EFT for all kinds of challenges. To this day, it is the primary tool I use to help clients change. It also had a profound effect in my own life and was the key tool that supported me in releasing the fears and beliefs fueling my self-sabotaging behavior.

Gary Craig continued to invite me to be a leading practitioner in his workshops, which meant I had to learn to use EFT for my fear of success. After presenting a workshop with him in Flagstaff, Arizona, Gary learned I had a fever and bad cold. He said, "If this is how you do with a fever, I'd love to see you on stage when you feel well." Mirroring my experience on the field hockey team, other practitioners were jealous of my being chosen to facilitate workshops with him. I was afraid of their envy, but I learned how to release my fear about their reactions and continued to shine in the field.

The first thing I healed in myself with EFT was my insomnia. The upside of my insomnia was that I felt *useful* when I was ruminating over problems, worrying about my family and patients, considering what to do with my career. Active worrying served a purpose – it kept me alert and on guard. The downside of letting it go? I feared I would be caught off guard. What if someone relapsed or yelled at me and I didn't see it coming? I was convinced I would miss something important if I wasn't worrying day and night. I couldn't articulate it at the time, but in hindsight I knew these were the reasons it was so hard to let go and have a good night's sleep. In addition, I didn't realize that my nervous system needed a reboot after the years of holding on to unexpressed traumas.

In the beginning of my EFT career, hypnosis clients were still being referred to me, and the bulk of my regular practice was still talk therapy. If I thought tapping could help my clients, I would offer them a five-minute peek into using the method. I would lead them through a few rounds of tapping to address their stress levels, and if they didn't like it or didn't experience positive results, I agreed to give them back the time at the end of the session.

After using tapping regularly for my clients' anxieties, I woke up one day and realized I had actually fallen asleep much earlier than usual – no racing thoughts, no nighttime anxiety keeping me wide awake. I was no longer ruminating late into the night, trying to solve impossible problems. EFT training will teach you that it's best to have a target to work on – *"my anxious thoughts keep me up at night."* But I hadn't worked on my insomnia directly, I had just been using tapping with clients for their anxiety and emotional conflicts. I would sit across from my clients and tap on myself while leading them through what to say and where to tap. I would help them with anxiety, anger, guilt, fear, and ambivalence. I was getting exceptional results with clients, but I didn't realize I was resetting my own nervous system in the process, and my insomnia disappeared. The EFT field calls this "Borrowing Benefits" – when your own issues get resolved even when you're not specifically focused or tapping on your personal challenge. It likely has something to do with mirror neurons, but it is a fascinating advantage when working in large groups.

Over the years of practicing, teaching, and using EFT, I went from yo-yo dieting up and down 25 pounds, to 20 pounds, then 15 pounds, then 10 pounds until finally I landed at a new set point. While I will always love to eat, I don't need to use food to numb my emotions, and I don't struggle with my weight anymore.

The main question I needed to ask and answer was: what was the extra weight doing for me? What was the upside of carrying that extra weight when I hated it so much? Did it protect me? The answer was simple – the best way to anesthetize my anxiety and grief was with emotional overeating. The downside of losing the weight was that I would surrender my security blanket and couldn't rely on food to numb myself anymore. I continued to tap on my stress, my anxiety, and the built-up traumas stored in my nervous system, and my weight finally stabilized.

I also cleared deep financial challenges with EFT. Most of the arguments in my family growing up centered around money challenges. I had always known and heard about financial stress and scarcity.

In the fall term of my freshman year at college, the check my father wrote for my tuition bounced. I wasn't allowed to buy books or attend classes, which was both shocking and embarrassing. In addition, I always had to work for extra money during my four years. I typed people's term papers, tutored French, waitressed and cleaned houses to help with expenses. I hated this necessity and became determined to solve my financial struggles.

Years later, when I was in private practice, I was adding up my income for my accountant and realized I had earned the exact amount as the previous year. This was a huge clue that I had an invisible ceiling on my income. Earning the same amount of money two years in a row is impossible for a private therapist. Holidays fall on different days, clients get sick, new clients show up, old clients leave – all these variables make it mathematically impossible. This revealed to me that there was an upside to keeping a lid on my income. After experimenting with tapping on my comfort zones, identity issues, and healing the fears around financial success, I doubled, tripled, and quadrupled my income. I stopped counting after I quintupled my income, and then wrote my first EFT success book – *Attracting Abundance with EFT* – to help others break through their financial comfort zones.

In the process of expanding my work, I became a trauma and PTSD expert, and still had plenty of traumas in my life that kept showing up for me to navigate. There were work and relationship surprises, bad news, my husband's two skiing accidents, three mammogram callbacks, but nothing prepared me for working at the intensive retreat with veterans organized by the founder of EFT. I had never heard stories of such atrocious traumas and violence or been around such human terror. For a solid week in a hotel, we treated veterans from Vietnam, Iraq, Afghanistan, and some of them brought their family members for support and treatment as well. The practitioners would lead each veteran through their traumatic memories, frame by frame, feeling by feeling, while using tapping for the visual or auditory cues and emotions that surfaced. Trauma by trauma, these veterans and their family members were released from PTSD and the horrors of war. The results were impressive. They started sleeping, no longer suffered from nightmares, reduced medications successfully under their doctor's supervision, and no longer felt the need for alcohol and drugs. It was life-changing for the veterans, but it was life-changing for me as well. I suffered from secondary trauma after hearing the details of these veterans' stories, so I needed a lot of tapping to process my own nightmares and visual memories of the tragedies I had heard. EFT was a healing solution for all of us.

I was also invited as an EFT expert to another intensive retreat organized by Gary Craig to help people with traumatic brain injuries and serious diseases. Since I wasn't a medical doctor, I couldn't "treat" something like a traumatic brain injury (TBI) or back pain, but as a psychotherapist, if the client agreed there might be a connection between their mental health and their body, I could work on the emotional conflicts connected to their ailments. This, too, was a life-changing experience as I watched people with TBIs, physical ailments, and debilitating symptoms release their emotional pain and traumatic memories and return to "normal" functioning.

These experiences continued to take my work and my own healing deeper. My life changed dramatically as a result of using and teaching EFT. I traveled all over the world teaching workshops to lay people, nurses, coaches, therapists, and doctors. I've taught multiple workshops in London, Amsterdam, Brussels, Paris, throughout Canada, Australia, and the United States.

There would always be stressful events and traumas both big and small to invite me to go deeper to release emotional distress. An old trauma I had to work on with EFT was the memory I mentioned earlier of spending the weekend with my parents on a sailboat on the Long Island Sound. Sound exciting? Not so fast. Sailing isn't fun anywhere near a hurricane. It was the 4th of July weekend, and while the weather report wasn't definitive about an emerging storm, someone, somewhere should still have convinced my father to cancel the trip. If you know anything about high waves, bad weather, being seasick or being terrified, you would have hated this trip. I know in my bones that this was the closest I have ever come to losing my life. In the middle of the hurricane, we had to attach our sailboat to a buoy marking the mouth of a harbor. This is strictly illegal according to nautical rules, but it was either that maneuver, or the sailboat would have capsized and the three of us would have drowned. Years later, I had to use EFT to work on the terror and trauma of enduring hours of unrelenting hurricane conditions. Specifically, I had to release the image of my father attached to a 30+ foot mast with a safety harness, swinging in the outrageous wind in a bright orange jacket that was seared into my memory and my nervous system.

And, of course, as life would have it, more stressful events and shocks kept coming.

When I was on vacation out in Colorado skiing, I received the call that my father had died in the middle of the night from a pulmonary embolism.

In spite of his hidden but emotional vow never to be close to anyone, in spite of his inability to express his deepest feelings, in spite of his reliance on alcohol for emotional escape and numbing, my father and I were very close. He was an alcoholic with a massive temper that scared me, and yet I knew how much he loved me.

Getting his body sent back to the USA, trying to wrangle a death certificate in English from the consulate in Mexico, and dealing with the aftermath of such a huge loss was overwhelming and added more stress to my nervous system. I was managing my intense job, flying back and forth to see my mother, and fulfilling workshop obligations that had been contractually arranged a year earlier. While on a business trip to Atlanta, I got a call from the funeral director: "Your father missed his connection in Houston."

"You mean his casket didn't make it in time?"

"Yes, he'll have to spend the night in Texas, and we'll get him on another flight tomorrow." I could not unsee this image. It added to my sense of helplessness, and I knew that the image tortured my mother.

My father's memorial service was scheduled for 2 pm at my parents' nearby church. Hundreds of friends and family members had gathered in the church to pay their respects, say goodbye to my father, and console my mother in her grief.

I'll cut to the chase. My mother had a cardiac event while getting dressed for my father's service. The paramedics arrived, tried to revive her, and rushed her by ambulance to the nearby hospital.

They pronounced her dead just before 2 pm.

Stunned and dazed, we left the tiny hospital for the church. I was shaking, in shock, and what I now recognize as completely traumatized and stuck in the freeze response.

My uncle (the minister) walked out between the choir stalls, motioned to the organist to stop the music, and calmly told the story to everyone waiting for my father's service.

"There will not be a service for David today because Charlotte collapsed. The girls accompanied the ambulance to the hospital, and she was pronounced dead just before 2 o'clock…" Gasps, yelps, lots of noise and commotion. Everyone was in shock.

We were inconsolable about losing my mother, and still trying to come to terms with my father's sudden death.

My mother and I were emotional soulmates; her long-term sobriety had allowed us to do the healing and repair work needed to keep our bond incredibly deep, regardless of her repeated relapses and my broken heart. Without the tapping, I don't know how I could have gotten through those first few days of immense grief, not to mention the next few years.

While the nightmare of grief continued, I went back to using food and busy-ness again to keep me afloat. And nothing could prepare us for the enormous job of cleaning out my parents' clutter-filled house. Nothing. I always knew they had a problem with clutter, and that I had inherited it emotionally, but when you clean out someone's house, you can no longer deny the depth of the problem.

After my parents' sudden deaths, life felt out of control and the pain was often excruciating. I gained 15 pounds again. Suffice it to say, I'm not sure where I'd be without tapping for the shock of these back-to-back losses. Tapping helped me heal the deep grief, eliminate the nightmares that tortured me by replaying the moments when I found my mother slumped on the floor, and regulated my nervous system so I could start thriving again.

Six months after their double funeral, I rounded the corner of my building in New York and burst out laughing about a comment a friend had said to me. I was stunned to realize that I hadn't laughed or felt that kind of lightness in six months. I had apparently turned an emotional corner, too. I'll never forget the surprise I felt at hearing my own laugh, feeling my body breathe, and then realizing how long it had been since I had felt any joy.

Expanding My Work

I continued to watch people sabotage themselves in my practice – and started to see how the need to feel safe drove self-sabotaging behavior. Why would they relapse now? What were they afraid of? Why would they (and I) gain the weight back? Why would they procrastinate when they knew it might threaten their job? I started to see the underlying pattern of needing to feel safe at any cost.

I also started being referred more clients with a history of trauma and saw how past traumas informed current self-sabotaging behavior. Despite the clear diagnostic criteria for trauma, only the individual can label their pain as traumatic or not. It's not how big the challenge was, or the clinical definition or criteria, it was how helpless and unsafe the event or circumstance made them feel. I learned the useful definition that *PTSD is a normal reaction to an abnormal event.*

When we don't make space to listen to our emotions deeply enough, the feelings and conflicts continue to show up in our bodies. The more you ignore them, the louder they get. In general, you would have said that I was in good physical condition for the first 25 years of my life. I had been a very healthy child, a strong athlete, never broke a single bone, and didn't get a cavity until I was 30. I had perfect attendance throughout my school years. It wasn't until later that my health started to show signs of weakness – the tumors, the fevers, and the polyp – all a reflection of carrying too many emotional burdens.

While I had finally landed in the right job and the right relationship, enjoyed my deep friendships and my improving health, my body kept calling for more release of the deep grief and anxiety. And that's what I kept doing – releasing and healing the grief, the pain, and the shocks I had stored in my nervous system. Talk therapy couldn't clear these; I needed an energy-based tool, such as EFT. I'm not asking you to stop talking. I'm inviting you to integrate a body-based energy technique like EFT to clear the traumas and stress patterns from your nervous system.

Consistently using tapping helped me heal my past emotional conflicts and release my limiting beliefs that kept me playing small. It also calmed me down enough to start a meditation practice. My anxiety had always prevented me from wanting to be still because it didn't feel good. In fact, it felt terrible because it allowed emotional pain and anxiety to surface. After being ripped apart by my parents' deaths, I healed enough of my emotional challenges to actually sit still and be quiet. It didn't feel good in the beginning, but I could tolerate it. Then I learned to enjoy it, and now I look forward to the peace and quiet.

I couldn't be more grateful for my clients, the work I get to do, and how my life has unfolded. I am honored that my clients trust me and ask me to witness their traumas and help them heal at the deepest levels. I have been told I have an unusually high capacity to "hold space" and witness other people's pain. This doesn't just come from being familiar with trauma, it comes from neutralizing the overload in my nervous system. Healing my early childhood experiences and my losses of my sister and parents helped me deepen my capacity for holding the emotional space for my clients' pain.

The Hope

We all have suffered unique hardships, losses, traumas, and upsetting events, and while my story may not be as dramatic as yours, and I may not have suffered as many horrific traumas as you have, we have one thing in common – we weren't able to or allowed to express our emotions when and how we needed to for deep healing to occur. We have also all felt guilt, shame, terror, anger, anxiety, and frustration in varying degrees, regardless of the event that triggered these emotions.

Once in a while, I binge-watch Netflix as a guilty pleasure, but my sabotaging behaviors have all but disappeared. I don't need to sabotage myself anymore because I've addressed the fears and limiting beliefs that supported the behavior in the first place. My fear of success and being visible isn't active anymore, I no longer fear what others think of my rocking the boat. I don't feel compelled to be perfect, and mild procrastination only shows up once a year at tax time. The space in my home and office are unrecognizable since releasing the extra clutter. I learned to ask for help and I say no when I need to. I have kept the extra weight off for years, and my schedule has plenty of time for recreation.

Most importantly, my self-care is my top priority. I will always have emotional challenges – they come with being human – but I have the desire and passion to be as healthy as possible and I have the best tools available to thrive. I don't know where I'd be if I hadn't uncovered the reasons I sabotage myself or the tools to heal those reasons.

When you treat the underlying problem – your fears, terror, traumas, and your feelings of guilt, grief, and helplessness – you don't need to people please, become addicted, or hide under the radar so someone's jealousy won't hurt you. I will always wish I had discovered EFT earlier so I could have addressed the old traumas, released my need to smoke and eat, and calmed down my nervous system with this cutting-edge tool rather than just talking about it for so long. If I had had the right tools way back then, I could have saved myself a lot of time and trouble. But I have them now. This book offers you the right tools to save you a lot of time and trouble as well.

In spite of being taught never to let my guard down or get my hopes up, I can't help being hopeful in my life and for you. Keep reading to unpack the fears and beliefs driving your self-sabotaging behavior. You'll find out how expensive these behaviors are to your happiness, and then you'll learn to use The Yes Code™ process and the spectacular stress relief tool of EFT to release the causes of your behavior so you can get the results you want and deserve, one yes at a time.

PART TWO
THE PROBLEM

In this section of the book, I will define self-sabotage, and examine the emotional, physical, financial, and spiritual costs of these behaviors to your success and, ultimately, your happiness. I will outline how to get better results in your life, and help you ask the right questions to get to the bottom of your self-sabotaging behavior. Finally, I will unpack the seven most common self-sabotaging behaviors and present client stories to show you before and after results.

CHAPTER 2

SELF-SABOTAGING BEHAVIOR DEFINED

The original definition of sabotage relates to wars and looking for clever ways to hurt the enemy, all for the "purpose" of destruction. *Self-sabotage* is when the conscious or unconscious purpose is to destroy *your own goals*.

Self-sabotage is defined by www.dictionary.com as follows:

The act or habit of behaving in a way that interferes directly with one's own goals, well-being, relationships etc.

Are you interfering with your own success?

As I said in the introduction, self-sabotaging behavior is like having one foot on the gas pedal while the other is on the brake. Part of you wants to move forward, but an equally powerful part of you is afraid of what might happen if you make progress. So you stay stuck where you are. Being stuck is evidence that your fear is stronger than your desire. That's when you start interfering with your own success.

"Driving" this way is a form of communication with yourself, and all communication is useful. If you keep saying you want to succeed in your job or in your personal life, but your behavior shows otherwise, it's a message that you need to pay attention to if you're going to make any positive changes in your life. It means there must be a conflict big enough to knock you out of alignment with the goal that you keep saying you want to reach. When you're out of alignment, you can't get to where you want to go.

Your "Drug of Choice"

In the agency where I worked with alcoholics, addicts, and their families, there was a question on the intake form: *What is your drug of choice?* This was meant to ask new clients, nine times out of ten, what would they choose if they were seeking an altered state: alcohol? cocaine? heroin? Many of my clients couldn't narrow it down and ended up writing "anything and everything" they could get their hands on.

Addictions to drugs, alcohol, food, drama, fixing others, and chasing shiny objects work to distract or numb us from dealing with serious emotional conflicts we need to address.

The other self-sabotaging behaviors do the same – they prevent us from dealing with serious emotional conflicts we need to address.

If you're afraid of standing out, being visible, or rocking the boat, you'll procrastinate. If you're afraid of meeting with someone's disapproval or you can't say no, you'll be a people pleaser and perfectionist. If you fear all of your emotions, you'll overeat, drink, or take drugs and neglect your self-care. If you're convinced you'll be left again, you'll pick a fight in your relationship; and if you feel safer surrounding yourself with stuff instead of people, you'll collect clutter.

I regularly used each of these self-sabotaging behaviors, but as you read about in Chapter One, the ones I used most often were addictions, self-care neglect, people pleasing, and procrastination.

Let's take a look at the list of the top seven self-sabotaging behaviors again.

1. **Procrastination**
2. **Perfectionism**
3. **People Pleasing**
4. **Addictions**
5. **Clutter**
6. **Relationship Drama**
7. **Self-Care Neglect**

Which ones are your "behaviors of choice"?

I know you want more out of your life. And if you have read this far, I know that you are personally interested in this topic. And if you're interested in this topic, it means you or a loved one has engaged in self-sabotaging behavior enough to frustrate or baffle you. You're looking for a solution.

Remember, it's not the economy; it's not your spouse; it's not the weather. It's you – you are the one who is in your own way. I've been in my own way so many times, I've lost count. As much as we'd like to point the finger at someone else, we are the only one responsible for staying on course or veering off the path and choosing detours that plague us. I can tell you why I care about releasing sabotage, and what I think it might do for you, but in the end, it will be your decision to make the changes you need to make so you can live the life you want to live.

What you need to uncover is what your self-sabotaging behavior is trying to tell you – scream at you in some cases – and then you can go about releasing this pattern you've developed to get in your own way. Remember, self-sabotage can be caused by an action or inaction, and you need to examine and interpret both.

A self-sabotaging behavior is what protects you from your fears and confirms your beliefs about yourself. You're actually trying to interfere with your forward progress, even when you say you're not. It's all about protection, and as a human being, what your nervous system perceives as emotional safety always comes first. The outside behaviors are being used to protect your insides.

Once you find the purpose of your self-sabotaging behavior – the point of the protection – you can get to work dismantling it and become more successful, productive, and fulfilled in your everyday life. Whenever I'm avoiding something I need to do, I feel the pull of frustration and heaviness. I feel the dread. I end up not feeling good about myself at all. But not feeling good about myself does nothing to propel me forward. I'm still stuck. *Aware of how I feel, but still stuck.*

This is the cycle we can stop – sabotaging ourselves, hating ourselves for it, and sabotaging ourselves again. Stopping this cycle means you're going to need to identify what problem your self-sabotaging behavior is trying to solve. Once you uncover the purpose it serves, you can clear these blocks and get the results you want.

Now, let's look at the tremendous cost of these self-sabotaging behaviors.

CHAPTER 3

THE COST OF SELF-SABOTAGING BEHAVIOR

Self-sabotaging behavior is very expensive, literally and figuratively. It costs you in all areas of your life, even though you may only associate the "expensive" part with your finances. There are many other losses you might suffer from as a result of your self-sabotaging behavior. Below is a thorough examination of these losses.

Financial Cost

If you procrastinate with projects at work, or about launching your website and products you sell, you will, of course, be *leaving money on the table*. It will be financially expensive for you. You block income coming in, and you may even incur additional expenses in the form of fees, penalties, or other types of "punishment" for being late. I was mentoring a coach who said she couldn't get her billing done. She was owed thousands of dollars in fees, but no bills sent to the clients meant no checks in the mail. She, of course, was having cash flow problems as a result of this. So, her behavior cost her money, time, and peace of mind.

If you were able to add up all the financial costs of delaying your projects from dragging your feet and procrastinating on finishing proposals or invoices to clients in any business, I can guarantee the cost would be sobering. If you don't get the proposal to your client, they can't sign on the dotted line. If you don't get your invoicing done in a timely fashion, your clients can't pay you. If you never create your online program or write your book, you obviously won't have any sales. And yet, thinking about leaving so much money on the table isn't enough to spur us to change our behavior or finally get the website launched, the product created, or the book written. This is where the "real" reasons come into play. Our underlying fears and beliefs override our common sense. If it's expensive not to complete the proposal, why do you continue to avoid finishing it? Because you're afraid of potential consequences connected with the completion.

Wasting Time

Time is the most precious commodity in our world, and we squander it every single day. And then we wake up decades later and ask: "Where did all the years go?"

Each of the seven primary self-sabotaging behaviors is a big drain on your time. If you're procrastinating with avoidance techniques like getting involved in "busy work," a lot of energy is going into wasting time and being busy for no good reason. My client admitted that her "To Do List was so long that it had its own To Do List."

Another form of self-sabotaging behavior – being involved in relationship drama – is also a time drain, as fights and arguments followed by spending time repairing the ruptures in your relationships takes effort and time.

Just think of what you could do with all that time if you set out to accomplish your goals without any detours or wasted hours getting involved in busy work that doesn't really matter. Again, even when thinking about the time you lose is upsetting to you, it's still never enough to make you change your behavior. Looking at time wasted is a logical and rational way to evaluate the expense of sabotage, but it's not the real problem that needs to be tackled.

Self-Esteem

Another form of "expense" from self-sabotaging behavior is loss of your peace of mind and self-esteem. When you sabotage your success, you feel it and know it in your gut. You usually trash yourself for it, which degrades your self-esteem and does nothing towards changing the behavior. Sabotaging behavior hurts your self-esteem because it hurts your sense of integrity. When you promise yourself, a friend, or your boss that you'll get something to them on time and don't follow through, you have broken your word. This can eat away at your self-esteem every day. Again, you'd think this "expense" would be enough to put a little fire under you to get things done. It isn't, because other fears and beliefs that are more important to your emotional safety override your desire to move forward.

And let's talk about your authenticity. There's no room for authenticity if you're saying yes when you want to say no. If you've betrayed yourself and your values by avoiding the conflict that might come from saying no, this will cost you. If you're a people pleaser and put the needs of others in front of your own, you'll pay the price at some point by feeling out of alignment, out of integrity, or seeing yourself as an imposter.

Physical Cost

The physical cost of self-sabotaging behavior depends on what kind of behavior you're engaged in. When you procrastinate, you create anxiety, and we know anxiety isn't good for any part of your body or brain.

The stress levels rise, causing a cascade of hormonal disruptions, and your body will eventually show the signs of these imbalances.

When you have difficulty saying no to others, you are constantly fighting your guilt and shame. These conflicts take up energy and drain your battery as well. When you feel overwhelmed by your clutter, you can also feel drained, confused, troubled, and helpless.

What about being addicted to drugs or alcohol? Wherever you are on the continuum of addiction, it is definitely unhealthy for your body to drink to excess, smoke, take drugs, or overeat. The behavior is costly to your physical body and will eventually show up as a health challenge. None of these feelings or behaviors are good for your body or soul. They cause physiological chaos in your body which may manifest as a weakened immune system, a susceptibility to catching every virus that's going around, extreme fatigue, irritability – you name it.

Think about your immune system. Mine was shot from anxiety and insomnia, worrying and overworking. I ended up with several chronic mysterious illnesses until I started taking better care of myself and stopped draining my battery by keeping the motor running day and night. There is no doubt that there is a physical cost to self-sabotage, and yet again, it doesn't provide enough of an impetus to make people change their behavior.

Emotional Cost

The emotional toll of self-sabotaging behavior is as big as, or even bigger than the financial expense in your life. Feeling afraid of failure, afraid of success, afraid to be clear, or afraid to rock the boat becomes a constant background noise that wears you down. You may end up feeling exhausted emotionally, physically, or even burned out and disconnected from yourself and others. This feeling of "running on empty" becomes all too familiar.

Depending on the types of self-sabotaging behavior you engage in, you may end up feeling anger, guilt, or resentment. All of these conflicts have to be expressed somewhere. In your sleep patterns? In your energy levels? In your sugar cravings? And what about the self-hatred you feel every time you don't follow through with a commitment you made? And how do you feel when you ignore your intuition and then feel trapped by a "should" you felt pressured to follow instead?

In addition to struggling with some of the "big" feelings such as anger, guilt, or resentment, you may also end up feeling numb and disconnected. Too much work, not the right results, avoiding what you need to do, spending time collecting clutter, and getting involved in relationship drama can all exhaust you emotionally. The result might be feeling emotionally spent or even feeling totally burned out. And while you're struggling with overwhelm or burnout, you may also feel a dull kind of numbness – nothing gets you high or low; nothing affects you anymore. Nothing is joyful, and you may be bordering on an actual depressive episode. This is very costly and of course, keeps you stuck in repetitive patterns.

The reverberations in your social life will also soon become apparent. You'll feel less like socializing, become less considerate of your friends and family, and lose the value of your social connections.

Spiritual Cost

Regardless of your religious or spiritual background, being entangled in your self-sabotaging behavior squeezes out any space for creating a spiritual connection. I've already mentioned how feeling ashamed of procrastination or clutter can make you judge yourself and stay isolated from others. This does not help you foster a connection to any form of spirituality, or stay in a spiritual or religious community from which you can take great comfort and solace. A client in one of my workshops said her clutter kept her from socializing with her spiritual community. The members took turns having coffee and meetings at each other's homes, yet she wouldn't let anyone visit because she was too ashamed of her clutter problem.

Remember, our need for safety always wins over our desire to reach our goals.

Add up the costs of your self-sabotaging behavior. Maybe it's time to change these patterns so you can move forward with ease and grace towards your vision of your best life. The cost of not changing will cause you to suffer with more of the same cycle that depletes you.

It's clear that self-sabotaging behavior is very expensive and costs you in every part of your life. And yet, understanding the cost has never been enough to make you change.

If it's so expensive, why would you do it?

Because there is something stronger and deeper keeping you tethered to the self-sabotaging behavior.

CHAPTER 4

THE KEY TO GETTING BETTER RESULTS

The key to getting better results in your life is to stop focusing so much on the behavior and start looking at the underlying feelings and beliefs that fuel the behavior.

Remember the old saying:

***If you keep doing what you've always done,
you'll keep getting what you've always gotten.***

This statement is as true as it is clichéd. No change leads to no change. Your results won't change if you don't.

We know the primary self-sabotaging behaviors, and we know how much they cost us in every part of our lives. So, what if you want different – or better – results?

As I've said, all the results that show up in our lives are driven by our emotions, our beliefs, and our behaviors. Therefore, if we want to get better results, we'll need to address one of these three areas. Our options are to:

1. Release our fears
2. Replace our limiting beliefs
3. Stop our self-sabotaging behaviors

It can sound fairly straightforward and simple. Just release your fear of being visible and start enjoying shining at work and at home. Replace a belief that success is dangerous with a belief that success is safe and secure, or stop collecting clutter and start enjoying the space and freedom in your life.

But if it were that easy, we'd all give up our self-sabotaging behavior and be well on our way to enjoying a more productive, happy, and fulfilled life.

Let's take a look at how these three ingredients contribute to the results we get in our lives.

Emotions

Fear, guilt, anxiety, grief, anger, hurt, frustration, resentment – they all keep us focused on the past or the future and prevent us from being present. If we are chewing on old anger, we are certainly staying stuck and not moving forward. All these emotional conflicts take up energy. For instance, if you continue to feel resentful and underappreciated at work, you won't be able to focus on what you need to accomplish, and you will be leaking valuable energy in the process.

If you stay attached to guilt from a past event connected to something you said or did, you will have trouble getting unhooked from this emotional state enough to move forward. Feeling guilty all the time will propel you to say yes when you want to say no. If you feel guilty for being relatively successful, you might notice that you sabotage yourself as a form of punishment for the guilt you feel. It scratches an itch for you... if you feel guilty for being or doing something bad, it can actually feel satisfying to punish yourself.

If you feel hurt from a terrible betrayal in your life, you'll tend to revisit the situation and go over and over the details without breathing any new life or insight into your current life. I've worked with people who are stuck with the feelings of betrayal from decades ago, wasting time trapped in a loop of self-sabotage because they haven't been given the tools to heal. They're still angry, can't imagine forgiving the person, and are reluctant to move forward for fear this lets the other person "get away with it." Being stuck emotionally keeps them from moving forward and is just another way of keeping their foot on the brake. These feelings might also lead to overindulging in alcohol, drugs, or food.

Fear is the most obvious emotion that blocks us from moving forward. Fear of failure, fear of success, fear of other people's reactions – all of these fears keep us stuck. If you're afraid of success, you'll chronically sabotage yourself so you keep a lid on yourself. You might be approaching an important stage of moving forward in your business, and then feel baffled as you watch yourself sabotage your progress.

If you fear other people's reactions to your progress, you'll make sure you return to your starting point time and time again. If shining or standing out feels unsafe to you, you will block this from ever happening. When we can't tolerate what attention the success might bring us, we are compelled to get in our own way.

If you neutralize your fear of shining and start feeling comfortable standing out, you will no longer "need" to sabotage your progress. There's nothing to protect. There is no longer any motivation to keep hanging on to conflicts that are holding you back.

Limiting Beliefs

Now for our limiting beliefs. All beliefs are limiting, as they direct how far you can go and when you should stop. If you believe you are a $75k a year earner, you'll land there repeatedly, in spite of economic changes or marketplace fluctuations. If you believe your set point for your weight is 140 lbs., you'll end up there, over and over again. If you believe no one from your background could be financially successful, you will be right. As the famous quote ascribed to Henry Ford states: *If you think you can or you can't – you're right.* The point is nothing's going to change in your life until you change your beliefs, since they act as a ceiling on your upper limits.

We all prefer to stay within our comfort zones. Being uncomfortable is often too much of an emotional stretch, so staying within the range we're accustomed to becomes our default position. Without questioning or stretching these comfort zones, we actually can't move forward. If we do, we are compelled to slide backwards again.

Your Behavior

What about your behavior? Unfortunately, this is where our culture has focused most of its attention – suggesting that if we change our behavior – our life will change and stay improved forever. While it's true that if you stop drinking, throw out your clutter, or stop people pleasing, your life will change, the bad news is that it never lasts. It can't last because you have only addressed a symptom and not the actual cause. Much like the doctors cutting out my breast tumor, my throat polyp, and the hemangioma in my hand, being focused solely on the symptom means you'll miss the opportunity to make lasting change.

Simply changing your behavior isn't enough to make permanent changes because your behaviors are driven by your fears and your beliefs.

Have you ever cleaned out your car, made vows to keep it neat, only to find it in bad shape a month later? That's because all you did is focus on the behavior, not the "why" of the clutter, which is usually trying to protect you. A client of mine felt safer when she had her special belongings with her at all times. She needed to feel her "stuff" around her. She admitted that her clutter also gave her an excuse to not to give anyone a ride.

How does sabotage help you feel safer? It protects you from an outcome you want to avoid – being judged, criticized, being called a failure, being seen as a threat. If your motivation only comes from changing behavior, your life will only change temporarily.

If you have any emotional conflicts about sticking with your new behavior, the "thanks, but no thanks" side of you will win. Remember, human beings are all about emotional safety, and if you don't feel safe with your new salary range, standing out at work, or going deeper into a romantic relationship, you will inevitably sabotage yourself unconsciously and end up back at the starting line.

There's an old saying in the 12 step recovery programs:

You need to change so much, the "disease" doesn't recognize you anymore.

Profound and true. This is why people quit smoking and start overeating. They haven't addressed the internal grief or void that makes them want to numb their feelings in the first place. This is why people give up using cocaine and start drinking. There's no real change, only a substitution of the "drug" or behavior of your choice. You need to make such fundamental changes, that it doesn't occur to you to pursue the self-sabotaging behavior anymore. You'll dissolve the emotional drive to pursue it because the need for protection has been eliminated. Procrastinating won't give you the protection it used to. When you resolve your fears, you won't need to prevent anyone from noticing that you're standing out.

So, how do we make the deeper changes that last?

Your Why and Your Why Not

I first heard the expression *"Your why has to be bigger than your why not"* from the famous success coach, Bob Proctor. In terms of safety, if you want to be promoted at work, but being promoted presents other complications around visibility and being judged or envied, then your *why* and your *why not* will compete with each other. Which one wins?

If you want to stop drinking but the last time you maintained a period of abstinence you remembered some painful childhood memories, your *why* will be weaker than your *why not*. While this may seem like just an excuse to angry family members, dealing with painful emotions and traumatic memories are what you've been protecting with your substance abuse all along. The only problem is that when it reaches a tipping point, you are no longer numbing your feelings, you are now feeding the addiction.

If quitting smoking poses problems for you because you experienced uncomfortable withdrawal symptoms the last time you tried to quit, your *why* won't be very strong and all those good reasons to quit smoking won't carry any weight. The surgeon general's warnings are irrelevant. If that's all it took to quit smoking, the tobacco industry would have died a long time ago.

The trick is, when you look at your behaviors through the lens of The Yes Code™ process, you will be able to figure out why you're not where you want to be and why you are protecting yourself from being there. You'll be able to see how it can feel like a good idea to stay stuck because of your fears, limiting beliefs, and memories. If you're still afraid of being visible, your nervous system will think it's a terrible idea to be successful. You'll keep sabotaging yourself because there's too much of an investment in playing small. If you value protection, and your nervous system still gets triggered at the thought of standing out, your *why not* will win. Remember, humans need to feel safe and protected, and if that means you shouldn't shine at work or amongst your peer group, your *why not* has more juice.

In the next chapter, I will offer you the best questions I've found to determine what you're afraid of and why you keep getting caught in the cycle of self-sabotage. Remember, this isn't about judging yourself, this is about getting to the bottom of why you would block your own success with one or more of the self-sabotaging behaviors. I promise there are good reasons according to your brain and your nervous system. Remember, we would never engage in destructive behavior unless there was a higher cause or gain.

CHAPTER 5

THE ROOT CAUSE OF SELF-SABOTAGING BEHAVIOR

What I know from decades of clinical practice with clients is that self-sabotaging behavior, no matter how much you hate it and beat yourself up for it, is considered positive by a part of you, or else you wouldn't need to use it.

I could look back at my life and see the benefit of sabotage even when I criticized myself and was ashamed of it. For years, I was too close to my own situation to even recognize that my negative behavior served a purpose. Something positive was coming from it, and I needed to let myself off the hook. I needed to get to the bottom of why I was involved in self-sabotage, but until I stopped beating myself up, I wouldn't be able to figure it out. Beating up on yourself always gets in the way of moving forward. (Yet another way to sabotage yourself.)

Hating ourselves makes no dent in solving the problem. But if you can identify the positive outcome of using one of the self-sabotaging behaviors, then you have increased your chances of making progress. Once I started framing self-sabotaging behavior this way for myself and for my clients – that sabotage is actually solving a problem – my clients and I started to relax and do the excavating necessary to find out what the *real problem* was. While procrastination, perfectionism, people pleasing, addictions, clutter, relationship drama, and self-care neglect are all problems in themselves, they're the actual result of a deeper problem – ***not feeling safe standing out, changing, or moving forward.***

Let's dive into the best questions to ask yourself to identify what you're afraid of and why you keep sabotaging yourself. In the first step of The Yes Code™ process, I ask you to *Clarify Your Vision* so you know what you want your life to look like and why you want what you want. Then I ask my favorite questions to help you understand the fears and beliefs that are fueling the self-sabotaging behaviors keeping you from reaching that vision.

When looking at your self-sabotaging behavior, there are two essential categories of questions that will help you uncover the fears and beliefs which fuel the behavior. We're all too focused on changing the behavior without looking at *why we do it* and what the positive part of the negative behavior is.

When a client seeks help from me with a desire to change a behavior or habit, I always ask the following two questions:

1. **What is the *upside* of your self-sabotaging behavior?**
2. **What is the *downside* of letting it go and reaching your goal?**

At first, clients balk at these questions and tell me there is no possible *upside* to doing something that slows them down. In time, and with more refined questions, all my clients have been able to come up with a reason (their *real why*) that they keep getting in their own way. An old memory often surfaces of a time when it wasn't safe to stand out or be visible.

Consider one of the self-sabotaging behaviors we have been discussing that you recognize and own in yourself. Choose one that slows down your progress or keeps you stuck. Then ask yourself the questions below. I have included several typical answers I have heard from my clients over the years about the *upside* of the behavior and the *downside* of reaching your goal.

I recommend keeping a journal and taking notes on what your answers are to these questions so you can clear the fears and beliefs in the next section when you start using EFT. (If you start to feel overwhelmed by memories, please consult your health care practitioner.)

What is the *upside* of your self-sabotaging behavior?

How does this behavior serve you?

_____

_____

_____

Some typical answers include:

- It serves me by keeping me hidden.
- It stops me from being exposed.
- It means I don't have to be out in public.
- It keeps others away from me.
- It keeps me from feeling any overwhelming emotions.

What are you trying to protect yourself from?

_____

_____

_____

- From their criticism
- From their scrutiny
- From rocking the boat in their world
- From their envy
- From feeling my own anger, hurt, and grief

What does this self-sabotaging behavior prevent in your life?

_____

_____

_____

- It prevents me from exposure.
- It prevents me from making a mistake.
- It prevents me from being vulnerable.
- It prevents me from being close to anyone.
- It prevents me from shining and being visible.
- It prevents me from feeling my most painful emotions.

How does staying small support you?

_____

_____

_____

- Then I don't have to show up for anyone.
- They will leave me alone.
- It means I can mind my own business.
- It means I don't have to change.
- I don't have to keep up with my success.

Why/How does staying under the radar feel safe to you?

_____

_____

_____

- I don't have to risk being known by anyone.
- They won't notice me.
- They won't ask me for anything.
- I can keep doing what I've been doing.
- No one will ask me questions I don't want to answer.

You may focus on a second self-sabotaging behavior and go through this list of *upside* questions again. For instance, if you were thinking of your procrastination when you first considered these questions, now reflect on your tendency to people please or your perfectionism and read through the questions and take notes again.

Now let's look at the *downside* question. I have provided several typical answers I have heard over the years from my clients. Again, fears, beliefs, and old memories of past events might surface. Keep a journal of your answers so you can clear them when you start using EFT on yourself in the next section of this book. (And if at any time you start to feel overwhelmed, please consult a health care practitioner.)

What is the *downside* of reaching your goal?

What consequences do you fear if you reach your goal?

_____

_____

_____

Some typical answers include:

- I'll have to change.
- I'll stand out too much.
- They'll be jealous of my success.
- I'll have to maintain it.
- I'll have to face some emotions I've been avoiding.

Who will be upset with your success?

_____

_____

_____

- My parents
- My siblings
- My friends
- My colleagues
- My competitors

What do you fear you'll need to change if you reach your goal?

_____

_____

_____

- My attitude
- My friends
- How I run my business
- How I run my home

Whose "boat" will you rock if you start to shine?

_____

_____

_____

- Everyone's boat
- My family's boat
- My peers
- My friends who aren't successful yet
- My sister's/brother's
- My own boat

What losses might you encounter if you reach your goals?

_____

_____

_____

- Loss of my comfort
- Loss of some friends
- Loss of my old ways of being
- Loss of excuses

Scan this QR code or visit www.TheYesCode.com for a complete list of effective upside/downside questions.

CHAPTER 6

SELF-SABOTAGING BEHAVIORS UNPACKED

Let's take a deeper dive into the seven self-sabotaging behaviors. Below I have detailed each of the behaviors and included client examples from my own practice. I have also described asking the upside/downside questions and shown you the clients' revealing answers. See if you recognize yourself in these examples.

Procrastination

I've never met someone who said that they didn't procrastinate at least occasionally at work or at home. And the reason behind procrastination is always the same – fear of what might happen if you complete the project.

If you're reading this book, I know you know how it feels to procrastinate. I would feel dread at the thought of doing certain tasks and get busy being busy instead. I have mopped the floors, cleaned the kitchen, even cleaned out a junk drawer to avoid what I don't want to do. But why don't I want to do it? Understanding the real fear is the key to the solution. The top two fears under the behavior of procrastination are (a) fear of failure and (b) fear of success.

Fear of failure

It's not that you *want to* sabotage yourself and your success. It's that your brain is telling you that you *need to* sabotage yourself or there will be some upsetting consequences. So, think about the upside/downside questions in the last chapter and why you would need to procrastinate. What does it do for you that could be seen as positive? How does it protect you? How does it serve you? We know it serves you in some unique way or you wouldn't need to do it.

Numerous clients over the years have said: "Don't be silly, this doesn't serve me. I hate it."

I know you hate it, but it provides cover for you from some outcome you fear, or you wouldn't do it.

Take my client, Jillian. She had great ideas, a great plan to get her coaching work out to many clients and had hired an expensive web designer. Every week when we checked in, she'd tell me "Not yet" on launching her website. The excuses started to pile up. After my asking repeatedly: "What is the upside, how does this serve you?" she eventually broke down and admitted that she was afraid she would go through all the effort to launch her beautiful new shiny website, and nobody would visit it or choose her services. She was afraid she'd be viewed as "a failure" and have wasted all the time and effort she put into it.

"What happened to your vision of helping so many people?" I asked her.

"I got derailed by my fear."

Once she identified she was procrastinating to avoid her fear of failing, she could address this fear and use EFT to collapse the need to procrastinate. She revisited her vision and connected to the joy she felt whenever she helped other people, launched her website, and started attracting clients.

Fear of Success

Everyone is afraid of change. We want to change but we don't want anything to be different. When you become more successful, there is no doubt that you will start to rock the boat of others around you. It's inevitable.

> ### *You're going to need to neutralize*
> ### *your reaction to their reactions,*
> ### *because they aren't going to change.*

Helping people who fear success has been a big part of my practice. Clients contact me because they know they are blocking their forward movement and feel sick and tired of the cycle. They're frustrated, irritated, and confused as to why they have such a strong desire to change, yet have an equally stubborn or deep part of themselves that is determined to get in their own way.

- If you start shining, is it going to upset someone?
- Will your promotion make someone jealous?
- Will your weight loss make someone envious and mean?
- Will your new relationship annoy your single friends?

When you've done solid emotional work on yourself, you will change for the better, and yes, people might get upset. Not all people, but likely someone close to you who hasn't been able to take the necessary steps for their own success will see that you've moved to the next level. They won't like it; *and more importantly, they'll let you know that.*

Jed wanted to be promoted in his Wall Street firm, but he knew there would be consequences. He was younger than a group of guys who had started two years before him, but he had become a bit of a favorite with the top bosses. He already took too much heat from his colleagues, and was definitely showing his conflict about being promoted by avoiding finishing his work on time.

"I've always wanted this job and to be playing at the next level. And I know I can do it if I'm given the chance."

So, of course I asked him: "What would be the downside of being promoted?"

"The other guys will give me so much crap; it won't be worth it. They already taunt me for being the favorite and suggest that my family connections got me this position."

We talked about how there was no way to change the behavior of others, and that his only way forward was to neutralize his fear of their jealousy. He was very uneasy about pursuing this professional path, but admitted that sabotaging his chances of the promotion by coming in late and not handing in a special project by the deadline was counterproductive.

Yes, self-sabotaging behavior looks counterproductive at the time, but remember, in your mind, it's for a good reason – some part of you is more afraid of succeeding than staying where you are. After using EFT to work on these fears about his colleagues being envious, jealous, and mean because of his professional advancement, Jed got back on track. He started behaving the way he wanted to; the way that would inevitably land him the promotion he had worked so hard for at the firm.

Perfectionism

Perfectionism plagues many people who grew up in a family where there was emotional dysfunction. To a small child, the message is to "do it better" and as a result, they will grow up striving to do better everywhere in their life. It's an insatiable need. Good enough is never good enough. The A- is treated like a national tragedy. Not being perfect on the outside to hide the imperfections going on inside the home was considered dangerous and potentially exposing for the family.

Perfectionism will smother any project or goal very quickly. If your written work has to be perfect, you'll spend hours and days crafting each sentence. This will lead to procrastination or being late when meeting deadlines. Needing to be perfect comes from a deep-seated fear and belief that you are flawed. Everyone thinks they are flawed in certain ways, but when it moves into troubling perfectionistic behavior, then it runs your behavior and ruins your goals. And not only do you feel flawed, you are also convinced that if you're perfect, you'll finally get "their" approval.

Callie said her boss had reprimanded her for being late on numerous projects. She feared it was going to get her put on probation or, worse, fired. She had been warned and had made a commitment to change her behavior and try harder. What Callie didn't see was that she was so compulsive about her perfectionistic behavior that it was impossible for her to change until she committed to doing some deeper emotional work. The impossibly high standards were getting in her way.

I asked her: "What is the downside of handing in your proposals on time?" Immediately she said, "If it's not perfect, I'll get into trouble."

"How old do you feel when you tell me that?"

"Honestly, about eight years old."

This made sense to me, because I know from my own life that perfectionism does not have its roots in adulthood. Callie tapped into a memory she had tried to forget but one that was driving her behavior. Her mother had a temper, so she felt she had to tiptoe around her all the time. This was exhausting, but she thought it would help her avoid her mother's anger. The only remedy in her eight-year-old mind was to do the household tasks perfectly. She was in charge of dusting, mopping, vacuuming, and cleaning out the kitty litter every day. When Callie did well with her chores, her mother would say "perfect" and her temper would temporarily subside. So Callie thought this was the formula – be perfect, do the tasks flawlessly, and mother calms down.

Of course, every once in a while, her mother's temper flared up anyway, confusing her belief that her airtight "pattern" would work. It left her feeling helpless and scrambling to be even more perfect in new ways.

Before Callie had found this formula for calming her mother down, she suffered from her mother's criticism about everything. One time her mother even said: "Nothing is right about you..." She criticized her choice of outfits, her hair, her homework, her messy room, how she spoke; nothing was good enough in her eyes.

Eventually, as her mother sank into a deeper and untreated depression, Callie thought cleaning the house to perfection, straightening her room, and vacuuming all the carpeting was the way to make her mother feel better and become less depressed. The vacuum marks in the carpets had to be all lined up, silverware drawer perfect, table set by 5:00 pm. Doing enough and getting it right gnawed at her daily.

Fast forward to her adult job. She hadn't discovered a formula for her boss. She was still under the assumption that if she handed in perfect proposals, she would get his approval. She neglected the necessary part about being on time.

Asking Callie the right questions helped her uncover how deeply flawed she felt, and that only a perfect performance could rescue her. With hard work and persistence using EFT, Callie was able to see her mother's projections, insecurities, and mental health issues for what they were and started taking responsibility for her own work in a healthy adult way.

People Pleasing

People pleasing is a very common self-sabotaging behavior. It means you put other people's needs ahead of yours; you value them over valuing yourself. It comes from feeling inadequate as you are, so you hope that pleasing others and putting their needs first will give you more self-esteem, and hopefully, other people's approval. The two primary forms of people pleasing show up as (1) you don't ask for help because you don't want others to think you need anything, and (2) you can't say no to anyone.

Don't Ask for Help

Asking for help can be very uncomfortable. If you are a people pleaser, asking for help is evidence that you aren't doing enough. In my family, you weren't supposed to ask for help, you were supposed to figure it all out on your own. More importantly, you weren't supposed to let anyone know that any event or stressor inside the family had caused a need for help and support from outside. I learned to please others by figuring it all out on my own, so I didn't have to ask for any help and risk either being a burden or airing our family's dirty laundry.

But asking for help can make the difference between solid mental health and spiraling dysfunction. Or between getting by on your paycheck and getting a better job that suits your skill level and pays for more than just the necessities of rent and food.

Amanda said she had been a "B+ student" at school but could have been an A student if she had asked for help more often. She recognized that she didn't ask for enough help in her adult life either. She said she was driven to find the answers to challenging work questions by herself. When I asked her what the downside would be of asking for help, she admitted that it would "reveal" her weaknesses.

"What weaknesses?"

"That I don't know it all…"

"And how could you know it all?"

"I don't know, but I just know I'm supposed to."

As a result, she took longer than her colleagues to complete work projects and ended up delivering what was due just minutes before the deadline. She didn't like how it felt, *but she preferred feeling this type of stress than the feared consequences of asking for help.*

We used EFT to work on her shame and embarrassment about asking for help and uncovered where it came from in her family of origin.

Her family was poor compared to the other families with kids she went to school with in the neighborhood. Her parents were ashamed, and equally angry about it, but made it clear that their kids shouldn't ask for help. They didn't want anyone to think they needed "charity." Amanda admitted that this behavior of never asking for help was emotionally expensive to her. She was starting to feel exhausted, burned out, and resentful about being overworked and underappreciated.

I suggested that she start small – ask for directions; ask for a favor from a friend or neighbor once in a while. This was awkward and painful for her, until she started to neutralize her shame with EFT and realize that most people around her were willing to ask for some kind of help, some of the time. Once she decided which areas of work were reasonable to ask for help in, she started recognizing a new template of what was acceptable. After working smarter, not harder, she developed a good balance between her independence and getting colleagues or friends to help her. She also started sleeping well again and enjoyed more of her life. What was important for Amanda was being asked the upside/downside questions so she could recognize why she was trying to protect herself. When using EFT, she focused on her fear of what other people would think of her if she asked for help.

Don't Say No

It took me a long time to figure out how to say no without all the guilt attached. Shouldn't I say yes to every favor that was asked of me? Shouldn't I be a good neighbor? Haven't I been given more than most people? The problem with being allergic to saying no to others is that you then rarely say yes to yourself. Not saying no when you need to will eat away at your sense of self, your balance, and your peace of mind. Now that's expensive.

Another client, Daisy, came to me to quit smoking. I asked her what the upside was of smoking and she answered immediately:

"It's the only time the kids will leave me alone. They know it's mommy time when I sit on the front porch and smoke like a chimney. I don't have to tell them no because they just know."

"Any other reasons?"

"Yes, it calms me down because it's quiet out there and I can think straight."

We worked together with EFT on the cravings, and the physical pleasure she would miss if she could no longer open the pack, handle a lighter, and blow smoke rings. But I knew that wouldn't be enough. She was going to have to learn how to say no and set boundaries with her kids, get additional childcare, and ask her husband to help out more if she wanted to remain a non-smoker. It was all true – smoking calmed her nerves and sent a message to the kids that they couldn't bother mommy while she was smoking because it was her space for quiet time. But she needed to find new ways to take care of herself and say no to their requests during certain times of the day. She used tapping to handle the cravings and withdrawal symptoms, neutralized her guilt, and became a non-smoker with the new skill of saying no and asking for what she needed. She said she had never been asked the *upside* question before, and that it made all the difference for her success.

Addictions

While there are as many kinds of addicts as there are substances and compulsive behaviors, there are some obvious hallmarks of addictive behavior. Go back to identifying the *point* of using whatever substance you're using. The point is to numb and shield yourself from the challenging emotions that you need to address. Numbing once in a while is understandable – a little Netflix binge won't hurt much if it's occasional. But if anyone tells you they only do cocaine recreationally, I recommend running for the hills. Recreational drug use eventually reaches a tipping point.

It's simple to spell out the criteria for addiction. For instance, the definition of addiction includes the following challenges:

- You get into trouble with the law (DWI, fender bender, altercation in a public place, etc.) as a result of your substance use, and *yet you keep using.*
- Your health suffers as a result of using substances (weight gain, blood pressure issues, nutrition problems, liver problems) and *yet you continue to harm yourself.*
- You swear off your addiction (give up drinking for a month, give up drinking for lent) and *yet you can't quite make it to your deadline.*
- Other people in your life confront you about your problem, and *yet you deny it's "that bad" and continue anyway.*

Look at the substances or behaviors you might be using addictively and examine which ones are causing a problem with your friends, family, or your health. Drinking a glass of wine with dinner isn't a problem if you can handle it and it doesn't turn into three drinks when you still have to put the kids to bed.

Overeating occasionally won't cause your clothes to be too tight, but extra weight is implicated in all the major health risks – heart disease, breast cancer, blood pressure, cholesterol. And think about why you would need to keep eating after your stomach is full. That would be like filling up your gas tank and then filling up your back seat and trunk with gas after the tank is full. You don't need more fuel.

Addictions will hurt you and everyone close to you. You can examine the behavior, but you'll get much further if you look at the feelings and beliefs underneath your drive to use the substances. The *downside* to giving up your substances is that you will have to confront and feel your grief, pain, resentment, or traumas. The *upside* to continuing using your substances is understandable – you won't have to feel anything painful from your childhood or your recent past, but the damage you'll be doing will be considerable.

When I asked Michael, "What is the upside of continuing to drink when you keep getting in so much trouble as a result?"

Michael said, "Now I get it – this is why I drank."

"What do you mean?" I asked.

"I can't stand the tension and the turmoil in my head."

Michael was only three months sober, but his feelings about his past had started to catch up with him. He was in AA, counseling, and was trying very hard to stay sober. When I asked him the downside of giving up his drinking, he said, "If I have to remember all my traumas and feelings, I'll just relapse again." Once he realized why he had been using alcohol, it helped make sense of his behavior, and he understood why stopping on his own had been fruitless; he had repeatedly relapsed because his emotions had been too intense to handle without his usual drinking. Michael needed an extra tool like EFT to help with his cravings, his fear, his emotional pain, and his grief. He kept up with the treatment and stayed sober. He stayed in touch over the years, kept up through my newsletter and made occasional referrals. I recently got an email from him announcing he had 30 years of sobriety.

Clutter

If you're included in the 54% of Americans who struggle with clutter, you'll know this is a complicated but effective way to sabotage your success. You also know on a deeper level that *it's not about your stuff*. It never is. It's about your emotional attachment to what you think your stuff represents. While Marie Kondo has a clearing clutter method of throwing an item out if it doesn't "spark joy," this unfortunately doesn't work for millions of people who couldn't care less if the item they're clinging to sparks joy or not. The items represent a different kind of survival and meet a much deeper emotional need. Someone with a clutter problem needs to answer the main questions – the upside of keeping it and the downside of letting it go – and work on the emotional attachment to their stuff that represents feelings, people, beliefs, and safety.

Beth said she was fed up with her clutter. It was getting in the way of everything – of moving forward, of having friends over to visit, of keeping herself physically safe from having an accident in her living room.

I asked Beth my favorite question: "What is the upside of keeping all your clutter?" She immediately admitted that it protected her and made her feel safe.

"Safe from what?"

"Safe from feeling exposed, small, and lonely."

Her clutter acted as a barrier between her and life, relationships, interactions with others, and from feeling her deep loneliness from her childhood. She actually felt safer when surrounded by boxes of books, paperwork, junk, and knick-knacks. "Space scares me. It means someone can get to me, hurt me, even see the real me."

Beth was able to identify how the terrible boundaries in her extended family made her feel unprotected. Her siblings and cousins felt they could have access to anything that was hers – toys, dolls, clothes, even her favorite coloring pens. She could remember the anxiety she felt when someone would come in her room and "touch" all her stuff. They would inevitably take something, break it, or not return it, and something beloved like a stuffed animal would end up on the kitchen floor or in the dog's water bowl after a game of monkey in the middle.

She said having all her stuff nearby made her feel in control, as if nobody could take anything anymore. But she was feeling increasingly trapped by the need to keep all her belongings close. Paperwork was never filed, books were stacked in massive piles and starting to fall over, her purse didn't zip shut anymore, and she could barely maneuver the kitchen.

"What is the downside of getting rid of the extensive paperwork, books, and stuff?" I asked.

"I'd feel exposed and unsafe…"

"And the upside again of keeping the clutter so close?"

"They can't take what's mine."

With the support of talking and tapping, Beth bravely examined the incidents from childhood with her older siblings and cousins and felt rage, resentment, and helplessness. She connected the dots and was able to make decisions about her piles of clutter, realizing they didn't actually keep her safe. She realized that she could keep herself safe now in new and healthier ways. Space no longer felt scary to her.

Relationship Drama

Relationship drama can show up in the form of rebellion, picking a fight, or choosing unavailable partners.

Return to the upside/downside questions: What is the upside of picking a fight? What is the downside of feeling calm and centered in this relationship?

Maria had a long history of trauma connected to caretakers leaving her, or in her father's case, dying. Her mother had an endless revolving door of new boyfriends who were often better at taking care of her than her mother was. But inevitably they got fed up with her mother's drug use and left them both. Maria admitted that she had no problem starting a relationship, but they all had a shelf life of about six months. Maria's relationships were often tumultuous, with Maria picking fights whenever she felt the stress of emotional closeness.

"What is the upside of starting a fight?" I asked.

"I create distance and resentment, and hopefully they'll break up with me."

I reminded her, "You have often expressed the desire to be in a long-term relationship."

"I thought I did, but I can't take it after a while."

Maria chose to dig deep and do a considerable amount of emotional work and healing relating to the people who had left her in her life. The amount of grief that came up while using EFT shocked her. She thought she had "moved on" but found out the old losses were as present as ever. She understood why picking a fight was a quick way to jumpstart the beginning of the end of her relationships. She also recognized why she chose unavailable men. She used EFT to release her feelings of grief, memories of being hurt, and her conviction that she would be hurt again in the future.

What led to her picking a fight was the anxiety she felt about feeling closer and more comfortable in her relationships. This is what surprised her boyfriends so much. They thought the relationship was going really well. And it usually was, but that just happened to be the trigger for Maria to feel the "need" to pick a fight and push them away. With time, and understanding the upside of why she needed to create such drama, Maria could tolerate more and more emotional intimacy and stopped sabotaging her relationships.

Self-Care Neglect

Are you guilty of neglecting your self-care, or putting yourself last on your list? This might be the most expensive sabotaging behavior of all. Sure, when I was young, I could get away with skipping exercise, eating crappy food, and ignoring healthy habits that would build emotional balance and physical health. But eventually, it caught up with me, and I promise it will catch up with you. My late nights, extroversion, and ignorance about health issues took their toll and set me up for some physical illnesses that were very expensive. In addition, I had no idea that earlier traumas had been stored in my nervous system, waiting to spill over into my physiology. And I'm not alone.

Take Holly, an athlete, a superstar at work, and a mom of two boys under the age of ten. Neglecting her self-care was starting to catch up with her when she contacted me. I asked Holly what was bothering her.

"I'm utterly depleted and exhausted, and I always feel as if I'm on the verge of getting sick. The kids are exhausting, my husband doesn't help enough, and I feel like I'm reaching my limit."

Holly was starting to show some mysterious physical symptoms. Her entire body ached, her muscles hurt even when she didn't exercise, she had headaches, brain fog, and generally felt unwell much of the time. She had some tentative diagnoses – fibromyalgia, chronic fatigue, maybe a form of Lyme – but any treatments she was given proved useless and she was starting to feel hopeless on top of being deeply exhausted. She said, "I'm bone-tired all the time and nothing helps, even when I get a good night's sleep – which is rare these days."

There was no doubt that her kids were a handful and that her husband could have been supporting her more, but the truth was, Holly's life was all about helping others, and putting her needs on the back burner. Before asking her the upside/downside questions, I asked her about her self-care practices. "What self-care? I don't have time for self-care. I can't afford the time," she replied.

I started by giving her short routines, nothing that would feel overwhelming to her already crammed schedule. "Will that be enough? Will it even make a dent?" I assured her that starting on the bunny slope was a good idea for her. I asked her to meditate five minutes a day, do EFT five minutes a day, and journal five minutes a day. In the beginning, it was hard for her to commit to these simple practices, but once she did, she felt the benefits during her first week. She used EFT on her exhaustion, her fear of slowing down, and her belief that she wasn't important enough to have self-care routines.

Once she had taken these initial steps, I asked her about the upside of running around helping everyone else and ignoring her own self-care. She said, "There's no upside, it's just what I was taught." Eventually, Holly admitted that her *need to be needed* is what crowded out everything else. So being the neighborhood super mom, the family go-to person, and the most loyal friend made her feel important. She had never felt she was "adequate enough" and thought being strong for everyone else was the answer to improving her self-esteem. I used EFT with her on her belief that she wasn't worthy unless she was being needed around the clock.

I, too, neglected my self-care for years, and it was beyond costly to my emotional and physical well-being. While I needed to do some deep digging in therapy, I also needed to craft self-care practices that I was willing to follow. EFT was the game changer as it restored my exhausted nervous system back to balance. With this balance in place, I could start with the basic building blocks of getting a good night's sleep and taking time to replenish my energy.

Another part of self-care is listening to your intuition. Have you been ignoring your intuition? If so, for how long? This is an extremely expensive part of self-care neglect. If you're like most people, you probably learned to shut down your intuition at an early age.

It is very costly emotionally, physically, financially, and spiritually to ignore your intuition. If you don't *follow your yes*, then how are you going to live the life you were meant to live? But what if you can't even find your "yes" much less follow it?

After doing extensive emotional healing with therapy and EFT around addictive family patterns, broken relationships, and choosing the wrong career, my intuition started to come back "online." The annoying noise and chatter that seemed to be on high volume in my head started to recede. I started hearing what my heart was trying to tell me, instead of just being connected to my left-brained logic. I started to feel what was *right* for me, no matter what my concerns were about other people's reactions. I started *knowing* what the next right step was for me personally and professionally. It wasn't without fear, but I started to make changes in my life and moved towards my purpose. It wasn't without hardship and conflict. But when you know, you know. What is hard for me to say out loud is that my intuition came back online so much, that I started to download "additional" information. In every workshop I've ever taught, all around the world, a participant or colleague would tell me that I am "channeling" information when

I'm on stage. This means even more information is coming to me in addition to tuning in to my basic intuition. I'm looking at the client, hearing their responses, and then I just "download" more information that I have no way of knowing. I used to deny it, but now I can't miss it. It doesn't mean your dead grandmother is talking to me. It just means I am allowing extra information to come through which allows me to help my clients even more.

The cost of not following my intuition? I once paid the very high price of signing a poorly thought-out contract while on an airplane. I had just presented a workshop outside of Paris for 300 people and had spent three days clearing participants' traumas. I came back to the hotel after the conference with a miserable head cold, and I felt disconnected to my deep "yes" about what was good for me. I was uncentered, had this miserable cold, but I signed the contract anyway. It cost me $20,000. They did a terrible job and did not deliver "as advertised." That was my fault – I knew something was off, but I ignored the "hits" I was getting that this wasn't a good match. I moved ahead anyway. Very expensive.

Tuning into your intuition is challenging with so much distracting noise around us. Getting the best answers for yourself takes time and effort. I call the process of tuning in, getting clear, and trusting your intuition *Finding Your Next Yes*.

Were you taught to hear and respect your intuition, your hunches, and your leanings? Or were you told you were silly, or worse, making things up? In the chapter detailing The Yes Code™ process, I will show you a quick way of starting to practice recognizing your internal yes and no answers.

Scan this QR code or visit www.TheYesCode.com for a video on how to recognize your "yes" and "no" answers.

So now you've read stories from clients who've been asked the upside/downside questions. While you, too, may say there is no upside to your self-sabotaging behavior and that *of course you want to reach your goals,* remember that there is always an upside to the negative behavior, or you wouldn't be doing it. All our behaviors serve a purpose, no matter how frustrating or dysfunctional they seem to us or our loved ones.

Finding out what that purpose is will allow you to start the process of changing your life.

It all boils down to your fears and your beliefs. Think about it: why else would you sabotage yourself if you weren't afraid of the consequences of reaching your goals? Why else would you keep telling people you want to reach your goals and then get distracted by the next shiny object? Fear. Fear of failure; fear of success; fear of rocking the boat; fear of criticism; fear of being abandoned; fear of being found out – the list goes on and on. And if you don't believe you deserve to be successful, you'll sabotage yourself as often as possible.

In this chapter, we examined the definition of self-sabotage and the cost of the top seven self-sabotaging behaviors. I offered you prompts and hints on how to find your own upside to sabotaging behavior and your own downside to reaching your goals. Now it's time for the solution.

Scan this QR code or go to www.TheYesCode.com if you'd like to access a more in-depth description of common fears and limiting beliefs.

PART THREE

THE SOLUTION

CHAPTER 7

THE YES CODE™

W e've talked about the seven most common self-sabotaging behaviors and about my personal history that led me to block my success. We've also examined the extensive and varied costs of not releasing your own self-sabotaging behaviors. Now it's time for the solution.

The Yes Code process is my signature coaching method that provides a structure for getting consistent results eliminating self-sabotaging behaviors. It is a step-by-step process to support you to get from where you are to where you want to go by clarifying your vision, clearing the blocks that are in your way, and finding the next best inspired actions, or what I call *finding your next yes*.

The Yes Code process provides an easier and faster way to reach your goals and get the results you want. Over the years, I've used the following simple three-step process on myself and with my clients and have found it to be efficient, effective, and life-changing.

Step One: Clarify Your Vision: The first step is to clarify your true vision and where you want to go in your life. If you're not clear about where you want to go or what your success will look and feel like to you, you won't know when you've arrived. When I ask clients to clarify their vision, most people start with stating what they don't want.

"I don't want to be in debt anymore."

"I'm tired of crappy relationships."

"I can't stand working at this company one more day."

That's a good start, but to set the stage for transformation, you'll need to identify the positive vision, not just what you don't want. Once your vision starts to take shape – how you want to feel, how your life will look, how you'll know when you get there – you'll be more inspired to make the necessary changes and your chance of getting to your destination increases dramatically. Those three statements above could be translated into the positive version as follows:

"I don't want to be in debt anymore" could turn into: "I'm looking forward to being debt-free so I can feel relaxed about my finances, have extra money in the bank to go out to dinner weekly with friends, and start a grown-up retirement account."

"I'm tired of crappy relationships" could turn into: "I want to be in a healthy, mutually respectful relationship with a partner who shares many of my interests, my values, and my love of the outdoors."

"I can't stand working at this company one more day" could turn into: "I look forward to having a job where I'm valued and appreciated, and where my hours are reasonable for my lifestyle."

While it's common practice to list everything you want to get rid of, you need to know where you want to go, not just what you want to leave behind. If you get in the car and just start driving away from something you don't want, who knows where you'll end up.

Here are more examples of stating your vision in terms of what you don't want versus what you do want your life to look like. Again, it's important to identify the positive vision because it is naturally more inspiring. Instead of saying, "I'm sick and tired of the extra weight," it's more helpful to imagine what you want as a result. For instance, "I want to lose weight so I can have the energy to play with my kids and enjoy taking walks in nature."

If your initial answer to clarifying your vision is, "I don't want to feel anxious anymore…" I would follow up and ask you what you want instead. How do you want to feel now that you are no longer struggling with anxiety? And how will your life change for you once you no longer suffer with anxiety? Will you be sleeping peacefully or enjoying new hobbies now that anxiety is no longer a challenge?

"I'm tired of being exhausted and not taking care of myself…" is a starting place – but why is that important to you? What will change when you start taking care of yourself? What will the benefits be? It's ok to start with the negative version of what you want to get rid of, as long as you eventually get to a version of your vision that is stated in the positive. Instead of saying, "I want to stop being a people pleaser," you could turn it around and say, "I want to have enough confidence to say no when I need to and set healthy boundaries at work and at home. I look forward to having that confidence and peace of mind."

A clear vision is also focused on how you want to feel, what you want your lifestyle to look like, and how you want to show up in your life and in the world. Your vision could include getting a car, a house, or a promotion, but it's important to understand why you want these things. What's the why behind wanting a promotion? How do you think it will make you feel? If you focus only on the "stuff," then you'll feel empty when you finally get it. There's a deeper and more important reason you want what you want, and once you identify that, you will fill out the picture and have more to aim for in your life. Helpful questions to ask when you're starting to clarify your vision are:

What results do I want in my life?

What will my success look like when I get there?

How will I know when I've arrived?

What will realizing my vision of success give me in my life?

It's helpful to add the reasons you want what you want. If your clear vision starts out with, "I want to quit my job because I'm tired of taking orders from my boss," it would be clearer if you said, "I want to start my own business so I can make my own hours and enjoy more of the profits." Then you can continue to explore why you want to start your own business. What will it give you that you don't have now?

Maybe your answer would be "freedom over my schedule" because that is important to you, or maybe having accountability and responsibility would feel satisfying to you.

Suppose you start by saying you're sick and tired of dating unavailable partners. So, what do you want instead? "I want to be in a committed relationship...because being in a committed relationship would give me the stability and peace of mind I'm looking for," or "I'm ready to settle down and start a family."

If you declare: "I want to have the three main rooms of my home cleared of clutter," then it would be important to identify what this looks like, how you'll feel and what it will give you when you get there – a feeling of being unburdened? More joy in your life? The space to entertain friends and family?

Being able to recognize how your success will be reflected to you is also critical. Will you see your success reflected in the amount of free time you have? In your healthier family relationships? Will your bigger bank account allow you to take your family on vacation every year? Or will you notice the changes in your inner emotional world of peace and confidence? Maybe you look forward to sleeping well, reacting less impulsively, and enjoying how you interact with others.

And how will you know when you've arrived? Again, this needs to be measured in specifics. Saying, "I want to feel better" or "I want to feel happy" isn't specific enough. What does happy look like to you, and how will you know when you get there? "I want to be healthy" may sound clear, but it is more engaging to identify the specifics – "I want to have enough energy to finally start an exercise program at my neighborhood gym." A clear vision with as many specifics as possible pulls you towards what you want. When you can see and feel the vision, it will feel fulfilling and satisfying when you get there.

To help you flesh out the specifics of a positive vision, ask yourself these questions:

1. What does my success feel like to me?

2. What emotions will I feel when I am successful?
3. How will I recognize it when I get there?
4. What will be different in my life when I have succeeded in realizing my vision?
5. How will I measure it? By my lifestyle changes, or my level of satisfaction and happiness? (For example: Maybe you can measure your decreasing tendency to people please because you've started to set boundaries at work and now you go home in time to have dinner with your family every night.)

Now that you have described a clear vision about how you want your life to look and feel once you've achieved the results you've detailed, it's time to identify the specific fears, beliefs, and memories that are blocking you from getting the results you want. This is the second part of Step One of The Yes Code.

Remember, you're only using self-sabotaging behavior as a way to keep you safe. So, if you say you want to be successful in business, but you're afraid to stand out, you will get in your own way to protect yourself.

Ask yourself what self-sabotaging behaviors are getting in the way of your results. Check the list of the seven most common self-sabotaging behaviors and identify which ones are blocking you from moving forward and living your vision.

1. **Procrastination**
2. **Perfectionism**
3. **People Pleasing**
4. **Addictions**
5. **Clutter**
6. **Relationship Drama**
7. **Self-Care Neglect**

For instance, maybe your procrastination is getting in the way of you being appreciated and noticed at work. If you are constantly missing deadlines, you won't be able to stand out and get the recognition you want.

Maybe you've noticed that your perfectionism keeps slowing you down. Your impossibly high standards make you check and recheck your emails so you never actually send the messages that would allow you to get to the next level in your business.

If saying no is too painful for you, you'll notice that your people-pleasing tendencies are leaving you exhausted and unable to find the time to take care of yourself.

It's also important to examine your theory about why you haven't achieved your vision yet. Do you blame the economy, your colleagues, or your partner for holding you back? Do you think this happens to everyone? Or just people in your family?

Since we know that self-sabotaging behavior is always protecting you from an outcome or consequence you fear, asking this next set of particular questions will get you focused on what behavior is getting in your way. Now we can move to the real heart of the matter – what you are specifically trying to avoid or protect yourself from by using these behaviors.

As we've explored in Chapter 5, there are two categories of questions to understand on a deeper level why you sabotage yourself: (1) Discovering the upside of staying the way you are, and (2) Uncovering the downside of reaching your goal or realizing your vision. You've already identified what behaviors are holding you back. With these two deeper questions, you will find out *why* you are using these self-sabotaging behaviors to hold yourself back.

Question One: *What is the upside of sabotaging yourself and staying stuck?*

1. What does your self-sabotaging behavior protect you from? (Procrastination might protect me from being visible.)

2. How might sabotaging behavior be keeping you safe? (I believe being a perfectionist keeps me safe from criticism.)

3. How does it serve you to keep getting in your own way? (Blocking my progress by creating relationship drama keeps me from being hurt.)

4. If you move forward, what reactions are you afraid of from other people? This might bring up a memory of a past event when someone else's reaction was hurtful or upsetting to you. (If I move forward, someone might try to attack me for my success.)

Question Two: *What is the downside of reaching your goal or vision?*

1. What might you be afraid of if you actually reached your goal? (Others might be jealous if I get my book published.)

2. How would reaching your goal rock the boat in your family or at work? (If I successfully lose the weight, my overweight cousin might feel threatened.)

3. Is playing small helpful in some way? (Being visible has always come with negative attention in my family.)

4. In what ways does standing out and shining scare you? This may bring up a memory of a past event. (The last time I stood out, something bad happened.)

When you have answers to these questions, you will understand the fears and beliefs that are fueling your self-sabotaging behaviors and keeping you stuck. If you don't feel safe in social situations, you might crowd your life with clutter to protect you from too much social contact. If you are afraid that reaching your goal will upset one of your siblings, you will find ways to block yourself from succeeding. If you don't believe you have what it takes to be successful, you'll fulfill this belief with your behavior.

Once we've identified the fears and beliefs (and the memories attached to them) that are keeping you from realizing your vision, we can move on to Step Two of The Yes Code. You will use the fears, beliefs, and memories that you identified in Step One to create EFT sequences to clear the need to protect yourself. I will teach you how to use EFT specifically on these fears, beliefs, and memories in the next chapter.

Step Two: Clear Your Blocks: In this next step of The Yes Code, you will use EFT to release the emotional blocks, limiting beliefs, and any memories associated with them identified in Step One that are in the way of reaching your goals. This is where the rubber meets the road, so to speak, and we get to pull the weeds that have been in your garden. Insight and awareness are fascinating but don't always lead to change. Clearing the fears and beliefs out of your nervous system and your consciousness is where the magic happens and will create the transformation you are looking for in your life.

In Chapters 9 through 15, I provide 40 tapping scripts targeting the fears, beliefs, and memories that are holding you back. I also include an additional four scripts in Chapter 16, Bonus Tapping Scripts.

Scan this QR code to visit The Yes Code™ portal at www.TheYesCode.com for video samples of EFT exercises.

Examples of fears or other emotions I will help you clear with EFT in order to move forward include:

1. I'm afraid of being visible.
2. I'm afraid of shining.
3. I'm afraid of success.
4. I'm afraid of failure.
5. I'm afraid of being judged and criticized.

6. I'm afraid to rock the boat.
7. I'm afraid of their jealousy.
8. I feel guilty saying no.
9. I'm afraid to ask for help.

You will also neutralize the limiting beliefs that keep you stuck in a pattern of self-sabotage. Common limiting beliefs that hold you back and trigger your self-sabotaging behavior include:

1. I believe I have to struggle.
2. I'm convinced I have to play small.
3. I believe I'm not worthy of success.
4. I'm convinced everyone will leave me.
5. I believe life has to be hard.
6. I believe in scarcity and lack.
7. I believe I don't have what it takes to succeed.
8. I'm convinced it's too late for me.

After you clear the fears and beliefs (and memories associated with them) that have been triggering your self-sabotaging behavior, you'll be ready for Step Three – *Find Your Next Yes* – so you can make a plan for your next inspired actions.

As you work through the EFT sequences, you may need additional practices to support you. I have found that making time for meditation, gratitude exercises and movement practices are deeply supportive while you're releasing the fears and beliefs that are holding you back. I provide details and suggestions for these additional healing tools in Chapter 17.

Step Three: Find Your Next Yes: After you've cleared your blocks in Step Two, we move on to Step Three where I will help you *find your next yes* by learning what an internal "yes" or "no" feels like to you so you can then act upon it. Once you know what feels right as your next step, you either make a choice to take that step, or you continue with tapping exercises to release any remaining fears or beliefs.

Do you know what your "yes" and "no" answers feel like to you?

Here's a quick way to tune into your "yes" and your "no."

Think of a color you absolutely love and picture a piece of clothing, book, or item in your home you have in that color. Focus on it and notice how you feel in your body. Peaceful? Happy? Settled? Calm? This would represent a feeling of "yes" for you. Now contrast that with thinking about a color you don't like and would never choose to wear, and notice how you feel when you tune into that. The response you get in your body would represent a "no" for you.

Now think of a person who you've had a conflict with recently, someone you don't trust, or with whom you've been disagreeing recently. Notice how you feel. Distracted? Upset? Irritated? This would represent a "no" feeling for you. Now think of someone in your life who can do no wrong in your eyes – maybe start with a pet, a niece or nephew – someone with whom you don't have any complicated inter-actions. And notice how you feel. Calm? Peaceful? Delighted? That feeling in your body would represent a "yes" for you.

Once you get accustomed to recognizing your internal yes and no answers, you'll be able to tune in to decisions you need to make and recognize your intuitive hits. You won't be making decisions for other people because of any fears you have about their reactions. Your intuition will come back online, and you will learn how to make the right decisions for yourself.

Sometimes your next yes is a good idea but overwhelms you. For instance, maybe you would say, "I'm finally ready to start an exercise program." If it overwhelms you, then you might want to break it down into the next yes step for today or this week. Maybe this means you research exercise programs, or you buy a new pair of walking shoes. If you know it's time to move on from your marriage, your next yes might be to set up a couples counseling session to discuss your needs and a plan for how to talk to the kids. In other words, calling the divorce lawyer isn't always the next best step.

Your next yes might also be as simple as downloading a meditation app or putting aside 10 minutes for your tapping exercises to continue clearing the fear you have about being visible. Once you get clear on what your next yes feels like to you, make a plan for when you're going to do it.

If it's clear that you need to have a conversation with your boss, is your next yes setting up the meeting, or is it practicing what you need to say during the meeting with a trusted colleague?

If you want to clean the clutter in your office, is the next yes buying organizing folders, or putting aside an hour each day to go through old paperwork? Picture doing it, and notice if there is any remaining resistance or "yes, but" attached to moving forward. And if there is, you can return to Step One and ask yourself the upside/downside questions to identify what fears or beliefs might still be in the way.

Important questions to consider are:

1. What feels like the next best step to take now?
2. If it's too big, what is a smaller step you could take instead?
3. Does it feel easy to imagine taking it?
4. Does it feel as if it's coming from motivation or inspiration?
5. Does it feel like a true "yes" for you? Or is it for someone else?
6. Can you easily imagine taking this next step?
7. Do you still feel afraid of moving forward?

If you feel comfortable, make a plan, and set a time and date for taking your next yes step to move forward. Write it down in your calendar or tell a friend, "I'm going to sign up for an online course to move my business forward."

If additional emotional blocks surface, go back and use the techniques in Step Two to release the fears and beliefs that are holding you back from finding your next yes.

Now it's time to take a deep dive into Step Two of The Yes Code and learn how to use EFT or tapping to remove your fears and beliefs that are fueling your sabotaging behavior.

CHAPTER 8

ALL ABOUT EFT ("TAPPING")

Now for the tool that changed my life and has changed the lives of thousands of people worldwide since it was created in the 1980's – the tool of Emotional Freedom Techniques (EFT) or what many people simply refer to as "tapping."

I have been a psychotherapist for 33 years, applying EFT, or tapping, for 25 of those years on myself and my clients. In my personal and professional experience, no other tool or "emotional technology" has ever come close to getting the results that EFT has for countless challenges from stress relief to migraines, and from phobias to abundance issues. In this book, we're going to focus on the following challenges that relate to self-sabotaging behavior:

- Fears
- Anxiety
- Guilt
- Abandonment
- Stress relief
- Relationship conflict

- Blocks to success
- Limiting beliefs
- Cravings
- Weight loss
- Addictions
- Upsetting memories

This one simple technique – EFT – can be used for all the fears, beliefs, past events, and memories that are causing you to sabotage yourself and block you from moving forward. Whether you are afraid of being hurt again or you are convinced you don't have what it takes, whether you were abandoned by loved ones or feel guilty saying no, EFT will target your automatic emotional reactions and release the stress response in your brain that surfaces when you tune into one of these feelings, beliefs, or memories of a past event.

The original method of tapping on acupuncture points was called Thought Field Therapy, and was created by a psychologist in California, Dr. Roger Callahan. Dr. Callahan found that by connecting to a client's acupuncture points through tapping with your fingertips, the brain would quiet down the fight or flight response (get "rewired") that was triggered when asking a client about a topic that was distressing. The usual anxious response would go away.

Then Gary Craig, a Stanford trained engineer and personal performance coach in California, simplified the complex "algorithms" of Dr. Callahan's original tapping prescriptions, and named his version of the tapping procedure, Emotional Freedom Techniques, or EFT. Most tapping practitioners have been using this simplified version of tapping since the 1990s.

What Is EFT or Tapping

So, what exactly is this technique? EFT is essentially a stress management tool. It has defined steps and a basic algorithm, originally called a recipe, where the clinician or the client uses their fingertips to tap on specific points on the face and body that correspond with traditional acupuncture points (acupoints) while repeating statements about the identified problem or distress. The location of the designated acupuncture points can be seen in the chart on the following page.

In EFT, a simple, unified algorithm is used no matter what you are focused on changing. If you want to change a feeling or belief, you're going to need to "call it up" in your mind first before tapping on these acupoints to relieve it. Similar to editing a word document, you'll need to open the file in order to make changes.

EFT includes identifying a problem, measuring the distress you feel connected to tuning into this problem, and then tapping on the acupoints to relieve the distress. Tuning into the problem activates your stress response in relation to the problem you have identified. This means the feelings and beliefs are now "available" to be "edited" by tapping on the acupoints.

Tuning into your distress activates your amygdala in your brain – the part of your brain we refer to as your "stress center" or your "smoke alarm." If the amygdala senses danger of any kind, it starts the alarm process and triggers your fight, flight or freeze response. It can totally hijack you when any stimulus outside of you reminds you of a past danger that is recorded inside of you. Tapping with your fingertips on the acupoints calms the physiological response in your body that is triggered by recalling a painful memory in the past – maybe a memory associated with standing out or shining – or by thinking of saying no to someone in the future. Tapping sends calming signals to the amygdala and rewires the responses you have traditionally experienced to your personal triggers. EFT also lowers cortisol, the primary stress hormone. All these effects take the emotional charge out of the topic you have chosen to release.

After decades of anecdotal success stories, some very dedicated clinicians and researchers have been tirelessly collecting data and completing studies that proved this method's effectiveness for fears,

Tapping Points

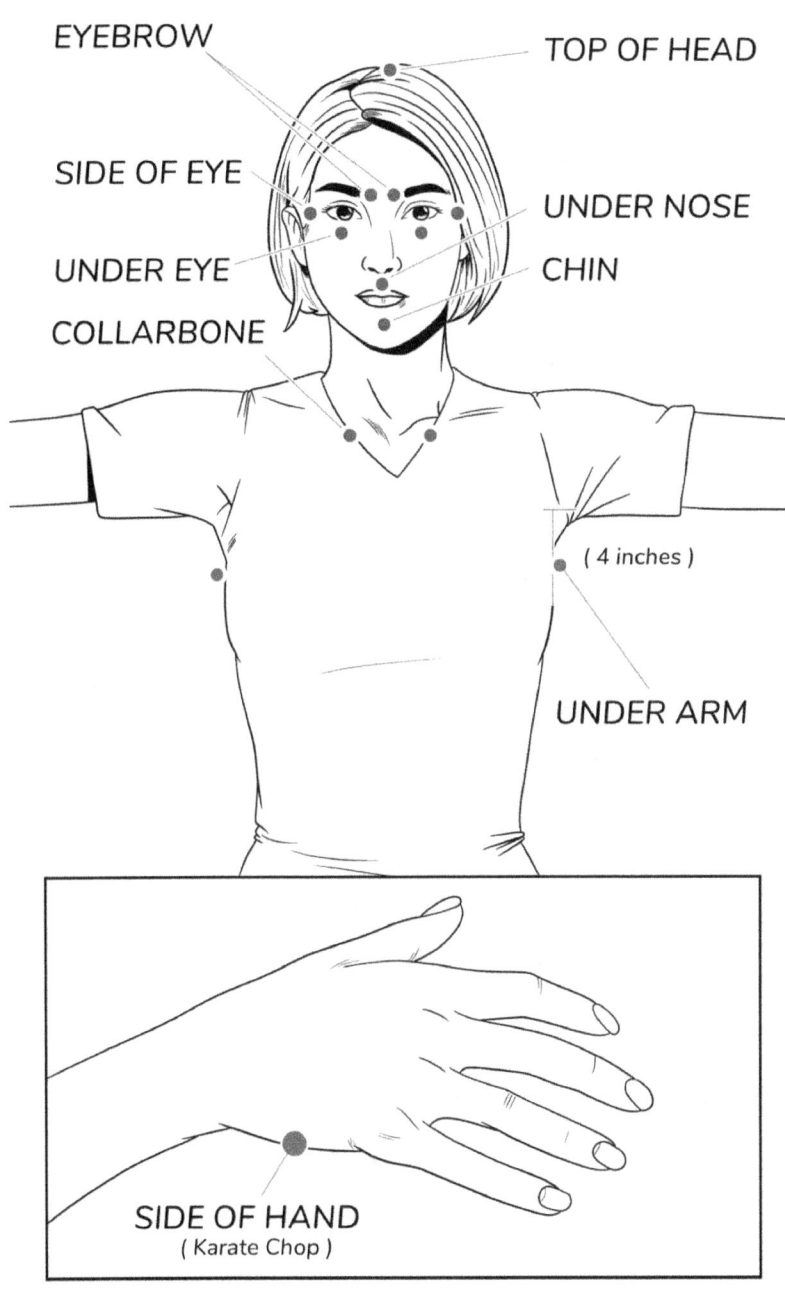

EYEBROW

TOP OF HEAD

SIDE OF EYE

UNDER NOSE

UNDER EYE

CHIN

COLLARBONE

(4 inches)

UNDER ARM

SIDE OF HAND
(Karate Chop)

Carol Look, LLC www.carollook.com | ask@carollook.com

cravings, and PTSD. Based on before and after responses, blood tests, saliva samples, and stress markers such as cortisol, the body of research studies has grown considerably. The research has changed the field and allowed Clinical EFT and tapping to become more widespread and accepted as a viable tool for clinicians and lay people for stress relief, anxiety, trauma treatment, weight loss and more.

Why and How It Works

The simple explanation is that combining tapping on the acupoints with focusing on the distress the person is feeling calms down the stress response – your fight or flight reaction – in your brain. Tapping on acupoints releases the emotional charge you normally experience when recalling a distressing event or thinking about a challenge in your future. For example, if you were afraid of speaking on stage, after doing a few rounds of tapping, the fear usually diminishes quickly and permanently. The rewiring in the brain happens quite quickly with skillfully-applied tapping rounds. Different practitioners refer to what occurs during this process of calming down our distress in a variety of ways – rewiring, reprogramming, reintegrating, resolving, or refocusing.

> *Stimulating acupuncture points (acupoints) by tapping on them while activating pertinent thoughts and feelings puts you at the keyboard as you reprogram the neural pathways that impact the quality of your life.*
>
> **David Feinstein and Donna Eden, *Tapping*[6]**

That's how simple an EFT or tapping session is – bring up a stressor, tap on acupoints, and release the charge associated with the stressor. We are literally reprogramming the brain and nervous system.

After many years of debate about how much of the success was attributable to the placebo effect, whether the clinician's personality mattered, and how ready the client was, it has been shown through multiple research studies including fMRI imaging, that tapping on the acupoints is the "curative agent" in the treatment.[7,8] For those of you interested in a deeper dive into the mechanism of how EFT works and the research behind this technique, I highly recommend must-read books in this field: Dr. Peta Stapleton's book, *The Science Behind Tapping*[9] and Dr. David Feinstein and Donna Eden's book, *Tapping: Self-Healing with the Transformative Power of Energy Psyhcology.*[10]

If at any time during this process you feel overwhelmed with the emotions associated with your memories, please consult your health care provider for additional support.

How to Use EFT Effectively

Once you learn the exact steps of EFT, the process is quite simple. When you follow the steps, you'll get results.

1. Choose your target.
2. Measure your fear or distress on the 0–10 point scale (10 is the highest level of stress or discomfort and 0 represents no stress or feeling neutral about the target).
3. Create a setup statement.
4. Tap on the acupoints while repeating the target you have chosen.
5. Re-test on the 0–10 point scale.
6. Repeat tapping rounds.

Choose Your Target

To start an effective round of tapping, you'll need to choose a clear and specific **target**. Effective targets can be an emotion, a belief, the memory of a past event, or a physical symptom. For the purposes of this book, we'll look at the first three. If at any time you are aware of a physical symptom connected to your fears, limiting beliefs, or memories of a past event, go ahead and tune into that part of your body while you complete an indicated tapping round.

Emotions:

- My fear of standing out or shining
- My fear of failing
- My fear of their jealousy
- My guilt about saying no
- My fear about letting go of my clutter
- My fear of my deeper emotions
- My fear of feeling my grief
- My hurt about what she said when I succeeded

Beliefs:

- I believe it's not safe to be successful.
- Being visible is dangerous.
- I need to look like I'm struggling.
- I can't handle letting go of my addictions.
- I'm too old to change.
- I'm convinced they'll attack me if I'm successful.
- All relationships are trouble.
- I believe letting go of clutter will feel unsafe.

Memory of a Past Event: (These memories would be connected to your fears and beliefs, causing you to sabotage yourself to stay safe.)

- The time my teacher humiliated me in front of the class.
- The time my friend was nasty when she was jealous.
- The time I felt hurt by their criticism.
- The time they made fun of me for being visible.
- The time she said I would never amount to anything.
- The time my father yelled at me for being a failure.

These statements listed above are just examples of clear targets.

Measure Your Stress Level

You've chosen your target – a feeling, belief, or memory – and now you need to measure how high your stress feels to you when you tune into it on the 0–10 point scale. On this scale, 10 represents the highest level of distress, and 0 represents a feeling of neutrality about the target.

The point of using the 0-10 point intensity scale, (originally called the "SUDs" level - subjective units of distress scale) is to accurately measure the baseline level of fear or stress that you feel about the original target so you can measure again after you have completed the treatment to make sure the tapping is working, or to figure out how to adjust your target.

For instance, if you are afraid to be visible because you worry that someone will attack you, you would measure how afraid you feel on the 0–10 point scale when you think of standing out and being visible.

Create Your Setup Statement

The **setup statement** includes a description of the fear, belief, or memory and a phrase of acceptance. Let's say you've chosen your target as the fear of being visible. And let's say you've brought it to mind and measured your distress on the 0–10 point scale, and it measures as a 7. In this example, the setup statement would sound like this: *"Even though I'm afraid of being visible, I deeply and completely love and accept myself anyway."* You will repeat this setup statement while you tap on the first acupoint, the side of the hand (or karate chop point.) But first, let's look at some classic setup statements.

These setup statements include a description of the problem (the target) and a phrase of acceptance. In the examples below, the targets are underlined. The original acceptance phrase used by clinicians world-wide was "I deeply and completely love and accept myself." Over the years, clinicians became more flexible with this phrase of acceptance to meet their clients' comfort levels. As a result, new practitioners and lay people use a wide variety of acceptance phrases at the end of their setup statements. The point is to pair the description of the problem with a statement of acceptance. Some people have objected to using "love" while others say there's no way they can accept themselves, so you'll see a variety of phrasing in the below examples. When in doubt, you can always default to "I deeply and completely love and accept myself" at the end of every setup statement.

> *Even though I feel afraid of being visible, I deeply and completely love and accept myself.*
>
> *Even though I feel afraid of being successful, I understand why and accept myself anyway.*
>
> *Even though I feel afraid of being seen as a failure, I accept who I am and how I feel about this topic.*
>
> *Even though I feel afraid of feeling any of my deep emotions, I accept who I am and how I feel.*
>
> *Even though I have really strong cravings for sugar, I deeply and completely accept myself and my reaction.*
>
> *Even though I feel afraid when I think of giving up my addiction, I accept who I am and how I feel about it.*

Even though I feel guilty when I consider saying no, I choose to feel calm and peaceful anyway.

Even though I feel afraid of asking for help, I accept who I am and where I learned this.

Even though I feel afraid I'm not going to be perfect, I accept my whole body and appreciate how strong it is.

Even though I'm convinced that I'll never get it right, I accept who I am and how I feel anyway.

Even though I'm convinced that being successful is dangerous, I accept who I am and where I learned this.

Even though I'm convinced I don't have what it takes, I accept who I am and how I feel.

Tapping On Acupoints

To begin, we use two fingers to tap on the side of the hand while repeating the setup statement two or three times. Then we proceed to the additional tapping points on the face and body. Most people tap with two fingers of their primary hand (I'm right-handed so I tap with the two fingers of my right hand). You can tap on one side of the face and body; it's not necessary to tap on both sides. And you don't need to tap very hard – not as hard as knocking on a door, but about as hard as tapping someone on the shoulder. All you need to do is make physical contact with the acupoint located right below the skin.

The next step is to isolate your original target, "I'm afraid to be visible again" and tap on the series of acupoints listed below while repeating this phrase. Here is a list of the remaining points where you will tap and repeat the original target you chose. (See tapping chart on page 121.)

EYEBROW
SIDE OF EYE
UNDER EYE

UNDER NOSE

CHIN

COLLARBONE

UNDER ARM

HEAD

The order of the tapping points works for simplicity, so if you change the order, it won't reduce the effectiveness of your tapping round. You may also change the wording (as long as you stay on the general topic) so that repeating "I'm afraid of being visible again" doesn't feel too monotonous to you when you're tapping on the series of points. Beginners can follow this protocol and repeat the exact same target phrase at each point and get excellent results.

Re-Test Distress

After completing the setup statement and one full round of tapping on each of the remaining acupoints – this is called a tapping round or tapping sequence – you will tune into your original target and measure the distress you feel again on the same 0–10 point scale. Usually, the initial feeling of fear or distress will have decreased a few points. If not, either reword the problem, get more tuned into the stressor you chose to work on, or keep repeating the original simple tapping round. Sometimes the target has moved – while you were first tuned into feeling afraid to be visible, you now feel stressed about how your colleague will respond to you when you tell her about your promotion. You may adjust the words to describe your target accordingly.

I will be providing more than 40 tapping scripts in Chapters 9-15 to address your fears, your beliefs, and memories of any past events connected with your self-sabotaging behavior.

If you'd like to review a video of how to use EFT (tapping), please scan this QR Code to go to The Yes Code™ book portal at www.TheYesCode.com.

To review, a typical tapping round or sequence includes the following steps:

- **Choose your target** (an emotion, a belief, or a memory of an event).
- **Measure your fear or distress** on the 0–10 point scale (where 10 represents the highest amount of distress or discomfort and 0 represents feeling neutral about the topic).
- **Create a Setup Statement** and repeat it out loud while tapping on the point on the side of your hand.
- **Tap on the remaining acupoints** while repeating your **target.**
- **Re-test your fear or distress on the 0–10 point scale.**
- **Repeat tapping rounds.**

Putting it All Together

Choose your target: In this sample tapping round below, I will be using *"I feel very stressed out"* as the target.

Measure how high your stress feels to you on the 0–10 point scale.

Create your setup statement: Even though I feel very stressed out, I deeply and completely love and accept myself anyway.

Start tapping on the side of your hand while you repeat the setup statement: Even though I feel very stressed out right now, I deeply and completely love and accept myself anyway. Even though I feel so stressed out, and I can feel it in my body, I accept who I am and how I feel.

Tap on the series of remaining acupoints while saying the target phrase (or variations of the original target).

> EYEBROW: I feel so stressed out.
>
> SIDE OF EYE: I feel very stressed out right now.
>
> UNDER EYE: I can feel it in my body.
>
> UNDER NOSE: I feel so much stress right now.
>
> CHIN: I feel so stressed out.
>
> COLLARBONE: This stress is really bothering me.
>
> UNDER ARM: I feel so stressed out.
>
> HEAD: The stress is really getting to me.

Re-test how high your fear about the target feels to you now on the 0–10 point scale. Continue tapping on this target until your distress decreases enough that you feel comfortable moving on to another target.

Scan this QR code to access templates for creating EFT tapping scripts on The Yes Code™ book portal.

Tapping Guidelines

I recommend to all my clients that they tap between 10-20 minutes a day, rain or shine. You may choose some fears and beliefs that trigger your self-sabotaging behavior, or something stressful that happened during the day. You could choose something that concerns you in the near future, or a memory of a past event. The point is to be clear when you're choosing your target and dedicate time to this daily practice.

If you are targeting a fear of standing out, and your intensity number starts at an 8 and then drops to a 4, you may feel ready to move onto another target. Some people insist on getting the fear down to a 0-1, but it's up to you. When you get to a low enough number, you'll feel ready to choose your next yes which may be to move onto another target that you know is blocking you. If there is still an emotional charge on the fear or belief you were tapping for, you have more work to do. Keep using the 0-10 point measurement scale until you feel confident that the fear, belief, or memory has subsided.

If you are struggling with work or family stress, use those topics as your targets and put aside tapping time every day.

If you're about to have a stressful meeting with your boss, I would tap several times before the meeting, including the day before.

If you're going to visit your family, and you're afraid they're going to criticize you, I would use the tapping for a couple of days before you go. Don't forget to measure your fear before and after the tapping.

If you have struggled with high cravings of any substance, I always tell my clients, "Don't wait until you're on your way to Dunkin' Donuts" because trust me, you won't do your daily tapping.

If particularly upsetting memories surface while you are tapping, please consult a qualified healthcare practitioner.

"Positive" Tapping

After a few decades of standard EFT exercises had helped thousands of people by making major shifts in emotional distress, some practitioners insisted that tapping while saying positive statements was a better idea than focusing on the problem. Their concern was that focusing on the problem might make it more stubborn or stick around. While this *hasn't* shown to be true – focusing on the problem does not make it more stubborn – practitioners started adding positive tapping into their sessions and many clients enjoyed it.

Focusing on the problem activates the fight or flight response in your brain, which is what we need to do before we can "edit it," thereby releasing its grip on your mind and mood. So, while I enjoy positive tapping – repeating positive, forward looking options – don't abandon the original form of tapping that effectively changes fears, beliefs, and memories that have been keeping you stuck in the cycle of self-sabotaging behavior.

After you have clearly identified your target, measured your distress, tapped for at least two rounds, and experienced the relief that comes with this process, you may go ahead and add positive tapping. (I have included a positive round after each regular tapping round for the examples in Chapters 9-15.)

After studying and using exercises around gratitude and appreciation, I created and added the simple practice of Gratitude Tapping and Thank You Tapping to my EFT work, and many practitioners have caught on to this variation. Again, wait until you've focused at least one round on the actual problem you're trying to reduce. Then you can proceed to a more positive tapping round, or one focused on gratitude. (I have included Gratitude Tapping scripts in Chapter 16.)

Scan this QR code or go to www.TheYesCode.com portal for examples of how to use Gratitude Tapping.

Now let's see The Yes Code process in action with our seven primary self-sabotaging behaviors.

CHAPTER 9

PROCRASTINATION

Below I have provided several client stories, a brief review of The Yes Code™ process for you, and multiple tapping scripts for the self-sabotaging behavior of procrastination.

Joel

I asked Joel to clarify his vision. He said that would be easy – he was tired of procrastinating and wanted to stop. I asked him what he wanted instead of just stopping procrastination. He said, "to follow through when I get an assignment and not care so damn much about everyone else's opinion." Joel struggled with procrastination because of his fear of failing. He knew it cost him raises and forward movement at work. Whenever he started working on one of his projects, all he could imagine was failing, so he started doing "busy work" to distract himself from what really needed to get done. He was paralyzed by this fear and felt stuck. He described himself as "treading water." I asked Joel, "What is the upside of your procrastination?" He said, "If I never finish my projects, then technically I can't fail." I asked him, "What is the downside of finishing a project?" He said, "That would give my boss an opportunity to see me as a failure and likely yell at me."

Joel's next yes step was to target his fear of failing and fear of being yelled at by his boss. Once he reduced this fear of failing with a tapping script, several specific events surfaced that he needed to address from his childhood. He remembered numerous times when his father criticized him for his chores around the house. He was called a failure repeatedly during his childhood. He also remembered a time when his teacher yelled at him for turning in a sloppy homework assignment. Then he remembered a time that his soccer coach said, "Why aren't you as fast as your older brother?"

Joel continued to use tapping to work on the fears and his memories of specific events that made him feel like a failure. He also used tapping to clear the fear of being unfavorably compared to his older brother. At first, he started to feel more neutral about completing his projects, and eventually felt eager and excited about them. He no longer "needed" to procrastinate because he didn't need to be protected from other people's reactions anymore. His next yes steps included keeping up with his daily tapping homework and making a clear accountability schedule for himself at work.

Janna

Janna was procrastinating on creating her new business cards and brochures for her massage business. She was spending way too much time on the wording, font sizes, and other details. When I asked her to clarify her vision of success, she said, "I want to make steady progress and stop getting in my own way." When I asked her what that would look like, she said, "I'd put one foot in front of the other until I built my business to the size I want. Then I'd enjoy creating my own schedule and putting aside money for vacations and retirement."

Her existing clients loved her work, but she didn't have enough clients to pay rent for the office. I asked her, "What is the upside of not getting your cards and brochures finished and printed?" She said, "I'm afraid I'll get too much business and be too successful." I asked her what being "too successful" would look like. She was worried her colleagues who were also struggling to get enough clients would be jealous and upset with her. Her belief was that she would become a target of their envy. I knew this wouldn't be a concern for Janna unless it had happened in the past. "When did this happen before?" I asked. When Janna worked in the corporate world, she had risen to the top of her company and her coworkers resented her; they even insinuated that she had slept with the boss to be promoted. She knew what it felt like to be a "target" because of standing out and shining, and she was afraid it would happen again.

After using EFT on this specific incident, her fears of standing out, and the belief that she would inevitably be resented by others again, Janna's next yes was to complete her cards and brochures, get them printed, and hand them out at local gyms. She got more business than she knew what to do with. She expanded her office, hired two employees, and felt deeply satisfied in her blossoming massage business.

Ellen

Ellen was definitely afraid to be visible, and her self-sabotaging behavior of procrastination showed up every time she neared the finish line with her book. She would find new and unique ways to procrastinate. In her book, she was revealing her story of betrayal and divorce and how her family upbringing contributed to blinding her to the problems in her own marriage. I asked her to clarify her vision. She said, "I want to finally finish my book and help other people with my story." I asked her, "What is the upside of sabotaging yourself every time you get close to finishing the book?" Her response was clear: "Nobody's going to like my version of events." She was convinced that being visible through publishing her book would be unsafe. Her immediate next yes steps were to use tapping, meditating, and journaling to clear her fear of other people's reactions to what she was writing. She was able to neutralize and release the fears of being visible, and finally sent her completed manuscript to her publisher.

Below are EFT scripts that will help you release the fears and beliefs behind your procrastination. I have included five of the most common fears that lead to procrastination and two of the most common limiting beliefs.

Follow the brief review for The Yes Code process below. Once you identify why you are procrastinating, you will be able to address those fears and beliefs and move forward. Whether you're afraid of failure or afraid of success, afraid of other people's jealousy, afraid your success will rock the boat, or afraid to be visible, your procrastination serves as a way to protect you. The Yes Code is the way out.

The Yes Code for Procrastination

Step One: Clarify your vision by answering: What do I really want my life to look like once I have stopped procrastinating? Why is this important to me? Then ask yourself: What is the upside of procrastinating? What is the downside of letting it go and achieving my vision? These questions will help you identify the fears and limiting beliefs that block your progress.

Step Two: Use the tapping sequences below to clear the fears and limiting beliefs that lead to procrastination. I have included scripts for five of the most common fears that make people procrastinate and two of the most common limiting beliefs.

Step Three: Once you've cleared your blocks, identify your next yes step by answering: What feels like the next best step to take now? If it's too big, what is a smaller step I could take instead? Then promptly take that action.

Fears:

1. **Fear of failure**
2. **Fear of success/shining**
3. **Fear of others' jealousy**
4. **Fear of rocking the boat**
5. **Fear of being visible**

Limiting Beliefs:

1. **My success will be disloyal**
2. **My success is unsafe**

TAPPING TARGET:
Fear of Failure

The fear of failure is an overarching fear – one of the umbrella fears under which many other fears fall. Since everyone talks and thinks about their fears differently, it's useful to target the fear of failure as a general starting target for your tapping rounds, but we also want to know *why* you have a fear of failing. For instance, are you afraid of criticism and judgement? Afraid of being humiliated? Then you can use these specific reasons as targets for your tapping rounds as well. For instance, you could start with fear of failing, and on subsequent rounds, you could use as your target: "The memory of being humiliated when I failed." The more specific you are, the clearer your target will be and the more potent the change will be.

When you think of completing a project that you have been procrastinating about and possibly failing at it, how do you feel? Measure your fear of failing on the 0–10 point scale, where 0 represents no fear or distress, and 10 represents the highest level of stress.

Then proceed to the tapping exercise below. Start by tapping on the side of your hand while repeating the setup phrase. Then move to tapping on the identified acupoints on the face and body. (If necessary, consult the tapping chart on page 121.)

SIDE OF HAND: Even though I'm afraid of failing, and I know it will feel terrible, I deeply and completely love and accept myself anyway. Even though I'm afraid of failing, I accept who I am and how I feel.

EYEBROW: I'm afraid of failing.

SIDE OF EYE: I remember what happened last time.

UNDER EYE: I'm afraid of failing.

UNDER NOSE: I know that would feel embarrassing.

CHIN: I'm afraid of failing.

COLLARBONE: I don't want to fail again.

UNDER ARM: I don't want to finish because I might fail.

HEAD: I assume I will fail because I always have.

Take a deep breath, and measure your fear of failing again on the 0–10 point scale. Notice whether the number measuring your stress has gone up or down, and write down any particular thoughts or memories that surfaced around this topic.

Start tapping again.

SIDE OF HAND: Even though I'm still afraid I might fail, I deeply and completely love and accept myself anyway. Even though I'm still afraid I will fail, no wonder I'm avoiding finishing the task, I accept how I am and how I feel.

EYEBROW: I'm still afraid I might fail.

SIDE OF EYE: I've failed so many times before.

UNDER EYE: I'm still afraid of failing.

UNDER NOSE: I've failed many times in the past.

CHIN: I hate failing.

COLLARBONE: I'd rather not do anything.

UNDER ARM: I hate failing.

HEAD: No wonder I won't finish this project.

Take another deep breath, and measure your fear now on the 0–10 point scale. Notice what happened to the intensity level and whether any other memories or thoughts surfaced. Now proceed to the round with more positive statements. Since you've already repeated the setup statement several times, you may skip tapping on the side of your hand this time. Simply begin with the eyebrow point.

> **EYEBROW:** I'm still afraid of failing.
> **SIDE OF EYE:** But maybe I won't fail this time.
> **UNDER EYE:** I haven't failed every time.
> **UNDER NOSE:** It's possible I won't fail.
> **CHIN:** It's possible I might learn something valuable.
> **COLLARBONE:** I want to finish the project and see how I do.
> **UNDER ARM:** It doesn't feel as intense anymore.
> **HEAD:** Maybe I could succeed instead of failing.

Take a final deep breath, notice your number on the 0–10 point scale, and make a note of what other memories and fears surfaced that you could use in later rounds of tapping. For instance, if you remember a time when someone actually called you a failure, you could create a tapping script where your target was: "The time he called me a failure." The setup statement would be: "Even though I remember when he called me a failure, I deeply and completely love and accept myself anyway."

TAPPING TARGET:
Fear of Success or Shining

Think of a time in your life when you were shining and enjoying it until someone poured a cold bucket of water on you. Do you remember it? Your body does, so that memory (and "trauma" with a small "t") is still inside of you, running the show, as all traumatic memories do. ***Remember, we are all about safety***. Anything we can do to keep ourselves safe rises to the top of our list. Even if it's behavior that makes us cringe.

Start by repeating the target phrase out loud: "I'm afraid to shine." Measure how high your fear is on the 0–10 point scale. Write down your number so you can chart your progress as you proceed with this process. Once you are no longer afraid to shine, or your intensity on the scale is a 3 or below, this fear won't be a contributing factor to your self-sabotaging behavior anymore.

As usual, we will start this exercise by tapping on the side of your hand – or the karate chop point – while repeating the setup statement two to three times. Then tap on all the other points listed, saying the phrases I have provided for you below.

> **SIDE OF HAND:** Even though I'm afraid to shine, and I don't want to stand out, I deeply and completely love and accept myself anyway. Even though I'm afraid to shine, what if they're mad about it, I accept who I am and how I feel.
> **EYEBROW:** I'm afraid to shine.
> **SIDE OF EYE:** What if they have a reaction?
> **UNDER EYE:** I'm afraid to shine.
> **UNDER NOSE:** It feels frightening to be exposed.
> **CHIN:** I'm afraid to shine.
> **COLLARBONE:** It feels safer to play small.
> **UNDER ARM:** I don't want to shine so much.
> **HEAD:** But I've always wanted to shine.

Take a deep breath, measure how high this fear of shining is on the 0–10 point scale, and tap for a second round.

> **SIDE OF HAND:** Even though I still feel some tension around my fear of shining, I deeply and completely love and accept myself anyway. Even though I'm still afraid to shine because I'm worried about their reactions, I appreciate who I am and where I learned this.

EYEBROW: I'm still afraid to shine.

SIDE OF EYE: I'm still worried about their reactions.

UNDER EYE: I'm still afraid to shine.

UNDER NOSE: What if they don't like it?

CHIN: What if they don't like me?

COLLARBONE: I'm worried about shining.

UNDER ARM: Maybe I should go back to playing small.

HEAD: I'm worried about shining.

Take another deep breath, and measure your fear of shining again on the 0–10 point scale. Now proceed to the tapping sequence with a more "positive" outlook. You may use the side of the hand again, or skip that step and move immediately to tapping on the series of points.

SIDE OF HAND: Even though I'm still afraid to shine, I realize they are entitled to their reactions, and I don't have to be bothered. Even though I know those old incidents are still bothering me, I've decided to let them go and mind my own business.

EYEBROW: I'm still slightly afraid to shine.

SIDE OF EYE: And that's ok.

UNDER EYE: Maybe I'm excited to as well.

UNDER NOSE: I'm not going to worry about their reactions.

CHIN: Their reactions are none of my business.

COLLARBONE: I don't care about their reactions.

UNDER ARM: They have nothing to do with me.

HEAD: I appreciate shining my light into the world.

Take a final deep breath, measure your fear of shining again on the 0–10 point scale, and assess whether you'd like to continue with this topic at another time, or whether it feels "finished" to you.

Scan this QR code or visit www.TheYesCode.com for a video of how to use EFT for the tapping target, Fear of Shining.

TAPPING TARGET:
Fear of Others' Jealousy

I've got news for you – if you make positive changes in your life, there will be some people who will absolutely be jealous of the new you and will prefer having you stay under the radar. We've all met those people. They don't want you to get ahead, so it suits them when you are overwhelmed, scattered, and inefficient. They get triggered when you stand out.

We can't stop other people from being jealous. We can't stop other people from being mean when they're jealous. *The only thing we can control is our reaction to their reaction.* So yes, you might be afraid they will be jealous. And yes, they might be mean when they're jealous. You can't do anything about their behavior which is based on their past traumas, insecurity, and upbringing.

Measure how afraid you feel on the 0–10 point scale about a friend, colleague, or family member possibly being jealous and being mean because of it. Start the tapping:

SIDE OF HAND: Even though I'm afraid they'll be jealous and lash out at me, I deeply and completely love and accept myself anyway. Even though I'm worried I can't handle their jealousy, I accept who I am and how I feel.

EYEBROW: What if they're jealous?

SIDE OF EYE: What if they can't handle it?

UNDER EYE: What if I can't handle their jealousy?

UNDER NOSE: I'm worried they'll be mean again.

CHIN: I'm worried they'll be nasty to me.

COLLARBONE: I don't like jealous people.

UNDER ARM: Jealous people scare me because they're mean.

HEAD: I don't know if I can handle their jealousy.

Take a deep breath, measure your fear on the 0–10 point scale, and notice any insights or thoughts about particular people whose reactions you fear most. Did the fear go up or down? Continue tapping.

SIDE OF HAND: Even though I'm still afraid of their jealousy, I choose to feel calm and peaceful. Even though I'm afraid they won't be able to handle my success, I accept who I am and how I feel.

EYEBROW: I'm still afraid of their jealousy.

SIDE OF EYE: What if they can't handle my success?

UNDER EYE: What if I can't handle my success?

UNDER NOSE: I'm still afraid of their jealousy.

CHIN: No wonder I try and hide.

COLLARBONE: I'm worried they'll react badly.

UNDER ARM: It's easier to play small.

HEAD: I'm worried they'll react badly to my success.

Take another deep breath, and evaluate your fear of someone being jealous because of your success on the 0–10 point scale again, and then proceed to the more positive statements below.

EYEBROW: I can handle their feelings.

SIDE OF EYE: I will focus on myself.

UNDER EYE: They can react any way they need to.

UNDER NOSE: I don't care if they're jealous.

CHIN: It's none of my business.

COLLARBONE: I want to do what I need to do.

UNDER ARM: It's true they might react.

HEAD: But I feel calmer about it already.

Take another deep breath, and measure your fear of their being jealous on the 0–10 point scale. Keep tapping if you need to in order to neutralize this fear and take note of any specific memories, fears, or beliefs that arise to use as your target in future tapping rounds.

TAPPING TARGET:
Fear of Rocking the Boat

Some people fear their success will rock the boat any time they enjoy an accomplishment in their life. Life feels safer when nothing changes. The mere thought of rocking the boat makes people feel tense and scared, and contributes to self-sabotaging behavior. Remember, we all just want to feel safe.

If this phrase hits home for you – I'm afraid to rock the boat – picture the person or people whose boat will be rocked by your success.

Measure your fear of rocking the boat on the 0–10 point scale. Make a note of your measurement so you can go back and measure your progress after your tapping. If this topic gives you any physical sensations in your body, you may tune into those as well.

Start tapping as indicated below:

SIDE OF HAND: Even though I'm afraid to rock the boat, no wonder I keep playing small, I deeply and completely love and accept myself anyway. Even though I'm afraid my success will rock the boat, I deeply and completely love and accept myself anyway.

EYEBROW: I'm afraid to rock the boat.

SIDE OF EYE: I don't want to rock the boat.

UNDER EYE: I'm afraid I'll rock the boat.

UNDER NOSE: I'd rather stay under the radar.

CHIN: I'm afraid to rock the boat.

COLLARBONE: Nothing good happens when I rock the boat.

UNDER ARM: I need to stay quiet and small.

HEAD: I'm afraid to rock the boat.

Take a deep breath, and measure your fear on the 0–10 point scale now. Are you still as afraid of rocking the boat? Does an old incident come to mind? Who are you most afraid of if you start to change and succeed?

SIDE OF HAND: Even though I'm still afraid to rock the boat, I deeply and completely love and accept myself anyway. Even though I was taught to never rock the boat, I deeply and completely love and accept myself and how I feel.

EYEBROW: I'm not allowed to rock the boat.

SIDE OF EYE: That message was very clear.

UNDER EYE: I'm not supposed to rock the boat.

UNDER NOSE: I need to stay small.

CHIN: I should stay small all the time.

COLLARBONE: I can't rock anyone's boat.

UNDER ARM: I need to stay small to avoid rocking the boat.

HEAD: I shouldn't rock the boat at any cost.

Take another deep breath, and measure your fear on the 0–10 point scale now. Did any new memories surface around this topic? Are there other people you need to picture that cause tension around this topic? You are welcome to change the wording and do your own tapping round that better suits your situation or take note of these memories and people to use as the target in your future tapping rounds.

Tap through the final round of more positive statements below:

EYEBROW: It's ok if I rock the boat.

SIDE OF EYE: I'm not trying to hurt anyone.

UNDER EYE: It's ok if I rock their boat.

UNDER NOSE: I won't get in trouble now.

CHIN: I'm an adult and I want to change.

COLLARBONE: I want to succeed.

UNDER ARM: I know I have what it takes to succeed.

HEAD: I appreciate the progress I've made.

Take a final deep breath, and measure your fear on the 0–10 point scale now. Keep using tapping on this topic until you recognize that you're not doing anything "to them" – you're just living your own life and if they have a reaction, it's their responsibility, and the solution belongs to them.

TAPPING TARGET:
I'm Afraid to Be Visible

While this tapping target seems identical to the fear of shining, I've had enough workshop participants tell me the two phrases feel different to them, so I will treat it as a separate fear.

Repeat this target phrase out loud and measure your fear on the 0–10 point scale: I'm afraid to be visible. You might imagine yourself being or feeling visible from a past event or connected to an event you are worried about in the future. Remember, safety wins, so if you've been hurt as a result of being visible, you will use this memory to hide and sabotage your success.

Picture it, feel it, and measure it on the 0–10 point scale. Proceed with the tapping sequence below:

SIDE OF HAND: Even though I'm so afraid to be visible, what if they hurt me, I deeply and completely love and accept myself anyway. Even though I'm afraid to be visible, it feels unsafe to me, I accept who I am and how I feel.

EYEBROW: I'm so afraid to be visible.

SIDE OF EYE: Isn't it dangerous?

UNDER EYE: Being visible feels unsafe.

UNDER NOSE: I'm afraid to be visible.

CHIN: If I hide under the radar, they can't yell at me.

COLLARBONE: I'm worried about being visible.

UNDER ARM: I don't want to be visible.

HEAD: Being visible makes me feel unsafe.

Take a deep breath, measure how high this fear is on the 0–10 point scale now, and continue tapping.

> **SIDE OF HAND:** Even though being visible still makes me scared, I deeply and completely love and accept myself anyway. Even though being visible feels very unsafe, I accept where I learned this and accept my feelings.
> **EYEBROW:** I'm still afraid to be visible.
> **SIDE OF EYE:** I'm worried about their reactions.
> **UNDER EYE:** Being visible makes me feel unsafe.
> **UNDER NOSE:** It feels scary to be visible.
> **CHIN:** No wonder I always hide.
> **COLLARBONE:** No wonder I stay under the radar.
> **UNDER ARM:** I don't want to be visible.
> **HEAD:** It feels too unsafe and scary.

Take another deep breath, and measure your fear of being visible on the 0–10 point scale. Has it gone down, stayed the same, or gone up? If it's gone up, tune in to a specific memory of when you were visible and felt hurt, and use that as your next tapping target.

> **SIDE OF HAND:** Even though I remember when this started, and it's still in my body's memory, I deeply and completely love and accept myself. Even though I'm still afraid to be visible because of what happened back then, I accept who I am and how I feel.
> **EYEBROW:** I know what made me feel this way.
> **SIDE OF EYE:** I remember how I got in trouble.
> **UNDER EYE:** I accept that it was a long time ago.
> **UNDER NOSE:** I'm an adult now, and I'm no longer unsafe.
> **CHIN:** But it still feels unsafe to be visible.
> **COLLARBONE:** I still feel safer under the radar.
> **UNDER ARM:** I want to let this go.
> **HEAD:** I'm no longer that scared person anymore.

Take another deep breath, and measure your fear on the 0–10 point scale, and proceed to the more positive tapping round below.

> **EYEBROW:** That was a long time ago.
>
> **SIDE OF EYE:** I feel that I am stronger now.
>
> **UNDER EYE:** They made a big mistake.
>
> **UNDER NOSE:** I didn't deserve to be in trouble for being visible.
>
> **CHIN:** I want to be free to be myself.
>
> **COLLARBONE:** I want to be myself and be visible.
>
> **UNDER ARM:** It's ok if they don't like it or me.
>
> **HEAD:** I appreciate my visibility now.

Take a final deep breath, and measure your fear of being visible on the 0–10 point scale. Assess whether you need more work on this particular fear or whether you feel good enough to set this aside and move on. You can always return to it at another time.

TAPPING TARGET:
I Believe Being Successful Is Disloyal

This is a heavy limiting belief that affects so many people, but they are often unaware of how powerful it is. When they ask themselves what the *downside* is of being successful, this belief often surfaces and feels undeniable. Your family didn't have to drill this into you; the message could have been quite subtle. All you need to know is that if this resonates with you, then it is true for you, whether they taught you this in a subtle way or hammered it into you. Somehow, you got the message that being successful would be seen and interpreted as a betrayal to your family or your background – that success would set you apart and you would no longer be "one of them." How you got the message is less important.

Measure how true this belief feels to you on the 0–10 point scale and start your tapping. If you remember what your family said about this specifically, go ahead and focus on the words or scene that surfaces for you.

> **SIDE OF HAND:** Even though I can't be successful because they'll see me as disloyal, I deeply and completely love and accept myself anyway. Even though being successful would be disloyal, I accept who I am and how I feel about this.
> **EYEBROW:** I can't be successful.
> **SIDE OF EYE:** It would be disloyal to them.
> **UNDER EYE:** I'm not allowed to be successful.
> **UNDER NOSE:** I can't be disloyal.
> **CHIN:** I don't want to be disloyal.
> **COLLARBONE:** No wonder I've been holding back.
> **UNDER ARM:** I'm convinced being successful is bad.
> **HEAD:** I'll be disloyal if I'm successful.

Take a deep breath, and measure how true this belief is on the 0–10 point scale now. If particular memories surface, go ahead and tap on those or continue with this next round.

> **SIDE OF HAND:** Even though I'm still convinced being successful would be disloyal, I deeply and completely love and accept myself anyway. Even though I'm still convinced that being successful would make me seem disloyal, I accept who I am and how I feel.
> **EYEBROW:** I still think being successful is disloyal.
> **SIDE OF EYE:** I'm still convinced I can't be successful.
> **UNDER EYE:** I shouldn't be successful.
> **UNDER NOSE:** I'm not supposed to stand out.
> **CHIN:** They'll think I'm disloyal.
> **COLLARBONE:** No wonder I've been holding myself back.
> **UNDER ARM:** I can't be disloyal by being successful.
> **HEAD:** I've always believed this.

Take another deep breath, and measure this belief on the 0–10 point scale. Watch for other memories to surface and go ahead and tap on them if necessary. Proceed to the positive round below:

> **EYEBROW:** I used to think it would be disloyal.
> **SIDE OF EYE:** I had a belief that my success would be disloyal.
> **UNDER EYE:** I'm ready to release that belief.
> **UNDER NOSE:** I'm ready to let it go.
> **CHIN:** I understand they taught it to me.
> **COLLARBONE:** I don't believe it anymore.
> **UNDER ARM:** I feel relieved I'm letting it go.
> **HEAD:** I appreciate that it's time to let this belief go.

Take a final deep breath, and measure your belief on the 0–10 point scale. Do as much tapping as necessary to neutralize this belief so you can move forward in your life with ease.

TAPPING TARGET:
I'm Convinced Success Is Unsafe

If you are convinced that success will be unsafe or dangerous for you, you will automatically slow yourself down, and procrastination is an easy way to do that.

Where do you think you might have learned this belief? Something must have happened to you when you were successful that led you to believe that standing out as a success would be punished instead of rewarded. What danger are you worried about? Measure how *true* this belief seems to you on the 0–10 point scale and proceed to the tapping sequences below:

> **SIDE OF HAND:** Even though I'm convinced that my success will be unsafe and dangerous, I deeply and completely love and accept myself anyway. Even though I'm convinced that

success will be unsafe and not worth the trouble, I accept who I am and how I feel.

EYEBROW: I'm convinced that my success is unsafe.

SIDE OF EYE: I learned this from my family.

UNDER EYE: I'm worried about being in "danger" if I'm successful.

UNDER NOSE: I am convinced my success will be unsafe.

CHIN: I'm worried about being successful.

COLLARBONE: What if I feel unsafe?

UNDER ARM: I believe my success might be dangerous.

HEAD: I learned to be careful about being successful.

Take a deep breath, and measure your belief again on the 0–10 point scale. How does the belief feel to you now – just as true? Or does it feel less true right now? You may have experienced something unsafe in your past, but you no longer have to fear the lack of safety as an adult. Continue using the tapping as detailed below:

SIDE OF HAND: Even though I'm still convinced that my success could be unsafe, I deeply and completely love and accept myself anyway. Even though I'm still convinced that I shouldn't be successful because it might be dangerous for me, I accept who I am and how I feel.

EYEBROW: I'm still convinced my success will be unsafe.

SIDE OF EYE: I believe success is dangerous.

UNDER EYE: I don't want to be unsafe.

UNDER NOSE: I'd rather stay hidden and safe.

CHIN: I still believe success is unsafe.

COLLARBONE: What if I get into trouble?

UNDER ARM: I'm still convinced success is unsafe.

HEAD: I believe I need to hide.

Take another deep breath, and measure how *true* this belief feels to you on the 0–10 point scale now. You may repeat these rounds as often as you wish until you no longer believe success is unsafe. Now proceed to the positive tapping round to help you move forward.

> **EYEBROW:** I appreciate my success.
>
> **SIDE OF EYE:** It seemed unsafe in the past.
>
> **UNDER EYE:** But I'm an adult and safer now.
>
> **UNDER NOSE:** I want to be successful.
>
> **CHIN:** I am releasing this old belief.
>
> **COLLARBONE:** I'm ready to feel good about my success.
>
> **UNDER ARM:** I feel better already.
>
> **HEAD:** I feel ready for my success.

I detailed many tapping sequences for the primary fears and beliefs that fuel your procrastination. As your next yes, I invite you to formulate your own sequences if a different fear or belief surfaced for you while completing these exercises. The key is to ask yourself what the upside of procrastinating is, or what the downside of reaching your goal is. This will help you identify why you would need to procrastinate and direct you towards creating exact tapping sequences to clear your fears and beliefs about standing out, being visible, and shining. In addition, consider what next yes steps would feel inspiring to you around moving forward in your business, family, or with your health.

Now let's proceed to the next self-sabotaging behavior.

CHAPTER 10

PERFECTIONISM

I have provided client examples of perfectionism, corresponding tapping sequences, and a review of The Yes Code™ process for you below.

Susan

When Susan came in for her first appointment, I asked her to clarify what she wanted for herself. She said she wanted peace of mind, emotional balance, and to stop feeling so resentful all the time. She admitted she was burned out, tired of being so self-critical, and had found herself feeling resentful and critical of others at work and at home.

More questions revealed that Susan had always feared her father's disapproval, and yet had become very disapproving and critical herself. Her father didn't just raise an eyebrow or say he was disappointed if he disapproved of her behavior. He would freeze her out for days on end. Just a few hours of this would feel like torture, and yet he often stretched it out until he was certain he had made his point. As a result, Susan became a perfectionist at work to avoid any disapproval from her boss or colleagues. I asked her, "What is the upside to being a perfectionist?" She calmly admitted, "If I could finally be perfect, I could stop anticipating and fearing anyone else's disapproval."

The pressure and stress levels had started to mount for Susan, and she'd started to be moody and reactive at work and at home. She resented everyone for their demands, even though she was the one who was setting unrealistic standards for herself. After a few out-of-proportion rants at colleagues who hadn't actually expressed any demands or disapproval, she realized she was acting inappropriately and needed to look at some of these old wounds with her father. When I asked her what the downside might be to letting go of her perfectionism, she said, "I have hidden behind my perfectionism like a shield, and I'm afraid if I let it go, I would be a total failure." In our tapping sequences, we targeted helplessness, sadness around her relationship with her father, her fear of criticism and her deep resentment of others. We also used setup statements such as: "Even though I'm convinced I'm a failure unless I'm perfect" and "Even though I feel anxious because I expect to be criticized all the time." Susan was shocked with how quickly the tapping sequences took the sting out of the old hurt connected to her father. "Where has this been all my life?" she said. She noticed herself being less reactive and prickly at work and was generally calmer.

Susan's next yes steps seemed simple once she cleared some of her old emotional pain. Her next yes was to continue to catch herself when she set unrealistic standards. She started to set appropriate deadlines at work and decided to start a self-care practice that included daily tapping and meditation.

Joan

When I asked Joan what her vision for her life looked like, she said she wasn't sure. All she knew was that she needed to relax more and stop looking over her shoulder all the time. Joan was terrified of making "another mistake." She felt she caused irreparable damage to her family when she instigated her divorce. While she warned her husband for years that she was unhappy and had asked him to go to couples counseling numerous times, he had refused. He said the communication problems were all her fault, and the divorce was all her fault, too. She told me, "I couldn't have lived in the marriage one more day!" She still thought it was a mistake that she could never take back.

This fear of making another mistake showed up as Joan becoming a perfectionist in her job, in her relationships with her adult children, and as a grandmother. This behavior annoyed her children, and they begged her to stop trying so hard to be perfect for them. She gave the grandchildren way too many gifts and tried to be the perfect host when they visited her. When I asked Joan what the upside was of trying to always be so perfect, she said, "then I can't be blamed for anything else." She said the downside of letting go of her perfectionism was that "I might be caught doing something wrong."

After using tapping on her fear of making another mistake, her guilt about breaking up the family, and her beliefs that she would always be blamed for being in the wrong, she was able to be at peace with the decision she made. Her worry about making a future mistake no longer bothered her, and she was able to put the divorce in perspective. She dramatically reduced her fear of having a candid conversation with her adult children and was therefore able to make one of her next yes steps initiating the conversation and "addressing the elephant in the living room." She was able to talk to them about how painful and devaluing the marriage had been for her.

Joan's additional next yes steps included being clear about her feelings when she communicated, setting up regular talking times with her children, and holding back on over-gifting to the grandchildren. She also tapped every day until she was able to forgive herself fully for the divorce.

The Yes Code for Perfectionism

Step One: Clarify your vision by answering: What do I really want my life to look like without my perfectionism? Why is this important to me? Then ask yourself: What is the upside of my perfectionism? What is the downside of letting it go and reaching my vision? These questions will help you identify your fears and limiting beliefs that block your progress.

Step Two: Use the tapping sequences below to clear your fears and limiting beliefs that led to your perfectionism. If your answers to the upside/downside questions revealed different fears or beliefs, use those answers as your tapping targets.

Step Three: Once you've cleared your blocks, identify your next yes by answering: What feels like the next best step to take now? If it's too big, what is a smaller step I could take instead? Then promptly take that action for yourself.

Below, I have designed tapping scripts for the four most common fears and the top two beliefs that fuel perfectionism. Review your list of the fears, beliefs, and memories you identified and choose the tapping scripts that speak to you most.

Fears:

1. **Fear of being judged and criticized**
2. **Fear of making a mistake**
3. **Fear of being exposed/found out/humiliated**
4. **Fear of their disapproval**

Beliefs:

1. **I'm convinced that being imperfect is dangerous**
2. **I'm convinced I'm not good enough**

I'm Afraid of Being Judged and Criticized

Being judged and criticized is a very common fear for perfectionists. I'm sure you remember a time when you were judged and criticized for your behavior or mistakes, and maybe even for being successful. Bring one of those memories to mind, and measure how afraid you are of being judged on the 0–10 point scale. You may have been hiding this memory for a long time, and it only showed up because your behavior of perfectionism was blocking you from moving forward. Or maybe it's been in the back of your mind for years. *It doesn't matter how severe the criticism was, it only matters how your nervous system recorded it.*

You can either measure your intensity about the specific incident on the 0–10 point scale, or measure your fear right now of being judged and criticized "again."

Go ahead and start tapping:

SIDE OF HAND: Even though I'm afraid of being judged and criticized because I remember how it felt last time, I deeply and completely love and accept myself anyway. Even though I'm afraid I'll be criticized again, I deeply and completely love and accept myself anyway.

EYEBROW: I'm afraid I'll be judged and criticized.

SIDE OF EYE: I remember how it felt in the past.

UNDER EYE: I'm afraid of feeling that way again.

UNDER NOSE: I'm afraid of being judged and criticized.

CHIN: That old memory feels terrible.

COLLARBONE: I'm afraid of being judged and criticized.

UNDER ARM: I don't want to hear it or feel it.

HEAD: No wonder I never feel perfect enough.

Take a deep breath, and measure your fear of being judged and criticized on the 0–10 point scale again. Notice what's happening in your body as well as with your thoughts. If the feelings about this first memory have subsided, you may bring up another old memory of when you were judged or criticized, either for being a failure or a success. Insert that memory into another tapping sequence such as, "Even though I remember when my soccer coach criticized me in front of the whole team, I deeply and completely love and accept myself anyway." You may also just insert the fear: "Even though I'm afraid of being judged and criticized again."

Continue tapping:

> **SIDE OF HAND:** Even though I remember how they judged and criticized me, and it felt terrible, I deeply and completely accept myself anyway. Even though I don't think I'll ever forget how it felt, and I'm afraid of it happening again, I accept who I am and how I feel.
>
> **EYEBROW:** It seems as if I'll never forget it.
>
> **SIDE OF EYE:** It really hurt when they criticized me.
>
> **UNDER EYE:** And I didn't see it coming.
>
> **UNDER NOSE:** I was so innocent back then.
>
> **CHIN:** I didn't know my behavior would bother them so much.
>
> **COLLARBONE:** I remember how terrible it felt.
>
> **UNDER ARM:** No wonder I'm still afraid of being judged and criticized.
>
> **HEAD:** That memory left quite a mark on me.

Take another deep breath, measure your fear of being criticized "again" on the 0–10 point scale (or measure the intensity about the original incident) and proceed with this more self-forgiving tapping sequence below.

> **EYEBROW:** I do remember being judged and criticized.
>
> **SIDE OF EYE:** But I'm tired of remembering it.
>
> **UNDER EYE:** They shouldn't have spoken to me that way.

UNDER NOSE: I took it to heart, but now I'm ready to release it.

CHIN: I'm ready to release the old pain.

COLLARBONE: I feel better about myself already

UNDER ARM: I always do the best I can.

HEAD: I appreciate who I am now and who I was back then.

Take a final deep breath, and measure your fear again on the 0–10 point scale. Make a note of whether you need to continue using this target or switch to another one. Additional setup phrases could be:

Even though I feel the pressure to be perfect, I accept who I am and how I feel.

Even though I'm convinced I still have to do it perfectly, I deeply and completely love and accept myself anyway.

Even though they taught me I had no choice but to be perfect, I deeply and completely love and accept myself anyway.

TAPPING TARGET:
Fear of Making a Mistake

I've made a zillion mistakes in my life – in my personal relationships, with my health, in business – you name it. I've had business flops, relationship flops, and challenging illnesses I didn't take care of in time. But with age and emotional maturity, I've come to love and accept myself anyway. I wouldn't be who I am right now – how happy I am, how wise I feel in spite of the scars, how I cherish my connections with clients, family and friends – if I hadn't made so many mistakes. Sure, I can still have a case of the regrets, but I'm ok with all that I did and how I'm living my life now.

Tune into your fear of making a mistake in the future – does it automatically trigger feelings about an old mistake you can't let go of, or are you just focused on avoiding making another one? Are you afraid of making "another big one" or are you afraid of the consequences? Are you afraid you can't come back from it? Measure your fear on the 0–10 point scale, and start tapping as indicated below:

> **SIDE OF HAND:** Even though I'm afraid of making a mistake, what if it's really bad, I deeply and completely love and accept myself anyway. Even though I'm afraid of making another big mistake, what if I can't come back from it, I accept who I am and how I feel.
>
> **EYEBROW:** I'm afraid of making a big mistake.
>
> **SIDE OF EYE:** I have to be perfect.
>
> **UNDER EYE:** I don't want to make a big mistake.
>
> **UNDER NOSE:** I'm so afraid of making a big mistake.
>
> **CHIN:** What if I can't recover from it?
>
> **COLLARBONE:** What if it's catastrophic?
>
> **UNDER ARM:** I'm so afraid of making a big mistake.
>
> **HEAD:** No wonder I keep trying to be perfect.

Take a deep breath, and measure your fear of making a mistake again on the 0–10 point scale. Did it decrease? Increase? Stay the same? If the measurement stayed the same, you are likely not tuned in enough or you've been distracted by something else. Tap again.

> **SIDE OF HAND:** Even though I'm still afraid of making another big mistake, I deeply and completely love and accept myself anyway. Even though I'm terrified of making a mistake and doing serious damage, I accept who I am and how I feel.
>
> **EYEBROW:** I'm still afraid of making another mistake.
>
> **SIDE OF EYE:** I'm not over the last one.
>
> **UNDER EYE:** I don't want to forgive myself for the big one.
>
> **UNDER NOSE:** I'm afraid of making another big mistake.
>
> **CHIN:** I don't want to forgive myself, what if I do it again?
>
> **COLLARBONE:** I'm afraid of making another big mistake
>
> **UNDER ARM:** No wonder I try to be perfect.
>
> **HEAD:** I'm afraid of making a mistake.

Take another deep breath, and measure your fear on the 0–10 point scale. Has anything changed? Are you still afraid of making a mistake? How high is your regret or guilt about the last "big one" you think you made? Take note of any specific memories, fears or beliefs that arise to use as the target in future tapping rounds.

Proceed to this gentler series of statements about forgiving yourself.

EYEBROW: I made big mistakes in the past.

SIDE OF EYE: And I want to forgive myself.

UNDER EYE: I learned a lesson.

UNDER NOSE: I am trying to forgive myself.

CHIN: I'm worthy of forgiveness.

COLLARBONE: I didn't know any better at the time.

UNDER ARM: I'm moving on and feel good about it.

HEAD: I deserve to be forgiven.

Take a final deep breath, and measure your fear of making a mistake on the 0–10 point scale. If it does not feel neutral enough, go ahead and make time to tap on this target again. If there is more than one "big one" that you think is contaminating or slowing down your progress, address each mistake separately as a tapping target and work on it until the fear and regret are low enough for you to move on.

Scan this QR code or visit www.TheYesCode.com for a video of EFT for the tapping target, Fear of Making a Mistake.

TAPPING TARGET:
Fear of Being Exposed/Found Out/ Humiliated

While many people refer to this as imposter syndrome, using those words for a tapping target won't work as well as using a more specific emotion. To have a more effective target, we need to look at the emotion or the belief that is supporting this syndrome.

If you feel afraid of being exposed or "found out," go ahead and measure that fear on the 0–10 point scale. You might tune into a specific event from your past where you actually felt exposed; use that as your tapping target. Measure how fearful you are about being exposed on the 0–10 point scale. Proceed with the tapping sequences below.

> **SIDE OF HAND:** Even though I'm afraid of being exposed or found out, I deeply and completely love and accept myself anyway. Even though I'm afraid they'll expose me as a fraud and I'll be humiliated, I deeply and completely love and accept myself anyway.
>
> **EYEBROW:** I'm afraid of being exposed.
>
> **SIDE OF EYE:** I'm afraid of being found out.
>
> **UNDER EYE:** That's why I try to be perfect all the time.
>
> **UNDER NOSE:** What if they find out I'm a fraud?
>
> **CHIN:** I'm afraid of being humiliated for being imperfect.
>
> **COLLARBONE:** I'm afraid of being exposed.
>
> **UNDER ARM:** What if I feel exposed?
>
> **HEAD:** I don't want to be found out, so I try to be perfect.

Take a deep breath, and measure how fearful you are about being exposed or found out on the 0–10 point scale now. Make a note of your number, and any other reactions you are having, and continue tapping.

> **SIDE OF HAND:** Even though I'm still afraid of being exposed and found out, so I have to be perfect, I deeply and completely love and accept myself. Even though I'm still afraid that I'll feel exposed and found out, I deeply and completely love and accept myself anyway.
>
> **EYEBROW:** I'm afraid of being found out and exposed.
>
> **SIDE OF EYE:** What if I feel exposed?
>
> **UNDER EYE:** I don't want to be found out.

UNDER NOSE: I'm afraid they'll think I'm a fraud.

CHIN: No wonder I try to be perfect.

COLLARBONE: I don't want to be exposed.

UNDER ARM: I'm afraid of being found out.

HEAD: I don't want to be exposed so I try to be perfect.

Take another deep breath, and measure your fear of being found out again on the 0–10 point scale. Has it gone down or gone up? Make a note of your number and of any other emotions or conflicts that surfaced to use in future tapping rounds.

Now tap on the more positive statements below, and notice any reactions you might have.

EYEBROW: I've been afraid of being found out.

SIDE OF EYE: But I feel more settled and calmer about it.

UNDER EYE: I used to feel afraid, but I'm calmer now.

UNDER NOSE: I appreciate what I have to offer.

CHIN: I appreciate that I'm feeling better already.

COLLARBONE: I appreciate that I want to feel normal, not perfect.

UNDER ARM: I'm no longer afraid of being exposed.

HEAD: I feel calmer about this whole topic.

Take a final deep breath, and measure your distress about this topic on the 0–10 point scale. Know that you can go back to this tapping sequence any time you wish and when any new memory of a past event or fear comes up for you.

TAPPING TARGET:
Fear of Their Disapproval

Feeling the heat of someone else's disapproval can be intense. It doesn't matter if you think you deserve to be on the receiving end of that heat or not. Once you have been at the other end of that, depending on how harsh it was and what the consequences were, you will fear being on the receiving end of it again. If the lesson is deep enough, you will morph into a perfectionist, trying desperately not to be the target of someone else.

Measure how afraid you are of getting someone's disapproval on the 0–10 point scale. You might decide you don't care at all. But if you're reading this book, you likely have at least a small amount of fear about it. Picture the person whose disapproval you fear, and start the tapping round below:

> **SIDE OF HAND:** Even though I'm afraid of their disapproval, I deeply and completely love and accept myself anyway. Even though I can't seem to do anything right, and I'm waiting for their disapproval, I accept who I am and how I feel.
>
> **EYEBROW:** I'm so afraid of their disapproval.
>
> **SIDE OF EYE:** I have to be careful and perfect.
>
> **UNDER EYE:** I need to really be perfect.
>
> **UNDER NOSE:** I'm afraid of their disapproval.
>
> **CHIN:** What if I do it wrong?
>
> **COLLARBONE:** What if they punish me?
>
> **UNDER ARM:** I can't take their disapproval.
>
> **HEAD:** I'll do anything to avoid their disapproval.

Yes, some people will "do anything" to avoid someone's disapproval. You can see why the sabotaging behavior of perfectionism takes hold in these instances.
Take a deep breath, and measure your fear of their disapproval on the 0–10 point scale again. Write down any extra thoughts or memories that come up for you so you can plug them into the tapping sequences another time.

> **SIDE OF HAND:** Even though I'm still afraid of their disapproval, I deeply and completely love and accept myself

anyway. Even though I'm so worried I'll get their disapproval, I accept who I am and how I feel.

EYEBROW: I'm still afraid of their disapproval.

SIDE OF EYE: What if they're disappointed in me?

UNDER EYE: I can't take it.

UNDER NOSE: I have to be perfect or else.

CHIN: I don't want to do anything they don't like.

COLLARBONE: What if I don't know what to do?

UNDER ARM: I'm tired of being so careful and perfect.

HEAD: I'm still afraid of their disapproval.

Take another deep breath, and measure your fear on the 0–10 point scale. Take any notes on what else surfaced for you – incidents, memories, fears of the future – and use them as targets for subsequent rounds of tapping. Proceed to the more positive round below.

EYEBROW: I'm tired of being scared.

SIDE OF EYE: So what if they disapprove?

UNDER EYE: It's none of my business.

UNDER NOSE: I don't think I care anymore.

CHIN: I was afraid of their disapproval.

COLLARBONE: I think I'm done with trying to be perfect.

UNDER ARM: I appreciate how well I'm doing.

HEAD: I appreciate how far I've come.

Take a final deep breath, and measure your fear of disapproval on the 0–10 point scale. Use any remaining "yes, but" as targets for your next tapping rounds.

TAPPING TARGET:
I Have to Be Perfect or I'll Be in Danger

Many perfectionists believe that if they're not perfect, it could be dangerous. Remember, your nervous system when you were a child likely recorded disapproval and being imperfect as far more dangerous than your adult nervous system would have. Unfortunately, being perfect is both unattainable and exhausting. Perfectionism, as a self-sabotaging behavior, serves as a false protection from danger because it only works until the next task, event, or fear.

Measure how true this belief is to you on the 0–10 point scale – I have to be perfect or else it's dangerous.

> **SIDE OF HAND:** Even though I think I have to be perfect or else it will be dangerous for me, I accept who I am and how I feel. Even though I'm afraid to be imperfect because I'm convinced it will get me into trouble, I accept who I am and how I feel.
>
> **EYEBROW:** I have to be perfect.
>
> **SIDE OF EYE:** Or I might be in danger.
>
> **UNDER EYE:** I could really get into trouble.
>
> **UNDER NOSE:** I have to be perfect.
>
> **CHIN:** But I'm so tired.
>
> **COLLARBONE:** I'm worried about being unsafe.
>
> **UNDER ARM:** I have to protect myself.
>
> **HEAD:** I have to be perfect.

Take a deep breath, and measure this belief again on the 0–10 point scale. How true does it feel to you? Does it bring back any memories from your childhood when you weren't perfect, or when someone told you that you should be? If it does, you could plug in that memory to an additional tapping sequence.

> **SIDE OF HAND:** Even though I'm still convinced that I have to be perfect, I accept who I am and how I feel. Even though I don't feel acceptable unless I'm perfect, I accept my feelings about this topic.
>
> **HEAD:** I have to be perfect.
>
> **EYEBROW:** Or else I'm not acceptable.

SIDE OF EYE: I might be in danger.

UNDER EYE: I have to be perfect.

UNDER NOSE: I feel such pressure to be perfect.

CHIN: The pressure is overwhelming.

COLLARBONE: All this pressure to be perfect.

UNDER ARM: I feel such pressure to be perfect.

HEAD: I don't want to get into trouble.

Take another deep breath, and measure how true this belief feels to you on the 0–10 point scale. You may continue with the above rounds or move on to the more positive wording below.

EYEBROW: I want to release the pressure.

SIDE OF EYE: I don't want to have to be perfect anymore.

UNDER EYE: So what if I get into trouble?

UNDER NOSE: I'm ready to release it.

CHIN: I'm tired of trying to be perfect.

COLLARBONE: I'm releasing the old belief about danger.

UNDER ARM: I'm ready to release it.

HEAD: I appreciate how hard I've tried.

Take a final deep breath, and measure how true this belief is to you now on the 0–10 point scale. Take some notes about what other events or memories surfaced and use them in subsequent tapping rounds.

TAPPING TARGET:
I'm Convinced I'm Not Good Enough

Perfectionists are on a quest to be perfect because they believe deeply that they are flawed, inadequate, and simply not good enough. Past experiences taught them that they couldn't live up to someone else's standards. They then take on the impossible task of reaching unrealistically high standards.

If you are someone who keeps trying to be perfect, try to measure this belief – I'm not good enough – on the 0–10 point scale. How true does it feel to you? Most people say it doesn't just feel true, it *is* true. That's the challenge with beliefs.

Try this tapping round below:

> **SIDE OF HAND:** Even though I'm convinced I'm not good enough, and maybe I never will be, I deeply and completely love and accept myself anyway. Even though I'm convinced that I've never been good enough to please them, I want to try and accept who I am and how I feel.
>
> **EYEBROW:** I've never been good enough.
>
> **SIDE OF EYE:** I still want to try.
>
> **UNDER EYE:** No wonder I want to be perfect.
>
> **UNDER NOSE:** I need to live up to their standards.
>
> **CHIN:** I need to be perfect.
>
> **COLLARBONE:** I want to try and be perfect.
>
> **UNDER ARM:** I hate not feeling good enough.
>
> **HEAD:** I'm tired of not feeling good enough.

Take a deep breath, and measure how true this belief feels to you now on the 0–10 point scale. Is it "true" that you're really not good enough? Or is it something your family taught you? Continue tapping below.

> **SIDE OF HAND:** Even though I'm still convinced I'm not good enough, and I never have been, I deeply and completely love and accept myself anyway. Even though I'm still convinced I never was and never will be good enough, I accept who I am and how I feel.
>
> **EYEBROW:** I've never felt good enough.
>
> **SIDE OF EYE:** I'm convinced I never will be.
>
> **UNDER EYE:** No wonder I try to be perfect.
>
> **UNDER NOSE:** I never felt good enough.
>
> **CHIN:** And I don't feel good enough now.

COLLARBONE: No wonder I try to be perfect.

UNDER ARM: I'm never good enough.

HEAD: Maybe I never will be.

Take another deep breath, and measure how true this feels to you on the 0–10 point scale. You may have learned this belief from your family, but it is not a fact. Keep tapping until you loosen this belief. When you do, you will watch your perfectionistic behavior subside. Now tap on the more positive statements below:

EYEBROW: They taught me I wasn't good enough.

SIDE OF EYE: But what if I always was?

UNDER EYE: I've never been good enough.

UNDER NOSE: I wonder if that's true.

CHIN: I don't think it's true anymore.

COLLARBONE: I wonder if maybe I am good enough.

UNDER ARM: It's possible I've always been good enough.

HEAD: I appreciate who I am.

Take a final deep breath, measure how true this belief feels to you on the 0–10 point scale and continue tapping when you notice any old perfectionist behaviors in operation.

I have detailed tapping sequences for very common fears and beliefs connected to perfectionism. I invite you to continue to create new tapping scripts that fit your situation.

Now that you have cleared many of your fears, beliefs, and memories that have caused you to be a perfectionist, what next yes steps feel inspiring to you? Plan on taking one or more of these inspiring next yes steps. If any remaining fears surface, it simply means you have more tapping to do.

Let's move on to the next self-sabotaging behavior.

CHAPTER 11

PEOPLE PLEASING

People pleasing as a self-sabotaging behavior shows up in two primary ways – you don't say no, and you don't ask for help. Both of these behaviors under the people pleasing umbrella protect you from a consequence you fear. You may be exhausted or worn out from not saying no or not asking for help, but you're still getting results you want on some level.

Here are some client stories about people pleasing, a review of The Yes Code™ process, and tapping sequences for fears and beliefs around this self-sabotaging behavior.

Marnie

Consider Marnie who always said yes at work no matter what her colleagues or bosses asked of her. She was definitely aiming to be employee of the year, but in the process, she was exhausting herself and becoming resentful. When I asked her to clarify the vision she had for herself, she said, "I just want to learn how to say no and not feel crappy about it." She wanted to feel relaxed at work rather than always looking to put out the professional fires in the office. She also said she wanted to set clear boundaries in some of her friendships; she admitted she was feeling taken advantage of because she always catered to their desires – what they wanted to do for fun, where they wanted to go for dinner, where to socialize.

After asking herself the upside and downside questions as to why she had so much trouble saying no, she identified several traumas from her childhood. She said her parents were deep into addiction and weren't present at all. She said if she didn't say yes to everything, "nothing would have gotten done." She did the cleaning, the cooking, and took care of her siblings as well. When I asked her the upside of saying yes all the time, she said, "I feel in control of the outcomes, and I don't have to wait for anyone else to forget or mess up." When I asked her what the downside was of letting go of this sabotaging behavior, she said, "It brings up too many childhood memories of my parents leaving me in the lurch – leaving me at parties, forgetting to pick me up from a friend's house, ignoring permission slips I needed for school trips. I'm convinced that I have to be the one in charge and in control, or everything will fall apart."

Marnie recognized the imbalance and the deep pain she felt from her parents' neglect. Neither parent had gotten clean and sober, and they had died alone and in incredibly poor health. After therapy and using tapping for her traumas, Marnie was able to see that her illusion of control was hurting her more than helping her. She identified her next yes as a commitment to continue to use tapping on her guilt and strengthening her ability to say no by practicing in small ways. She started saying no when she needed to and set strong boundaries at work and in her relationships, and though she ruffled some feathers, she stayed in her job and her friendships improved.

Jack

Jack never said no to anyone and never asked for help either. He didn't like the term *people pleaser* but understood that's what he was doing – pleasing others to protect himself. When I asked him what the upside was of avoiding asking for help, he said: "I need to be independent. I never want to rely on anyone else." I asked him what the downside was of letting go of this protective behavior, and he said, "I would feel too vulnerable if I needed help from someone else." Regarding never saying no, I asked him the same questions. Jack said, "I like being indispensable to others, it makes me feel worthwhile. And if I start saying no, they'll rely on someone else instead of me." Jack laughed at the irony that he never wanted to be dependent, and yet enjoyed it when others depended on him.

I asked Jack about his family history. Apparently, his parents had a very contentious divorce after years of fighting in front of their kids. One day, he came home from school and his father had packed up and disappeared and left his mother to explain the situation to the kids. He knew it wasn't logical, but he blamed himself for arguing with his father about chores the night before, believing he caused the final decision between his parents. He admitted that he got his value from his mother saying how dependable and reliable he was. She regularly compared him to his "good-for-nothing" father, and he wanted to uphold this image and reputation.

Jack's clarified vision of what he wanted in his life included the ability to ask for help and the wisdom to know when he should say no. He wanted to be less indispensable and have more two-way relationships. He admitted he didn't trust anyone, and thought they'd eventually leave him.

After clearing his fears, bitterness, and beliefs about why people wouldn't stick around, he was able to identify his next yes of dating friends of friends rather than fishing around on dating sites. He began finding more balance in his relationships and started the first "real" relationship he had had in his adult life.

The Yes Code for People Pleasing

Step One: Clarify your vision by answering: What do I really want my life to look like if I no longer engage in people pleasing? Why is this important to me? Put it in terms of something positive, so rather than, "I just want to stop people pleasing," consider what you want instead. Then ask yourself: What is the upside of my people pleasing? What is the downside of letting it go and enjoying my vision? These questions will help you identify your fears, limiting beliefs, and memories of old events that block your progress.

Step Two: Use your answers to the upside/downside questions and the tapping sequences below to clear your fears, limiting beliefs, and memories that lead to people pleasing. I have included scripts for three of the most common fears and three of the most common limiting beliefs that lead to people pleasing behavior.

Step Three: Once you've cleared your blocks, identify your next yes by answering: What feels like the next inspired step to take now? If it's too big, what is a smaller step I could take instead that would still feel like a yes?

Fears:

1. **I'm afraid to ask for help.**
2. **I'm afraid to say no.**
3. **I feel guilty saying no.**

Beliefs:

1. **They'll leave me if I say no.**
2. **Asking for help is dangerous.**
3. **I have to be in control.**

TAPPING TARGET:
I'm Afraid to Ask for Help

For so many of us, asking for help was a no-no in our families. Naturally, we grew up with the attitude that we should do it ourselves, even when we don't know how.

Measure your fear of asking for help on the 0–10 point scale. What do you imagine happening if you do ask for help? What might others say?

> **SIDE OF HAND:** Even though I'm afraid to reach out and ask for help, I deeply and completely love and accept myself anyway. Even though I'm afraid to ask for help, I accept who I am and how I feel.
>
> **EYEBROW:** I don't want to ask for help.
>
> **SIDE OF EYE:** I feel so uncomfortable.
>
> **UNDER EYE:** It makes me feel inadequate.
>
> **UNDER NOSE:** I hate asking for help.
>
> **CHIN:** I don't want to ask for help.
>
> **COLLARBONE:** I don't know what to do about this problem.
>
> **UNDER ARM:** I can't even ask for a little help.
>
> **HEAD:** I feel stuck when I need help.

Take a deep breath, and measure how afraid you still feel on the 0–10 point scale when you repeat the target phrase out loud: *I'm afraid to ask for help*. Now either repeat the sequence above, or change the wording to fit the specific reasons why asking for help bothers you.

> **SIDE OF HAND:** Even though I have always been reluctant to ask for help, I deeply and completely love and accept myself anyway. Even though I'm afraid to ask for help, I accept who I am and how I feel.
>
> **EYEBROW:** I still feel afraid to ask for help.
>
> **SIDE OF EYE:** I'm still afraid to ask for help.
>
> **UNDER EYE:** I don't like how it looks.

UNDER NOSE: I learned not to ask for help.
CHIN: I feel afraid when I need to ask for help.
COLLARBONE: All this fear is in my body.
UNDER ARM: I'm afraid to ask for help.
HEAD: I feel a lot of fear around this topic.

Take a deep breath, and measure your fear of asking for help on the 0–10 point scale again. Make note of any memories or additional fears that arise to use as targets in future tapping rounds before proceeding to the more "positive" solution-oriented outcomes below.

EYEBROW: I'm still not good at asking.
SIDE OF EYE: But I feel a little better already.
UNDER EYE: Maybe I could ask for a little help.
UNDER NOSE: Maybe it's a good idea.
CHIN: Everyone asks for help sometimes.
COLLARBONE: I feel calmer about this issue.
UNDER ARM: I like feeling calm about asking for help.
HEAD: It feels so much better to ask for help.

Take another deep breath, and measure your original target statement – I'm afraid to ask for help – on the 0–10 point scale. If other aspects surface, go ahead and create another tapping round for those aspects. For instance, if you are afraid of others thinking you're stupid or inadequate, your setup phrase would sound like this: "Even though I'm worried they'll think I'm stupid if I ask for help, I accept who I am and how I feel." And then the target phrase that you would repeat on all the other points would be: "I'm worried they'll think I'm stupid," or variations on that theme.

TAPPING TARGET:
I'm Afraid to Say No

Now we need to address the idea of setting good boundaries at work or at home. This brings up the behavior of saying no, which is very difficult if you're a people pleaser. If you say no to someone, or set a boundary, what do you fear? What might change in the relationship? What might be threatened? Will they dislike you because you won't do what they ask? Will they resent you? Will you resent them?

On the 0–10 point scale, measure how afraid you feel when you think of saying no to someone who asks you for a favor or to do something extra at work. If keeping a particular person in mind helps you focus (boss, friend, or partner), go ahead and picture saying no to them to get your initial measurement. Then start tapping as follows:

> **SIDE OF HAND:** Even though I'm afraid to say no, because they won't like it at all, I deeply and completely love and accept myself anyway. Even though I'm afraid to say no, I accept who I am and how I feel.
>
> **EYEBROW:** Don't ask me to say no.
>
> **SIDE OF EYE:** I'm afraid to say no.
>
> **UNDER EYE:** I hate saying no.
>
> **UNDER NOSE:** I know they won't like it.
>
> **CHIN:** I don't want to say no.
>
> **COLLARBONE:** It scares me to say no.
>
> **UNDER ARM:** I'm afraid to say no.
>
> **HEAD:** Please don't ask me to say no.

Now take a deep breath, and with one particular person or incident in mind, measure your distress when you think of saying no on the 0–10 point scale again. Any movement? Any insights? Swap out the person you were picturing if you think that might get you more focused on this fear. We want you to be "in it" in order to find the right words as you tap to decrease the anxiety. Continue tapping:

SIDE OF HAND: Even though I'm still afraid to say no, I appreciate that it's difficult and that I'm doing the best I can. Even though I'm still afraid to say no, I accept all of me anyway.

EYEBROW: It still scares me to say no.

SIDE OF EYE: I don't want them to be mad.

UNDER EYE: I remember what happened last time.

UNDER NOSE: I don't want to say no.

CHIN: I'm afraid to say no.

COLLARBONE: I know this fear gets me into trouble.

UNDER ARM: I always avoid saying no.

HEAD: I'm afraid to say no to anyone.

Take another deep breath, and measure your fear of saying no with particular people or certain circumstances in mind on the 0–10 point scale. Hopefully you are feeling a decrease in the anxiety or more insight into why you feel so afraid. Jot down any insights to use in future tapping rounds.

At this point, you could either continue tapping on the target as listed above, or move to the more positive tapping round below.

EYEBROW: I'm still afraid to say no.

SIDE OF EYE: But I feel calmer already.

UNDER EYE: It's true they won't like it.

UNDER NOSE: But I can handle that now.

CHIN: I want to want to say no.

COLLARBONE: I deserve to say no.

UNDER ARM: I feel better already.

HEAD: I can learn to say no when I need to.

Take another deep breath, measure the intensity of the fear on the 0–10 point scale, and either continue to tap on this fear or choose another related tapping target.

Scan this QR code or visit www.TheYesCode.com for a video of using EFT for the tapping target, Fear of Saying No.

TAPPING TARGET:
I Feel Guilty When I Say No

Do you feel guilty at the thought of saying no to someone? Feeling guilty about saying no is different than being afraid to say no. Some people feel terribly guilty, and the guilt traps them into saying yes way too often. If you feel guilty at just the thought of setting better boundaries and saying no, try this next tapping exercise.

> **SIDE OF HAND:** Even though I don't say no because it makes me feel too guilty, I deeply and completely love and accept myself anyway. Even though I feel so guilty whenever I say no, it's too uncomfortable, I accept who I am and how I feel.
>
> **EYEBROW:** I feel so guilty when I say no.
>
> **SIDE OF EYE:** I think my responsibility is to say yes.
>
> **UNDER EYE:** I can't say no without feeling guilty.
>
> **UNDER NOSE:** I can't say no.
>
> **CHIN:** It makes me cringe with guilt.
>
> **COLLARBONE:** I avoid saying no because of my guilt.
>
> **UNDER ARM:** I feel too guilty when I say no.
>
> **HEAD:** No wonder I feel trapped.

Take a deep breath, and measure your level of guilt on the 0–10 point scale when you think of saying no, and proceed to the next tapping round:

> **SIDE OF HAND:** Even though I still feel guilty when I think of saying no, I accept who I am and how I feel. Even though

I still feel guilty when I think of saying no to someone, I accept how I feel and where I got this fear.

EYEBROW: I hate feeling so guilty.

SIDE OF EYE: I've always felt guilty.

UNDER EYE: I feel so guilty saying no.

UNDER NOSE: My guilt traps me every time.

CHIN: I wish I could say no.

COLLARBONE: I feel so guilty saying no.

UNDER ARM: I always feel guilty.

HEAD: I know how they feel is not my responsibility.

Take a deep breath, and measure your level of guilt when you say the target statement out loud. Did you notice the guilt decreasing? Any new insights coming up? Any particular people who "make you" feel more guilty than you already do? Use any new information to revise your tapping targets and keep working on this issue. In other words, if you can say no to colleagues at work but not your sister, imagine saying no to her and measure your guilt about that scenario. Your new setup statement could be: "Even though I feel too guilty to say no to my sister, I deeply and completely love and accept myself anyway." Your new target phrase for the other tapping points would be: "I feel guilty when I think of saying no to my sister...I can't say no to her."

Below is another tapping round with positive wording suggesting you have made some progress about being trapped by your guilt. Tap on it if it feels right to bring in the positive statements at this time. Remember, you don't need to get your guilt down to a zero, just down low enough that you feel ready to move on.

EYEBROW: I still feel guilty.

SIDE OF EYE: I'm learning to say no.

UNDER EYE: I appreciate how far I've come.

UNDER NOSE: Their reactions are not my responsibility.

CHIN: I want to say no calmly.

COLLARBONE: I think I could start to say no.

UNDER ARM: I appreciate that this is getting easier.

HEAD: Saying no is good for both of us.

Take a deep breath, and measure your feeling of guilt on the 0–10 point scale when you imagine saying no. Again, you may picture different people in your life who cause you distress around this topic. Keep tapping on each situation that comes up where you know you need to say no, but you say yes instead just to keep the peace.

TAPPING TARGET:
They'll Leave Me If I Say No

These next two beliefs about the possible consequences of saying no are rooted in deeper trauma. Most people aren't afraid someone will leave them if they say no unless they've experienced this as a threat or as a real scenario from their past. In other words, most people would agree it's uncomfortable to say no, but not that they will be abandoned or left if they say no.

Measure how true this belief feels to you on the 0–10 point scale. Maybe you did experience this as a threat or a real life situation, so you became a people pleaser and avoid saying no as a way to protect yourself from someone else leaving you. If so, take notes on the specifics of the memory and use the information as a target for your next tapping round. If at any time the feelings feel too intense for you, please stop the tapping, and seek additional support for yourself from your mental health care provider or from a qualified EFT practitioner.

SIDE OF HAND: Even though I'm convinced they'll leave me if I dare to say no, I accept who I am and how I feel about this. Even though I'm certain they'll leave me if I say no, I accept who I am and how I feel.

EYEBROW: I'm convinced they'll leave if I say no.

SIDE OF EYE: I'm sure they'll just leave me.

UNDER EYE: I feel trapped and can't say no.

UNDER NOSE: No wonder I always say yes to them.

CHIN: I'm worried they'll just leave me if I say no.

COLLARBONE: I feel so stuck.

UNDER ARM: I know they'll leave me if I say no.

HEAD: I'm worried they'll leave me if I dare to say no.

Take a deep breath, and measure this conviction or belief on the 0–10 point scale again. It will likely bring up an old incident for you. You could change the wording of the setup statement, or keep tapping as I've indicated below. For instance, your new setup statement might be as follows: "Even though I expect to be left if I say no, I accept who I am and what happened back then." Then your target phrase could be: "I still expect to be left."

SIDE OF HAND: Even though I'm convinced they'll leave just like last time, I accept who I am and how I feel. Even though I remember what happened the last time I said no, I accept who I am and how I feel.

EYEBROW: I remember how it felt last time.

SIDE OF EYE: I learned never to say no.

UNDER EYE: I remember how scared I was.

UNDER NOSE: I remember what happened when I said no.

CHIN: I remember what happened last time.

COLLARBONE: I learned never to say no again.

UNDER ARM: No wonder I don't say no to anyone.

HEAD: I always fear they'll threaten me.

Take another deep breath, and measure how true or distressing this belief feels to you now on the 0–10 point scale. Do you still expect someone to leave you if you say no? If you feel ready, go ahead and tap with the more positive statements below.

EYEBROW: That was then, and this is now.

SIDE OF EYE: Maybe I don't have to be left.

UNDER EYE: Maybe I can say no more often now.

UNDER NOSE: I'm ready to say no.

CHIN: I used to be scared, but I'm letting go.

COLLARBONE: It feels freeing to let go of that fear.

UNDER ARM: I'm ready to start saying no now.

HEAD: I'm ready to let go and start saying no.

Take a final deep breath, and measure this belief on the 0–10 point scale. Does it still feel true? Keep tapping until you release this expectation and can start practicing saying no.

TAPPING TARGET:
Asking for Help Is Dangerous

If the thought of asking for help actually feels dangerous to you, it is likely you were punished or scolded for asking for help as a child. It's not natural to be afraid to ask for help, so you would have learned that belief in your family or at school. Measure how true this belief feels to you on the 0–10 point scale. If a particular memory comes to mind when you were punished, you could use that memory for your tapping sequence.

Suppose you asked for help with your homework, but your parents were preoccupied with something else at the time and criticized you. This could be a memory to use as a tapping target. Your setup statement for the side of your hand would sound something like this: "Even though I remember them getting mad at me when I asked for help back then, I deeply and completely love and accept myself anyway." Then you would use: "They got mad at me when I asked for help" as the main phrase for the additional tapping points.

Try this Tapping sequence below:

SIDE OF HAND: Even though I'm afraid I'll be punished again for asking for help, I accept who I am and how I feel about it. Even though I'm convinced it would be dangerous to ask for help, I accept who I am and how I feel about this topic.

EYEBROW: Asking for help feels dangerous.

SIDE OF EYE: I remember what happened last time.

UNDER EYE: I don't want to ask for help.

UNDER NOSE: I assume I'll get into trouble, again.

CHIN: It feels dangerous to ask for help.

COLLARBONE: I know it could get me in big trouble.

UNDER ARM: Asking for help feels dangerous.

HEAD: No wonder I always do everything by myself.

Take a deep breath, and measure how true this belief feels to you on the 0–10 point scale. Keep tapping as indicated below.

SIDE OF HAND: Even though I'm still convinced that asking for help is dangerous, I accept who I am and how I feel. Even though I'm still certain that it's dangerous to ask for help, I deeply and completely love and accept myself now.

EYEBROW: It still feels dangerous to ask for help.

SIDE OF EYE: I might get into trouble again.

UNDER EYE: It still feels dangerous to ask for help.

UNDER NOSE: But I really need help.

CHIN: I'm tired of expecting danger.

COLLARBONE: Maybe it's no longer dangerous.

UNDER ARM: Maybe I could start to ask for help.

HEAD: I'm still convinced it could be dangerous.

Take another deep breath, and measure how true this belief feels to you on the 0–10 point scale. Keep tapping as indicated above if this belief still feels very true to you, or proceed with the more positive tapping phrases below.

EYEBROW: I was convinced asking for help is dangerous.

SIDE OF EYE: I'm starting to feel better about it.

UNDER EYE: It was dangerous in the past.

UNDER NOSE: But it's safer for me now.

CHIN: I deserve to ask for help.

COLLARBONE: I deserve to get help.

UNDER ARM: It's time for me to get the help I deserve.

HEAD: I'm ready to move forward and ask for help.

Take a final deep breath, and measure the belief again on the 0–10 point scale. If you have other memories of it being dangerous to ask for help, go ahead and tap on a revised setup statement: "Even though I remember another time when they yelled at me instead of helping me, I deeply and completely love and accept myself now." And then you could use phrases on the additional tapping points such as, "I remember learning that asking for help was dangerous," and "It was dangerous back then."

TAPPING TARGET:
I Have to Be in Control

Does this belief feel true to you on the 0–10 point scale? What would happen if you relinquished control and let other people occasionally take the lead at work or at home? Start tapping:

SIDE OF HAND: Even though I'm convinced I need to be in control, I accept who I am and how I feel. Even though I believe I'm the only one who can do it and do it well, I accept who I am and how I feel.

EYEBROW: I'm convinced I'm the only one.

SIDE OF EYE: I have to do it all.

UNDER EYE: Nobody else will do it well enough.

UNDER NOSE: If I don't do it, it won't get done.

CHIN: I need to be the one in charge.

COLLARBONE: I don't want to let go.

UNDER ARM: I have to be in charge.

HEAD: I need to be in charge all the time.

Take a deep breath, and measure how true this belief feels to you now on the 0–10 point scale. Does this cause anxiety or fear when you think of letting go of control? Continue tapping.

> SIDE OF HAND: Even though I'm sure that I'm the only one who can be in control, I accept who I am and how I feel. Even though they taught me that it was all up to me, I accept who I am and how I learned this lesson.
>
> EYEBROW: I can't let go of control.
>
> SIDE OF EYE: It wouldn't be safe.
>
> UNDER EYE: I have to be in control.
>
> UNDER NOSE: I need to be in control.
>
> CHIN: I don't want to let go.
>
> COLLARBONE: It feels dangerous to let go.
>
> UNDER ARM: I can't let go of control.
>
> HEAD: Something bad might happen.

Take another deep breath, and measure how true this belief feels to you now on the 0–10 point scale. If any of the phrases above really hit home, you could create your own tapping sequence just for that belief. For instance, you could use this setup statement: "Even though I'm convinced that I can't let go of control or something bad will happen, I deeply and completely love and accept myself." Then you could just repeat the target belief, "I can't let go of control or something bad will happen," on all the remaining points on the face and body.

If you feel ready, proceed to the tapping round with more positive phrases about letting go:

> EYEBROW: I used to need control.
>
> SIDE OF EYE: But now I want to let go.
>
> UNDER EYE: I feel safer letting go.
>
> UNDER NOSE: I don't need to be in control anymore.
>
> CHIN: I'm ready to let go.
>
> COLLARBONE: It feels safe to let go now.

UNDER ARM: I can let go of control now.

HEAD: I appreciate feeling safe letting go.

Take a final deep breath, and measure how true this still feels to you now on the 0–10 point scale.

People pleasing is a frustrating sabotaging behavior that will definitely hold you back. There is no doubt it is keeping you safe by providing protection from these fears and beliefs listed above. Keep working through your fear and your guilt until you realize it's both healthy and appropriate to set good boundaries, ask for help, and say no when you need to.

After you have used tapping for the most obvious fears, beliefs, and memories for yourself, consider what your next inspired step – your next yes – feels like for you and plan on taking it. If it causes more fear, go ahead and do more tapping for your fear.

CHAPTER 12

ADDICTIONS

Whether you feel you are addicted to alcohol, drugs, food, or destructive behaviors, addictions get in your way of living a full and satisfying life. Using substances will sabotage your success very quickly.

One of the dominant fears for someone who is using substances is that they fear feeling *any of their feelings*. They've locked their emotions away behind the numbing effects of drugs, alcohol, and food for so long, that they're not even sure what's lurking behind this wall. Many addicts will tell you that's what got them started drinking or using drugs in the first place – their feelings were too intense to handle. Someone offered them a drink when they were a teenager and voila, their social anxiety was solved. Remember that the definition of an addiction is that the behavior gets you into trouble – with the law, your family, at work, or with your health – yet you continue to abuse the substances or engage in the risky behavior.

If you are engaged in substance abuse, emotional overeating, or any addictive behavior, ask yourself expanded upside/downside questions:

- How does using this substance protect me?
- What am I afraid of if I don't have access to it anymore?

- What would be the downside of giving it up?
- What am I afraid of if I give up food/alcohol/drugs?

I have provided several client cases below, followed by a review of The Yes Code™ process for you. Then I've written out scripts for the most common fears and limiting beliefs for people engaged in addictions.

Jonnie

Jonnie was an alcoholic and had relapsed many times after short periods of sobriety. When I asked him to clarify his vision, he didn't just want longer term sobriety, he wanted to stop feeling tortured by his shame. When I asked him to describe the positive version of that vision, he said, "I'd like to forgive myself and finally feel at peace."

He described his family as a "trainwreck" and said both parents were alcoholics, and his father was physically violent with him and his two brothers. I asked him what the upside was of relapsing; how did it serve him? Jonnie said, "Every time I get sober for more than a few weeks, the pain, hurt, shame, and rage comes screaming back. When it reaches a certain intensity, that's when I start thinking it's a better idea to drink than to feel any of these feelings." The downside to getting sober was obvious to him – he'd have to remember and feel emotional conflicts he had been avoiding for years. He'd have to address his painful memories of his parents' divorce, the terror and shame of changing schools and being an outcast, and the shame of ruining his first marriage with his drinking.

After intensive therapy and tapping for his self-hatred, shame and rage, Jonnie started putting together longer periods of sobriety. He identified that his next yes was getting a sponsor in Alcoholics Anonymous, something he had previously resisted. He eventually earned his three-year chip and made great headway in forgiving himself for the damage he had caused to friends and family members, as well as to himself. Without expressing his feelings or using a tool such as tapping to reduce the panic in his brain, Jonnie couldn't have put any sobriety together. It just felt too unsafe to feel his emotions.

Annie

Annie was 40 pounds overweight. She said her cravings were totally unmanageable and she just couldn't stop eating. She would diet, then binge, and end up weighing a little more each time she went on the roller coaster. When I asked her to consider Step One of The Yes Code – to clarify her vision – she said she wanted to be "craving-free" and relaxed around food and mealtimes, which usually made her feel anxious and uptight. She knew she could lose the weight if she released her intense cravings.

I asked her what the upside was of carrying around all this extra weight. She said, "It keeps me from feeling my grief about losing my grandmother." She was convinced that the downside of losing the weight was that she would "drown in her own grief." Her grandmother was her only protector and "friend" in her family. Everyone else had criticized her and told her she was too sensitive, too slow, too something. Her grandmother died when she was a kid, and she started overeating then. After using tapping on her fears of feeling the grief and on the grief itself, she noticed other layers of feelings that needed tapping, too. She realized that overeating made her feel "connected to her grandmother" as they often had meals and snacks together. She was also very angry at her parents because not only had they criticized her, but they also hadn't been very kind to her grandmother and showed very little empathy to Annie about this tremendous loss. Once she used tapping to work through these layers of emotions she had been numbing with food, she was able to identify her next yeses of finding a reasonable food plan, working with an accountability partner, and starting a gentle exercise program. She lost the weight and continued to tackle ongoing stress in her life with the tapping.

The Yes Code for Addictions

Step One: Clarify your vision by answering: What do I really want my life to look like when I stop using drugs and alcohol? Why is this important to me? Then ask yourself: What is the upside of continuing to use my drug of choice? What is the downside of getting sober (losing the weight) and reaching my vision? These questions will help you identify your fears, limiting beliefs, and memories that block your progress.

Step Two: Use the answers to the upside/downside questions and the tapping sequences below to clear your fears, limiting beliefs, and memories that keep you using your drug of choice.

Step Three: Once you've cleared your blocks, identify your next yes by answering: What feels like the next best step to take now? If it's too big, what is a smaller step I could take instead that would still feel inspiring?

I have included three tapping scripts for fears and feelings, and three tapping scripts for common beliefs that often surface for alcoholics, addicts, and people who emotionally overeat.

Feelings:

1. **Fear of feeling my emotions**
2. **Guilt and shame over my behavior**
3. **Stress over cravings**

Beliefs:

1. **It's too late to recover after all the damage.**
2. **I don't have what it takes.**
3. **I'm not worthy of success.**

TAPPING TARGET:
Fear of Feeling my Emotions

Sometimes a person who gets sober can't identify what specific emotions they are afraid of feeling. All they know is that they don't want to feel anything intense. If that resonates for you, measure how afraid you are of feeling your emotions on the 0–10 point scale, and try this tapping sequence below:

> SIDE OF HAND: Even though I'm afraid of feeling my emotions, I deeply and completely love and accept myself anyway. Even though I'm afraid of feeling any of my emotions, I don't want to go there, I accept who I am and how I feel.
>
> EYEBROW: I don't want to feel anything.
>
> SIDE OF EYE: I'm afraid to feel my big emotions.
>
> UNDER EYE: I'm afraid to feel anything.
>
> UNDER NOSE: I don't want to stop using, I might feel too much.
>
> CHIN: I can't take the stress of my emotions.
>
> COLLARBONE: I can't take the intensity of my emotions.
>
> UNDER ARM: I've tried before.
>
> HEAD: I failed at feeling my emotions.

Take a deep breath, and measure your fear again on the 0–10 point scale. Continue tapping:

> SIDE OF HAND: Even though I'm still afraid of feeling my emotions, I choose to appreciate who I am and that I'm trying. Even though I'm still afraid of feeling intense emotions, that's why I started using drugs/alcohol/food in the first place, I accept who I am and how I feel.
>
> EYEBROW: I'm still afraid of feeling my emotions.
>
> SIDE OF EYE: They're too intense for me.
>
> UNDER EYE: I'm afraid of feeling too much.
>
> UNDER NOSE: I can't handle it.

CHIN: I've never been able to handle them.

COLLARBONE: I'm afraid they will overwhelm me.

UNDER ARM: I'm afraid of feeling any of them.

HEAD: I'm terrified of my intense emotions.

Take another deep breath, and measure your fear now on the 0–10 point scale. If your number is still intense (above a 7) then go ahead and repeat this round again. If you're ready to acknowledge that you've made some progress and could handle some positive tapping, proceed to the round below:

EYEBROW: I am doing better every day.

SIDE OF EYE: I can handle feeling a little bit at a time.

UNDER EYE: I don't have to feel everything today.

UNDER NOSE: And now I have the tools.

CHIN: I was afraid but now I'm calmer about it.

COLLARBONE: I was afraid but now I feel better.

UNDER ARM: I can handle a little bit of emotion.

HEAD: I feel stronger about this topic.

Take a deep breath, and measure how afraid you feel of feeling your emotions on the 0–10 point scale now, and then continue tapping.

TAPPING TARGET:
I Feel Guilty and Ashamed of My Behavior

Many addicts and alcoholics feel guilty for the damage they've caused when drunk or using drugs. They have ruined relationships, caused financial headaches, and generally behaved immaturely and selfishly. They may have been verbally or physically abusive and may have treated other people very poorly. Once they face their guilt, it can feel quite intense, and they might have cravings again and struggle with the urge to relapse.

Measure how guilty you feel on the 0–10 point scale about something you did (or didn't do) because you were too involved in your addiction to show up or remember.

> **SIDE OF HAND:** Even though I feel so guilty for what I did, I accept who I am and how I feel. Even though I feel so guilty for what I did, I accept myself and accept responsibility now.
>
> **EYEBROW:** I feel so guilty.
>
> **SIDE OF EYE:** I can't take the guilt.
>
> **UNDER EYE:** I feel so guilty.
>
> **UNDER NOSE:** It makes me feel terrible.
>
> **CHIN:** I know I was so selfish.
>
> **COLLARBONE:** I know I didn't care about anyone else.
>
> **UNDER ARM:** I feel so guilty.
>
> **HEAD:** I wish I didn't feel this way.

Take a deep breath, and measure your guilt on the 0–10 point scale now. Continue tapping. You may take more than one of these issues or incidents that you feel guilty about and do tapping on each of them separately.

> **SIDE OF HAND:** Even though I still feel guilty about what I did when I was using drugs/alcohol, I deeply and completely love and accept myself. Even though I still feel guilty about what I did, I accept who I am anyway.
>
> **EYEBROW:** I still feel guilty.
>
> **SIDE OF EYE:** I was so selfish.
>
> **UNDER EYE:** I still feel guilty.
>
> **UNDER NOSE:** I shouldn't have done it.
>
> **CHIN:** But I wasn't thinking straight.
>
> **COLLARBONE:** I still feel guilty.
>
> **UNDER ARM:** I was so immature and selfish.
>
> **HEAD:** I wonder if I will ever forgive myself.

Take another deep breath, and measure how you feel about this particular incident now on the 0–10 point scale. If the number hasn't budged at all, consider the upside/downside questions again: What might be the upside of holding onto all your guilt? What might be the downside of letting it go? Then proceed to the more positive tapping round.

> **EYEBROW:** I didn't treat them well.
>
> **SIDE OF EYE:** It's time to forgive myself.
>
> **UNDER EYE:** I want to move on.
>
> **UNDER NOSE:** I want to forgive myself.
>
> **CHIN:** I did a terrible job in the past.
>
> **COLLARBONE:** But it's behind me now.
>
> **UNDER ARM:** I want face it and forgive myself.
>
> **HEAD:** I choose to move on.

TAPPING TARGET:

Stress Over Cravings

While cravings feel "real" to people who have them, they are actually a byproduct of built-up emotional stress. When I ask people what the downside is of not drinking or eating a favorite food, they usually admit that they'd have to feel very uncomfortable, so they never let themselves be without their substance of choice.

If you're having a craving now for a particular food or for alcohol, go right to the tapping sequence below. Or, you could think about a food that you usually crave and imagine it in detail in your mind.

Try this tapping sequence on a craving you have:

> **SIDE OF HAND:** Even though I have a strong craving for this substance, I choose to feel calm and relaxed about it. Even though I really want this substance right now, I choose to feel calm and peaceful.
>
> **EYEBROW:** I desperately want this substance.
>
> **SIDE OF EYE:** I can feel the craving.

UNDER EYE: I want it right now.

UNDER NOSE: It feels intense to me.

CHIN: I don't want to feel this craving.

COLLARBONE: I just want to eat/drink/use.

UNDER ARM: I have such a strong craving right now.

HEAD: I don't know if I can control myself.

Take a deep breath, and measure your craving on the 0–10 point scale. Has it decreased? Do you feel the same about it? Keep tapping until your craving is low enough that you have a choice about whether you want to consume it or not.

SIDE OF HAND: Even though I still have this craving, I deeply and completely love and accept myself anyway. Even though I still feel this strong craving, I accept who I am and how I feel.

EYEBROW: I still have this craving.

SIDE OF EYE: I can feel the craving.

UNDER EYE: I still want it right now.

UNDER NOSE: It feels a little lower to me.

CHIN: I feel a lot of stress.

COLLARBONE: I feel stress with the craving.

UNDER ARM: I hate these strong cravings.

HEAD: I have such a strong craving right now.

Take another deep breath, and measure how strong your craving is now on the 0–10 point scale. If you feel ready, go ahead and proceed to the more positive tapping sequence below.

EYEBROW: I feel so much calmer.

SIDE OF EYE: I can take it or leave it.

UNDER EYE: I don't need to have it right now.

UNDER NOSE: It doesn't feel as intense to me.

CHIN: I don't feel so anxious about the craving.

COLLARBONE: I feel calmer about this.

UNDER ARM: I feel so much better right now.

HEAD: I feel calm and stable.

Take a final deep breath, and remember that you can come back to this tapping sequence whenever you need to. I recommend you do tapping before every social event where there is food or alcohol, and before every meal. If more feelings, memories, or beliefs surface that seem difficult to handle on your own, please consult your health care practitioner for extra support.

TAPPING TARGET:
It's Too Late to Recover

Many alcoholics and addicts will tell you that it feels too late for them. They've hurt family members, ruined their relationships at work, and damaged their health as well. But it's never too late to make amends and start using tapping to clear your fears and your beliefs.

SIDE OF HAND: Even though I'm convinced it's too late for me because I've done too much damage, I deeply and completely love and accept myself anyway. Even though I'm convinced it's too late for me – I've done too much damage – I accept who I am and that I'm trying to recover.

EYEBROW: I'm convinced it's too late for me.

SIDE OF EYE: I've done too much damage already.

UNDER EYE: I don't know if it's worth it.

UNDER NOSE: It feels too late for me.

CHIN: I believe it's too late.

COLLARBONE: I just want to give up.

UNDER ARM: Why bother trying?

HEAD: It's too late for me.

Take a deep breath, and measure how true this belief feels to you now on the 0–10 point scale. No matter how many times you've relapsed or lost and regained the weight, it's never too late.

Keep tapping:

SIDE OF HAND: Even though I still believe it's too late for me, I deeply and completely love and accept myself anyway. Even though I'm still convinced it's too late for me to recover, I accept who I am and how I feel.

EYEBROW: I still believe it's too late.

SIDE OF EYE: I've done too much damage.

UNDER EYE: I'm still convinced it's too late.

UNDER NOSE: Too much time has passed.

CHIN: I'm convinced it's too late.

COLLARBONE: I don't believe I can do it.

UNDER ARM: I am convinced it's too late.

HEAD: I've just done too much damage to myself and others.

Take another deep breath, and measure how true this belief feels to you now on the 0–10 point scale. This one may be a very stubborn belief that could keep you sabotaging yourself because you cleverly use it as an excuse to keep eating or drinking. Keep tapping, and if you feel ready, go ahead and use the more positive tapping sequence below:

EYEBROW: What if it's not too late?

SIDE OF EYE: What if I can make amends?

UNDER EYE: Maybe I can recover.

UNDER NOSE: I want to start living my life.

CHIN: I'm willing to start trying.

COLLARBONE: And I will consider forgiving myself.

UNDER ARM: I'm ready to start fresh.

HEAD: I'm ready to have new beliefs.

Take a final deep breath, and measure how true this belief feels to you now on the 0–10 point scale. You may repeat these tapping sequences at any time you need to.

TAPPING TARGET:
I Don't Have What It Takes

This target is more general, but still works well if that's how you feel about yourself. It's important to find out where you learned this. What experiences taught you that you don't "have what it takes?" Do you feel flawed or inadequate? Get as specific as possible and tailor the tapping sequence below as needed.

First, measure how true this belief feels to you on the 0–10 point scale. Then proceed to the tapping.

> **SIDE OF HAND:** Even though I believe I'm flawed, and I don't have what it takes to attract success, I deeply and completely love and accept myself. Even though I'm convinced that I'm missing something, and success is not for me, I accept who I am and how I feel.
>
> **EYEBROW:** I'm convinced I'm flawed.
>
> **SIDE OF EYE:** I don't have what it takes.
>
> **UNDER EYE:** I think something is wrong with me.
>
> **UNDER NOSE:** I feel flawed and broken.
>
> **CHIN:** I don't have what it takes.
>
> **COLLARBONE:** I feel flawed and inadequate.
>
> **UNDER ARM:** I don't have what it takes to attract abundance.
>
> **HEAD:** I'm convinced I don't have what it takes.

Take a deep breath, and measure how true your belief feels now on the 0–10 point scale. Does it feel any lighter? Did other thoughts or beliefs surface?

Continue tapping:

SIDE OF HAND: Even though I still believe that I don't have what it takes to attract what I want, I deeply and completely love and accept myself anyway. Even though I'm still convinced that I'm flawed and don't have what it takes, I accept who I am and how I feel.

EYEBROW: I've never had what it takes.

SIDE OF EYE: That's what I was taught by them.

UNDER EYE: But what if I do have what it takes?

UNDER NOSE: Maybe they were wrong.

CHIN: What if I am enough?

COLLARBONE: I'm almost ready to believe I am enough.

UNDER ARM: I'm willing to believe I have what it takes.

HEAD: I'm ready to attract success into my life now.

Take another deep breath, and measure how true your belief feels on the 0–10 point scale now. Proceed with the more positive statements below.

EYEBROW: What if I do have what it takes?

SIDE OF EYE: What if I definitely have what it takes?

UNDER EYE: I love knowing I'm not flawed.

UNDER NOSE: Nothing is wrong with me.

CHIN: I do have what it takes.

COLLARBONE: This is just an old belief.

UNDER ARM: I'm ready to let this go.

HEAD: I'm ready to release this old belief.

Take a final deep breath, and measure how true this feels to you now on the 0–10 point scale. Consider what belief could replace this negative one, write it down, and repeat it to yourself while tapping. For instance, you could do one full round of tapping while saying, "I do have what it takes."

I'm Not Worthy of Success

If you do not feel worthy of success, there is no way to achieve it. Success will be incongruent with your beliefs, and you can't *get there*. Remember, our beliefs are compulsive; we have no other choice but to live them out in our lives.

Were you ever told you're not worthy of success? Who in your life believed this or communicated this to you? If a specific incident comes to mind, measure how upsetting it feels to you on the 0–10 point scale. And then measure how true this belief feels to you. Again, because it is a belief, you might doubt that it could change.

Start tapping below:

> **SIDE OF HAND:** Even though I don't think I'm worthy of success, I just don't deserve it, I deeply and completely love and accept myself anyway. Even though I don't feel worthy of success, I accept who I am and how I feel.
>
> **EYEBROW:** I'm just not worthy of success.
>
> **SIDE OF EYE:** Why would I be?
>
> **UNDER EYE:** They said I wasn't worthy of success.
>
> **UNDER NOSE:** I'm convinced I'm not worthy.
>
> **CHIN:** I've never had it anyway.
>
> **COLLARBONE:** I'm not worthy of success.
>
> **UNDER ARM:** Nothing can change this.
>
> **HEAD:** I'm simply not worthy.

Take a deep breath, and measure this belief on the 0–10 point scale. Is anything changing? Has it gone down? Did you get any other specific images or memories of an event that contributed to this belief in your life? If so, take note of them and formulate additional tapping sequences for yourself. For instance, if you remember a family member saying something like, "you never do it right," your new setup statement would be, "Even though I'm convinced I'll never do it

right, just like she said, I choose to accept who I am and how I feel."
Continue tapping:

SIDE OF HAND: Even though I still don't think I'm worthy
of success, I deeply and completely love and accept myself
anyway. Even though they taught me that I wasn't worthy, I
accept who I am and how I feel.

EYEBROW: They taught me I wasn't worthy of success.

SIDE OF EYE: I don't believe I am worthy of success.

UNDER EYE: I know exactly where it came from.

UNDER NOSE: I'm not worthy of success.

CHIN: I don't think I'm worthy.

COLLARBONE: I'm convinced I'm not worthy.

UNDER ARM: There are many reasons why I'm not worthy of
success.

HEAD: I don't believe I'm worthy of success.

Take another deep breath, and measure this belief on the 0–10 point
scale. Now start the positive tapping round below:

EYEBROW: What if I am worthy of success?

SIDE OF EYE: What if I've been worthy all along?

UNDER EYE: What if I am already worthy?

UNDER NOSE: I don't believe I'm not worthy anymore.

CHIN: I think I might be worthy of success.

COLLARBONE: What if I've always been worthy?

UNDER ARM: I might have been worthy all along.

HEAD: I will give them their belief back, it's not mine.

Take a final deep breath, and measure how true this belief feels to you
now on the 0–10 point scale. Keep tapping until this belief is neutralized enough to feel flat or unimportant. Consider what belief you
would like to replace it with and tap while you are saying the new,
positive belief out loud. If you get any pushback from your thoughts –
"this isn't true" – keep tapping on the phrase "this isn't true" and then

continue tapping while saying your new belief until the new belief feels true.

If you've done enough tapping on your fears and beliefs, you will notice that your behavior starts to change. Now you can find your next yes and take inspired actions for your life.

CHAPTER 13

CLUTTER

In this chapter, I have provided several client stories about clutter, a review of The Yes Code™ process, and multiple scripts for the feelings and beliefs that are often underneath the self-sabotaging behavior of collecting clutter.

Andrea

Andrea came to a Clearing Clutter with EFT workshop I hosted and had some follow up sessions with me. I asked her to clarify the vision of what she wanted. She said she wanted to be free of the clutter and mess that had always surrounded her. I asked her what she wanted instead. She said, "Peace of mind, quiet, and the ability to make some new choices in my life." Andrea was the middle child of five kids and experienced shortages in food, clothing, and attention when growing up. She said the first two kids got everything material, and the last two got all the attention because they were the youngest. She always felt she had been stuck in the middle and there wasn't anything left for her after her siblings from "above or below" got what they needed. She was convinced there would never be enough of anything she wanted, and she admitted that she believed in lack and scarcity.

Andrea's clutter problem had reached a tipping point. She had tripped over a pile of books in her living room and ended up with stitches in her leg and a sprained wrist. She came to me to try and understand where her clutter problem came from and how to get rid of it.

I asked her what the upside was of keeping all the clutter around her. She paused, and burst out, "Well, at least it's mine and I get to have all of it!" While her experience of lack was true for her in her childhood, it didn't have to continue to be true in her adult life. I asked her, "What is the upside of holding onto the belief that there would always be lack in your life?" She said, "If I continue to believe this, then I won't have to get my hopes up and be disappointed when I don't get what I want." After understanding that she was holding onto the clutter because of the belief she needed to protect herself, we tapped on setup statements, such as: "Even though I don't have to share my stuff with anyone, I deeply and completely love and accept myself," and "Even though my stuff keeps me safe, I accept who I am and how I feel." Tapping became fun for her and she released the need to hold onto so much unnecessary stuff. By using tapping on her fears and beliefs, she realized that the clutter gave her a false feeling of being safe and provided for but wasn't in fact helping her in her relationships or health.

Letting go of her beliefs around the *meaning* of clutter helped her let go of the actual clutter. It wasn't overnight, but her next yes was to make a solid plan to clean out her apartment one pile at a time. She later reported she was actually enjoying letting go of so much clutter and no longer felt unsafe as a result.

Ruth

Ruth contacted me about her clutter problem. I asked her to clarify her vision for her life, and she said: "I want to have peace in my home. I want to be able to invite people over without shame. I don't want to feel so attached to all this crap I have." When I asked her what the upside was of holding onto everything, she admitted, "When I'm preoccupied with my clutter and what to do with it all the time, I don't have to look at some old traumas and painful experiences." The upside was obvious to her; it distracted her from serious emotional work she knew she needed to tackle. Then I asked: "And the downside of letting it go?"

"Then I would be really clear, and that scares me. I'd be clear about my emotions, my dissatisfying job, and the reality of some of my troubled relationships." Ruth was surprised to hear herself admit she was afraid of being clear, but when she said it out loud, it resonated deeply with her. She understood that the distraction of her clutter had kept her safe from feeling deep emotional pain. Now that she knew what the underlying culprit was – trying to avoid emotional pain – we used tapping to target her fear of talking about her old traumas from childhood. With the fear subsiding with each tapping round, she was able to tell me about abusive situations she endured, and she was able to process the feelings and memories that she had been avoiding. She learned to be present with all her tangled emotions from her past. When she felt she had made enough progress with addressing what she had been afraid to face, she felt less attached to her stuff, and was able to make considerable headway in sorting, giving away, and getting rid of her clutter.

The Yes Code for Clearing Clutter

Step One: Clarify your vision by answering: What do I really want my life to look like when I let go of my clutter? Why is this important to me? Remember to state your vision in positive terms rather than just describing what you don't want. Then ask yourself: What is the upside of collecting clutter? What is the downside of letting it go and enjoying my vision? These questions will help you identify your fears, limiting beliefs, and any associated memories that block your progress.

Step Two: Use the answers to the upside/downside questions and the tapping sequences below to clear your fears, limiting beliefs and memories that lead to your collecting clutter.

Step Three: Once you've cleared your blocks, identify your next yes by answering: What feels like the next inspired step to take now? If it's too big, what is a smaller step I could take instead that would still feel inspiring?

Below, I have designed tapping scripts for the two most common fears and the top two most common beliefs for people who hold onto clutter.

Fears:

    4. **I'm afraid to be clear.**
    5. **I'm afraid of space/emptiness.**

Beliefs:

    1. **There won't be enough for me.**
    2. **I believe in lack and scarcity.**

TAPPING TARGET:
I'm Afraid to Be Clear

Remember that remaining unclear could be a possible upside to staying overwhelmed and cluttered. It could actually help you avoid conflicts in your life that are painful. Ask yourself again what your fears are about being clear – what might change? What might you need to examine if you become clear?

Maybe you're worried about what your emotional clarity might cause you to decide. Maybe there are changes ahead if you stop feeling overwhelmed and start being clear. Go back to the classic questions to uncover what's really going on:

- What is the upside of staying emotionally unclear?
- What is the downside of getting emotionally clear?
- How does it serve you to "not know" your next steps?

Measure the level of your fear of being clear on the 0–10 point scale when you say the target statement out loud, *I'm afraid to be clear*. Then proceed to the tapping sequences below.

> **SIDE OF HAND:** Even though I'm afraid to be clear, I deeply and completely love and accept myself anyway. Even though I'm afraid to be clear, I don't want to face what I'm avoiding, I accept who I am and why I'm afraid.
>
> **EYEBROW:** I'm afraid to be clear.
>
> **SIDE OF EYE:** What if I have to make changes?
>
> **UNDER EYE:** I'm afraid to be clear.
>
> **UNDER NOSE:** Maybe others won't like it.
>
> **CHIN:** Maybe I won't like it.
>
> **COLLARBONE:** I'm afraid of what might have to change.
>
> **UNDER ARM:** I'm afraid to be clear.
>
> **HEAD:** Maybe that's why I hold onto my clutter.

Take a deep breath, and measure your fear of being clear on the 0–10 point scale again. Maybe certain relationships came to mind, or changes you want in your professional life got your attention during this round of tapping.

If this is the first time you've considered whether being clear is solving a problem or not, take some time to journal about it and ask the questions again.

- What is the upside of staying unclear?
- Who might be upset if I'm really clear?
- What is the downside of being clear?
- What might change if I'm clear?
- What relationships might end if I'm clear?

Continue tapping:

> **SIDE OF HAND:** Even though I'm still afraid of being clear – what if I don't like what it feels like? – I accept who I am and how I feel. Even though I'm still afraid of being clear, it might rock the boat, I accept who I am and how I feel.
> **EYEBROW:** I'm still afraid of being clear.
> **SIDE OF EYE:** What if I feel painful emotions.
> **UNDER EYE:** I'm afraid to be clear.
> **UNDER NOSE:** I prefer to hide behind my clutter.
> **CHIN:** I'm afraid to be clear.
> **COLLARBONE:** I'd have to make too many changes.
> **UNDER ARM:** I know I'd need to make too many changes.
> **HEAD:** I'd rather stay unclear, it feels safer.

Take another deep breath, and measure this fear of being clear again on the 0–10 point scale. Try one more tapping round targeting the consequences of being clear:

> **SIDE OF HAND:** Even though I'm afraid my clarity will rock the boat, I accept who I am and how I feel. Even though they're not going to like how I change when I'm clear, I accept who I am anyway.
> **EYEBROW:** I'm afraid my clarity will rock the boat.
> **SIDE OF EYE:** I know how powerful I am when I'm clear.
> **UNDER EYE:** I'm afraid of being crystal clear.
> **UNDER NOSE:** They're not going to like it.
> **CHIN:** I might make a big change once I become clear.
> **COLLARBONE:** I'm worried I'll be inspired to leave.
> **UNDER ARM:** I'm worried about being too clear.
> **HEAD:** I know how powerful I can be when I'm clear.

Take a deep breath, and measure your fear of being clear again on the 0–10 point scale. You may use this tapping sequence every time you feel yourself slipping into that *I don't know what to do* area. Consider whether it's protecting you from making changes or rocking the boat.

Before using the more positive round below, continue taking notes on why you might be afraid to be clear. Consider what circumstances or relationships might be threatened if you become crystal clear about what next steps to take in your life. For instance, if you feel afraid of being judged for asking for help for your clutter, an additional setup statement would sound like this: Even though I'm afraid to ask for help because I'll be judged for my clutter, I deeply and completely love and accept myself anyway.

When you feel ready, proceed to this next round that includes more positive statements about being clear.

EYEBROW: I appreciate being clear.
SIDE OF EYE: I love being clear.
UNDER EYE: Being clear gives me so much energy.
UNDER NOSE: They might be upset with my clarity.
CHIN: It's none of my business what they think.
COLLARBONE: I need to be clear for me.
UNDER ARM: I deserve to be clear.
HEAD: I love being so clear now.

Take another deep breath, and measure your fear of being clear on the 0–10 point scale. Maybe there is no more fear when you consider being clear about your job, but there's a lot of fear around being clear about the direction of a particular relationship. Continue using setup phrases that have specific targets and keep tapping until it feels safe and productive to be emotionally clear. For instance, you might use revised setup statements like these:

Even though I'm afraid to know what I want, I deeply and completely love and accept myself.

Even though I'm worried they won't like my clarity, I accept who I am and how I feel.

Take a deep breath and measure your fear of being clear again on the 0–10 point scale. You may use this tapping sequence every time you need to make a decision and you feel yourself fading into a lack of emotional clarity.

Scan this QR code or visit www.TheYesCode.com for a video on how to use EFT for the tapping target, Fear of Being Clear.

TAPPING TARGET:

I'm Afraid of Space and Stillness

Without clutter, your space would definitely be calmer and quieter. Does that scare you? What is the upside to holding onto all this clutter? For instance, you might feel calmer when you are surrounded by physical items. What does it block you from feeling? Consider whether you appreciate that the chaos of your clutter interferes with experiencing old grief, fear, or loneliness.

Measure this fear for yourself on the 0–10 point scale. Start tapping below:

SIDE OF HAND: Even though I'm afraid to be in a quiet space, I deeply and completely love and accept myself anyway. Even though I'm afraid to be in a quiet space, I accept who I am and how I feel.

EYEBROW: I'm afraid to be quiet.

SIDE OF EYE: I'm afraid of space.

UNDER EYE: What if painful feelings surface?

UNDER NOSE: I don't want peace and quiet.

CHIN: That would scare me.

COLLARBONE: I don't want to feel my emotions.

UNDER ARM: I'm worried about space and stillness.

HEAD: I'm worried about too much quiet and space.

Take a deep breath, and measure how afraid you feel of being in a quiet space now on the 0–10 point scale.

> **SIDE OF HAND:** Even though I'm still afraid of having a quiet, calm space, I accept who I am and how I feel about it. Even though I'm still afraid to be too quiet and to have too much space, I accept who I am and how I feel.
> **EYEBROW:** I'm still afraid of the space.
> **SIDE OF EYE:** I'm still afraid of the quiet.
> **UNDER EYE:** I don't want feelings to surface.
> **UNDER NOSE:** It's why I like my clutter around me.
> **CHIN:** I'm afraid of too much space.
> **COLLARBONE:** I'm afraid to be still and quiet.
> **UNDER ARM:** I'm afraid I'll feel something painful.
> **HEAD:** I feel safer with all my stuff around me.

Take another deep breath, and measure how afraid you feel now on the 0–10 point scale of having too much space and quiet around you. Proceed to the positive tapping round below:

> **EYEBROW:** I can appreciate space now.
> **SIDE OF EYE:** I can handle quiet now.
> **UNDER EYE:** I appreciate my emotions that surface.
> **UNDER NOSE:** I can appreciate I was using my clutter as protection.
> **CHIN:** I am ready to release some clutter.
> **COLLARBONE:** I am ready to let go of some of my stuff.
> **UNDER ARM:** I feel ready to be still and quiet.
> **HEAD:** I appreciate how far I've come.

Take a final deep breath, and measure how you feel about having space around you without your clutter on the 0–10 point scale. Continue tapping on variations of this theme. Make note of any specific memories or feelings of discomfort that arise and use them in future tapping sequences.

TAPPING TARGET:
There Won't Be Enough for Me

If you are convinced that there won't be enough for you, ask yourself where you learned this belief. What experiences in your childhood led you to believe this in your adult life?

Do you believe there won't be enough for you? What is the focus of this belief? Money, food, clothing, attention, time? If you can quantify how true this feels to you, measure it on the 0–10 point scale.

Proceed to the tapping rounds below:

> **SIDE OF HAND:** Even though I'm convinced there won't be enough for me, I deeply and completely love and accept myself. Even though there was never enough before, so there won't be enough now, I accept who I am and how I feel.
>
> **EYEBROW:** There won't be enough for me.
>
> **SIDE OF EYE:** There never was enough for me.
>
> **UNDER EYE:** So why would there be enough now?
>
> **UNDER NOSE:** There was never enough for me.
>
> **CHIN:** I'm assuming there won't be enough for me now.
>
> **COLLARBONE:** There was never enough for me.
>
> **UNDER ARM:** I'm sure there won't be enough for me.
>
> **HEAD:** There was never enough for me.

Take a deep breath, and measure how true this feels to you now on the 0–10 point scale. Continue tapping.

> **SIDE OF HAND:** Even though I'm still convinced there won't be enough for me, I deeply and completely love and accept

myself anyway. Even though they taught me there wasn't enough for me, I accept who I am and how I feel.

EYEBROW: There was never enough for me.

SIDE OF EYE: I learned not to get my hopes up.

UNDER EYE: Why get disappointed?

UNDER NOSE: There was never enough for me.

CHIN: I'm convinced there won't be enough now.

COLLARBONE: I'm sure there won't be enough for me now.

UNDER ARM: I assume there won't be enough.

HEAD: Oh well, at least I won't get disappointed.

Take another deep breath, and measure how true this belief feels to you now on the 0–10 point scale. Proceed to the positive tapping round below:

EYEBROW: What if there could be enough now?

SIDE OF EYE: What if the past doesn't have to stay true?

UNDER EYE: What if there is enough for me now?

UNDER NOSE: It's true there wasn't enough in the past.

CHIN: What if this doesn't have to be true anymore?

COLLARBONE: I'm looking forward to having more than enough.

UNDER ARM: I appreciate relaxing about this topic.

HEAD: I love knowing there is enough for me now.

Take a final deep breath, and measure how true this feels to you now on the 0–10 point scale. Make notes of any other beliefs or thoughts that you might need to tap on to continue to neutralize this limiting belief.

TAPPING TARGET:
I Believe in Lack and Scarcity

If you truly believe this – that there is lack and scarcity everywhere – you will sabotage yourself to make this come true. So even if you're offered abundance, you won't accept or receive it. Your brain and mind can't contain the concept because it is not in alignment with your belief. You won't allow yourself to have what you don't believe is possible.

If this is a belief for you, where do you think you learned it? You could use a setup statement that sounds like this: Even though they taught me there was only lack, I deeply and completely love and accept myself anyway.

How did you get the impression that there's scarcity everywhere? How does this belief protect you? What would be the downside of letting go of this belief? A client of mine said he never wanted to get his hopes up, so letting go of this belief felt threatening to him. A setup statement for tapping might sound like this: Even though I'm afraid to believe in abundance, so I don't want to let go of my belief in scarcity, I deeply and completely love and accept myself anyway. If you started to believe in abundance instead of scarcity, what would change in your life?

Measure how true this belief feels to you on the 0–10 point scale. Proceed to the tapping below and see if you can change your beliefs about this topic.

> **SIDE OF HAND:** Even though I believe in scarcity, there's not enough of anything anywhere, I accept where I learned it and accept myself anyway. Even though I believe that everything is in short supply, I accept myself anyway.
>
> **EYEBROW:** I believe in scarcity and lack.
>
> **SIDE OF EYE:** That's what they taught me.
>
> **UNDER EYE:** I believe in scarcity and lack.
>
> **UNDER NOSE:** That's what I learned.
>
> **CHIN:** I believe in scarcity and lack.
>
> **COLLARBONE:** There's not enough of anything.
>
> **UNDER ARM:** I don't believe in abundance.
>
> **HEAD:** There's not enough anywhere.

Take a deep breath, and measure how true this belief feels to you on the 0–10 point scale. Keep tapping.

> **SIDE OF HAND:** Even though I don't believe in abundance, I only believe in scarcity, I deeply and completely love and accept myself anyway. Even though I'm convinced that everything is in short supply, I accept who I am and how I feel.
>
> **EYEBROW:** I don't believe in abundance.
>
> **SIDE OF EYE:** I only believe in scarcity and lack.
>
> **UNDER EYE:** Abundance is a foreign concept to me.
>
> **UNDER NOSE:** Everything seems scarce to me.
>
> **CHIN:** I believe in lack and scarcity.
>
> **COLLARBONE:** I know where this came from.
>
> **UNDER ARM:** And I believe it deeply.
>
> **HEAD:** I believe in lack and scarcity.

Take a deep breath, and measure how true this belief about lack and scarcity feels to you on the 0–10 point scale now. Continue tapping on the positive phrases below.

> **EYEBROW:** What if there is abundance, but I can't see it?
>
> **SIDE OF EYE:** What if there is plenty around me?
>
> **UNDER EYE:** What if scarcity and lack are just concepts?
>
> **UNDER NOSE:** What if this isn't true?
>
> **CHIN:** I want to believe in abundance.
>
> **COLLARBONE:** I want to believe there is enough.
>
> **UNDER ARM:** I love knowing there is enough.
>
> **HEAD:** I appreciate how much abundance is available.

Take a final deep breath, and measure how true this belief feels to you on the 0–10 point scale. Make notes of anything else that surfaced – phrases you heard, relatives who believed this, or events that taught you to believe in lack and scarcity. Use these phrases and events in future tapping sequences to continue to eradicate this belief. For instance, you might create these setup statements:

Even though I learned about scarcity from my family...

Even though my mother always said there wasn't enough...

Even though they ran out of _____ before I could have any...

I have addressed some of the most common fears and beliefs that could be the source of collecting clutter, and given you solid guideposts for tapping to release the need to surround yourself with stuff you don't need. Now that you've cleared some of these feelings and beliefs, consider what might be a reasonable next yes step for you, and make a commitment to follow through. If at any time more fear arises, create a new tapping target and setup statement for yourself.

Now let's proceed to the next self-sabotaging behavior.

CHAPTER 14

RELATIONSHIP DRAMA

I have provided client stories for the self-sabotaging behavior of relationship drama, a review of The Yes Code™ process, and several scripts for the fears and beliefs that are common for people who need to create relationship drama.

Mia

Mia had run from every adult romantic relationship she had been in since she was 19 years old. She said she knew when it was time to leave. When I asked Mia what the upside was of leaving these men, she said: "It was always better to leave first instead of being abandoned by them." Mia had been abandoned by both her father and mother at key times in her life. Just as she felt she could trust them, they wouldn't show up for a special occasion or important event for her. She developed a belief that nobody ever stayed, no matter what. And the more her boyfriends professed their love for her and promised they would stick around, the faster she found an excuse to leave them.

When I asked her to clarify her vision for her future, Mia said her vision was to stay in a long-term romantic relationship and stick out the hard times as well as the easy times. She found that when her partners had an issue with her, she felt extremely defensive and felt blamed the way she did when her parents used to blame her for things she didn't even do.

Mia's next yes steps before she entered another relationship were obvious to her – she needed to be consistent with her therapy work and tapping to clear the old pain from her past and feel less fearful about intimacy. She knew she wanted to break down her tough exterior shell and take risks regarding love and connection. After tapping on old traumas related to being abandoned, she was able to open up more to all her relationships. She also used tapping for her guilt of leaving so many boyfriends behind. She finally felt worthy of finding true connection and deserving of a stable and healthy relationship.

Adam

When I asked Adam to clarify what he wanted out of seeking help, he said: "For once in my life, I want to stop being blamed for everything." His vision was to get a real job and start to feel a healthy sense of responsibility. Adam was the eldest of three boys, and his parents held him responsible for the younger siblings, even though he was only three years older than his closest brother. He was never able to stay for tryouts for soccer, he was never able to volunteer for after school activities, and he barely had enough time to do his own homework. In addition to taking on too much responsibility, he was also often unfairly blamed for everything that went wrong.

I asked him what he understood about his self-sabotaging behavior. He said he knew he was rebelling against his parents even though they were "long gone." His rebellion showed up mostly at work – he was hired for menial jobs with very little responsibility and said that suited him because the upside of sabotaging himself was: "I can't be held responsible or blamed for anything serious!" I asked him what the downside was of stopping the rebellion. He said he feared he would become deeply depressed without the "energy" of fighting. But he was tired of the pattern and wanted to stop rebelling against his parents and start feeling accountable to himself and others.

He was reluctant at first to do the tapping as it seemed too "out there" for him. I taught him how to use the tapping for his anger about being blamed for conflicts he didn't cause and his need to fight and rebel all the time. Eventually, he was diligent with his tapping homework and created a clear vision for himself of taking appropriate responsibility for his life. His next yes was to enter a vocational school so he could acquire new skills to help him get better paying jobs with more balanced responsibilities.

The Yes Code for Relationship Drama

Step One: Clarify your vision by answering: What do I really want my relationships to look like? Why is this important to me? Then ask yourself: What is the upside of creating relationship drama or rebelling? What is the downside of letting go of the drama and reaching my vision? These questions will help you identify your fears and limiting beliefs that block your progress.

Step Two: Use the answers to the upside/downside questions and the tapping sequences below to clear your fears and limiting beliefs about relationships.

Step Three: Once you've cleared your blocks, identify your next yes by answering: What feels like the next best step to take now? If it's too big, what is a smaller step I could take instead?

I have grouped the tapping sequences below into typical fears and beliefs for people who sabotage themselves with rebellion or relationship drama.

Fears:

1. **Fear of being abandoned/rejected**

2. **Fear of being blamed**
3. **Fear of being controlled**

Beliefs:

1. **I'm not worth loving.**
2. **Everyone leaves anyway.**

TAPPING TARGET:
Fear of Being Abandoned

One of the feared consequences of being in an adult relationship is to be abandoned the way you may have been in your childhood. If your parents didn't have stable attachment styles that made you feel secure, you will expect to be abandoned in your adult relationships. That may sound like strong language to you if you've never been abandoned or rejected, but millions of people have both experienced this in their past and fear it in their future. As a result, they create relationship drama so they can *quit before they get fired.*

If this target speaks to you, go ahead and measure your fear of being abandoned or rejected on the 0–10 point scale. Proceed with the tapping sequence below:

SIDE OF HAND: Even though I'm afraid I'll be abandoned for who I am, I deeply and completely love and accept myself anyway. Even though I fear being rejected because I'm not good enough, I deeply and completely love and accept myself anyway.

EYEBROW: What if they abandon me because of what I've done?

SIDE OF EYE: What if I get abandoned because of who I am?

UNDER EYE: I remember getting abandoned last time.

UNDER NOSE: It felt terrible.

CHIN: I learned hard lessons from being abandoned.

COLLARBONE: I am always vulnerable to being left behind.

UNDER ARM: It's not worth being rejected.

HEAD: I don't want to be abandoned.

Take a deep breath, and measure your fear on the 0–10 point scale now. Does this bring up a specific incident when your behavior caused you to feel abandoned or rejected? Take some notes and write down your own targets for a tapping sequence. For instance, if you misbehaved at home or at school and the punishment felt like abandonment, your setup statement could be: "Even though I felt abandoned back then, I deeply and completely love and accept myself." And your target phrase could be: "I remember being abandoned…" or "I can't be abandoned again."

SIDE OF HAND: Even though I remember being rejected and abandoned, I deeply and completely love and accept myself anyway. Even though I'm afraid I'll be abandoned or rejected again, I deeply and completely love and accept myself anyway.

EYEBROW: I'm afraid of doing something wrong.

SIDE OF EYE: What if I don't see it coming?

UNDER EYE: What if they abandon me again?

UNDER NOSE: What if I get left again?

CHIN: I have to be very careful.

COLLARBONE: I don't want to be rejected or abandoned.

UNDER ARM: I better leave them first.

HEAD: I'm worried I'll be abandoned again.

Take another deep breath, and measure your fear on the 0–10 point scale. Any difference? Any new memories? Usually, as you work through an old memory, it starts to get neutralized. It will no longer be stuck in your body's memory and no longer haunt you. Proceed to the more positive statements below:

EYEBROW: I was abandoned as a child.

SIDE OF EYE: I blamed myself.

UNDER EYE: Maybe it wasn't my fault.

UNDER NOSE: I don't think it was my fault.

CHIN: But I feel calmer about it already.

COLLARBONE: I want to make changes.

UNDER ARM: I don't need to run away all the time.

HEAD: I appreciate how far I've come.

Take a final deep breath, and measure your fear on the 0–10 point scale. Make notes for future tapping targets connected to this fear or to the history around being abandoned or rejected.

TAPPING TARGET:
Fear of Being Blamed and Punished

Most people have been blamed or punished for something they weren't responsible for in their lives. Your adult reactions will depend on how *big* the incident was and how consequential the punishment was.

Measure how afraid you feel of being blamed and punished on the 0–10 point scale. You may also recall an event where you were blamed or punished for something specific and measure the fear around that as well. This would make the target a *past event* rather than something you're afraid of in the future. For instance, you could use a setup statement, such as: "Even though I feel resentful when I remember being blamed for something my brother did, I accept who I am and how I feel." And then your target phrases would be, "I feel resentful about it…I remember being upset…It wasn't fair" and phrases along those lines.

Start tapping:

SIDE OF HAND: Even though I'm afraid of being blamed and then punished, I deeply and completely love and accept myself anyway. Even though I'm afraid of being blamed and punished for something I didn't even do – no wonder I hold myself back – I accept who I am and how I feel.

EYEBROW: I'm afraid of being blamed.

SIDE OF EYE: They never listen to my side.

UNDER EYE: I'm afraid of being blamed.

UNDER NOSE: What if they blame and punish me (again)?

CHIN: I'm afraid of being blamed.

COLLARBONE: I hate it when they don't listen to me.

UNDER ARM: It's just easier to be alone.

HEAD: No wonder I keep holding myself back.

Take a deep breath, and measure the fear again on the 0–10 point scale. If a memory of a specific incident surfaces, you may go ahead and focus on that as your target. For instance, maybe you got unfairly blamed for an incident as a child. Your setup statement could be: "Even though I was unfairly blamed for something that wasn't my fault, I accept who I am and how I feel." Then your target phrase for the additional points could be: "It wasn't fair" or "I was unfairly blamed."

SIDE OF HAND: Even though I remember when they blamed and punished me last time, I deeply and completely love and accept myself anyway. Even though I'm afraid they're going to blame and punish me again, I deeply and completely love and accept myself anyway.

EYEBROW: I'm still afraid they'll blame me.

SIDE OF EYE: They won't listen to my side.

UNDER EYE: What if they do it again?

UNDER NOSE: No wonder I'm holding myself back.

CHIN: I'm afraid I'll be blamed.

COLLARBONE: I'm afraid they'll punish me.

UNDER ARM: No wonder I won't put myself out there.

HEAD: I'm afraid I'll be blamed and punished again.

Take another deep breath, and measure how afraid you are of being blamed and punished again on the 0–10 point scale. Continue tapping on the more positive phrases below.

> **EYEBROW:** I'm afraid I'll be blamed again.
>
> **SIDE OF EYE:** But I want to get over this old event.
>
> **UNDER EYE:** I don't think it was my fault.
>
> **UNDER NOSE:** I'm ready to move on from it.
>
> **CHIN:** I'm an adult now, and I don't need to worry about this.
>
> **COLLARBONE:** It doesn't matter if they blame me.
>
> **UNDER ARM:** I'm ready to take that risk.
>
> **HEAD:** I'm already feeling calmer about being with others.

TAPPING TARGET:
Fear of Being Controlled

Many people have felt controlled by others. They often think the only way out of this trap is to be fiercely independent to a fault – they become rebellious and controlling themselves.

Measure how high your fear of being controlled is on the 0–10 point scale. Start tapping below:

> **SIDE OF HAND:** Even though I'm tired of them controlling me all the time, I deeply and completely love and accept myself. Even though I'm tired of being controlled, I accept who I am and how I feel.
>
> **EYEBROW:** They've always tried to control me.
>
> **SIDE OF EYE:** I'm tired of being controlled.
>
> **UNDER EYE:** They've always tried to control me.
>
> **UNDER NOSE:** I want them to leave me alone.
>
> **CHIN:** I'm angry that they always controlled me.
>
> **COLLARBONE:** Leave me alone.
>
> **UNDER ARM:** I want to feel free of them.
>
> **HEAD:** I want to feel free instead of controlled.

Take a deep breath, and measure your fear again on the 0–10 point scale. Note if any old incidents surface when you felt controlled by others. If an old incident surfaced, go ahead and formulate your own tapping sequence. Your setup statement could sound like this: "Even though I remember when they tried to control me back then, I accept who I am and how I feel…" Then your target phrases could be: "They tried to control me back then… I remember when they tried to control me…"

Continue tapping:

> **SIDE OF HAND:** Even though I still feel angry about being controlled, I deeply and completely love and accept myself anyway. Even though I still fear they are trying to control me, I accept who I am and how I feel.
>
> **EYEBROW:** I don't want to be controlled.
>
> **SIDE OF EYE:** I'm tired of being controlled.
>
> **UNDER EYE:** Leave me alone.
>
> **UNDER NOSE:** I'm tired of being controlled.
>
> **CHIN:** I'm afraid they'll keep doing it.
>
> **COLLARBONE:** Stop controlling me.
>
> **UNDER ARM:** I rebel when I think I'm being controlled.
>
> **HEAD:** I hate being controlled.

Take another deep breath, and measure your fear on the 0–10 point scale again. Tap on the more positive statements below:

> **EYEBROW:** They did control me back then.
>
> **SIDE OF EYE:** It's changing now.
>
> **UNDER EYE:** They can't control me anymore.
>
> **UNDER NOSE:** I'm an adult now, and I'm independent.
>
> **CHIN:** They can't control me anymore.
>
> **COLLARBONE:** I have good boundaries.
>
> **UNDER ARM:** Even if they try, it won't work.
>
> **HEAD:** I appreciate feeling free now.

Take a final deep breath, and measure this fear on the 0–10 point scale again. If you find yourself particularly angry at a parent or someone in authority who regularly controlled you, go ahead and create a new tapping round for that target. The setup statement could sound something like this: "Even though I'm angry at my father for always controlling me, I accept who I was back then and who I am now." And then the target phrase for the other acupoints would simply be: "I'm angry at him for controlling me...I still feel angry at him..." and more variations on that theme.

TAPPING TARGET:

I'm Not Worthy of a Successful Relationship

If you do not feel worthy of a successful relationship, there is no way to create a loving and balanced partnership. Success will be incongruent with your beliefs, and you won't be able to "get there." Remember, our beliefs are compulsive, and we end up living out our beliefs in our lives.

Were you ever told you're not worthy of a successful relationship? Who in your life believed this or communicated this to you? If a specific incident comes to mind, measure how upsetting it feels to you on the 0–10 point scale. And then measure how true this belief feels to you. Again, because it is a belief, you might doubt that it could change, but repeat the tapping sequences anyway.

> **SIDE OF HAND:** Even though I don't think I'm worthy of a successful relationship, I just don't deserve it, I deeply and completely love and accept myself anyway. Even though I don't feel worthy of a successful relationship, I accept who I am and how I feel.
>
> **EYEBROW:** I'm just not worthy of a successful relationship.
>
> **SIDE OF EYE:** Why would I be?
>
> **UNDER EYE:** They said I wasn't worthy of any success.
>
> **UNDER NOSE:** I'm convinced I'm not worthy.

CHIN: I've never had a successful relationship anyway.

COLLARBONE: I'm not worthy of success.

UNDER ARM: Nothing can change this.

HEAD: I'm simply not worthy.

Take a deep breath, and measure this belief on the 0–10 point scale. Is anything changing? Has it gone down? Did you get any other specific images or memories of an event that contributed to this belief in your life? Continue tapping:

SIDE OF HAND: Even though I still don't think I'm worthy of a successful relationship, I deeply and completely love and accept myself anyway. Even though they taught me that I wasn't worthy, I accept who I am and how I feel.

EYEBROW: They taught me I wasn't worthy of a successful relationship.

SIDE OF EYE: I don't believe I am worthy of success.

UNDER EYE: I know exactly where it came from.

UNDER NOSE: I'm not worthy of a successful relationship.

CHIN: I don't think I'm worthy.

COLLARBONE: I'm not worthy of a successful relationship

UNDER ARM: There are many reasons why I'm not worthy.

HEAD: I don't believe I'm worthy of a successful relationship.

Take another deep breath, and measure this belief on the 0–10 point scale again. Now start the positive tapping round below:

EYEBROW: What if I am worthy of a successful relationship?

SIDE OF EYE: What if I've been worthy all along?

UNDER EYE: What if I am already worthy?

UNDER NOSE: I don't believe I'm not worthy anymore.

CHIN: I think I might be worthy of success of all kinds.

COLLARBONE: What if I've always been worthy?

UNDER ARM: I might have been worthy all along.

HEAD: I will give them back their belief, it's not mine.

Take a final deep breath, and measure how true this belief is to you now on the 0–10 point scale. Keep tapping until this belief is neutralized enough to feel untrue to you. Consider what belief you would like to replace it with and tap while you are saying the new, positive belief out loud. For instance, if you'd like to replace this old belief with a solid new one such as: "I now believe I'm worthy of a successful relationship," then complete another tapping round using this statement while you tap on all the acupoints.

TAPPING TARGET:
Everyone Leaves Me

If you were repeatedly left as a child, and nobody had your back, you will grow up and expect people to leave you – bosses, partners, family members and even close friends. In an attempt to protect you from this, you will try and do what Mia did – quit before she got fired. It's a natural response and when it's unexamined, it will dictate the direction of all your relationships. Remember, the number one goal of a human being is to feel and be safe.

Does this belief feel true to you on the 0–10 point scale? If you have any expectations that this is just what happens with everyone, it will be enormously helpful for you to tap and erase this belief.

> **SIDE OF HAND:** Even though I'm convinced that everyone will leave me, they all did before, I accept who I am and how I feel. Even though I'm convinced everyone will just leave me anyway, I accept who I am and that this is just true.
>
> **EYEBROW:** They always leave me.
>
> **SIDE OF EYE:** They always have.
>
> **UNDER EYE:** It will just be the same now.
>
> **UNDER NOSE:** I better leave first.
>
> **CHIN:** I know they're going to leave me.
>
> **COLLARBONE:** I'm not worth sticking around for.

UNDER ARM: Everyone leaves me anyway.

HEAD: Why bother staying.

Take a deep breath, and measure the truth of this belief to you on the 0–10 point scale. Does it still feel true? If one particular breakup or abandonment is still sticking in your mind, go ahead and tailor the tapping sequence to fit that event. For instance, your setup statement could sound something like this: "Even though I didn't see it coming when _____ left me, and it still hurts, I deeply and completely love and accept myself. Even though I vowed never to trust anyone again, I accept who I am and how I feel." Then your target phrases when you tap on the remaining points could be: "I never got over _____ leaving me…I still feel betrayed…I still feel hurt…I'll never trust again."

Continue tapping:

SIDE OF HAND: Even though they always leave me, so why bother, I accept who I am and how I feel. Even though everyone always leaves me, I accept who I am and how I feel now.

EYEBROW: I don't trust anyone to stay.

SIDE OF EYE: They always leave me.

UNDER EYE: They'll leave again.

UNDER NOSE: They always leave me.

CHIN: I better not let down my guard.

COLLARBONE: I know they're going to leave, too.

UNDER ARM: I better leave first.

HEAD: It's safer that way.

Take another deep breath, and measure how true this belief feels to you on the 0–10 point scale. You can create new setup statements to match your experiences and continue tapping until this belief no longer bothers you. Then proceed to the more positive statements below when you feel ready.

EYEBROW: Not everyone left me.

SIDE OF EYE: But some did.

UNDER EYE: I made a vow to never trust anyone.

UNDER NOSE: Some people might be trustworthy.

CHIN: What if I trusted again?

COLLARBONE: I don't have to expect to be so hurt.

UNDER ARM: I'm ready to trust again.

HEAD: I'm looking forward to trusting again.

Take a final deep breath, and measure how true this belief feels to you now on the 0–10 point scale. Continue tapping as needed.

Now that you have cleared several fears, beliefs, and memories that have kept you entangled in relationship drama, what would your next yes be? Take some time to list options, tap on any remaining fears about taking inspired actions, and continue your journey. You can always revisit these original scripts and tap on them again or create your own scripts.

Scan this QR code for The Yes Code™ portal or visit www.TheYesCode.com for directions on how to create your own EFT tapping scripts.

CHAPTER 15

SELF-CARE NEGLECT

We can't possibly be as successful as we want to be if we neglect our self-care. Eventually, our neglect will catch up with us, and one or more parts of our lives will break down – our health, our relationships, or how we run our business. The areas in our lives that need care are: our physical health, our mental health, our spiritual development, our intuition, our sexual health, and the health of our relationships. When you consider Step One of The Yes Code™ process – *Clarify Your Vision* – make sure you're not just focusing on your desired financial success, but focusing on being emotionally and physically healthy as well.

I have provided client stories, a review of The Yes Code, and several tapping scripts for the fears and beliefs that contribute to self-care neglect.

Nora

I asked Nora to clarify the vision she had for her life and lifestyle. What did she want and what did she want her life to look like? She started by telling me what she was tired of, what she was scared of, and how she felt trapped. Nora was a self-proclaimed workaholic. She knew it was starting to wear her down, and she came to me when her husband complained about her long hours at work and her doctor raised concerns about both her blood pressure and being prediabetic. She admitted she thought she could get away with working around the clock.

When I asked her, "What is the upside of being a workaholic?" She said, "Being so busy all the time allows me to feel important." She had never felt good enough in her family, and she thought being an overworked lawyer gave her prestige as well as financial success. She knew her excessive busyness was causing problems in many areas of her life, but she couldn't seem to stop. I then asked, "What would be the downside of giving it up?" She said, "Then I'd have to deal with some big conflicts in my marriage and my relationships at work." Her friends at work complained that she was always canceling on them at the last minute, and they were starting to feel resentful and unappreciated. Her husband described her as "checked out" and way too engaged at work instead of with him. By working so much, Nora was conveniently too busy to pay attention to these upsetting conflicts.

Eventually, Nora was able to clarify the vision she wanted for her life. "Balance!" She wanted balance with her family, at work, and with her health. After answering the upside/downside questions, she was able to pinpoint what she was running from and why. We tapped on her fears of facing her feelings, her low self-worth and where it came from, and the looming conflicts she would need to address in her relationships, such as her friends' disappointment with her lack of consistency and her husband's description that she was checked out.

One of the effective tapping targets for Nora was, "I'm afraid to feel my feelings, so I work too hard instead." Another target that really hit home for Nora was, "I'm afraid they'll be mad at me." Nora was diligent with the tapping homework I gave her in between sessions and was able to identify her next yes in several areas of her life, including blocking out time to go home at a reasonable hour to have dinner with her husband, and being the one to set and keep lunch dates with her work colleagues. Both her friends and husband deeply appreciated her efforts to spend more time with them.

Nora was able to pare down her work hours on a regular basis, carve out time for her family, and tend to the health warnings from her doctor. Another next yes for her was to watch her diet more carefully, and she started to take daily gratitude walks. She released the feeling of running from her feelings, balanced her marriage and life, and still enjoyed her position as a top lawyer in her firm.

Derek

Derek came to me because he'd had a third panic attack at the office. He worked very hard and kept long hours. The boss heaped praise on anyone who stayed late and came in early. Derek also played even harder after work and was starting to feel exhausted. When I asked him to clarify his vision for what he wanted, all he could say was, "I'll do anything to stop the panic attacks." I asked him if he had any self-care practices. He said: "What do you mean?" which gave me the information I needed to proceed.

I asked him about the upside – how it served him – to work and play too hard as it was clearly starting to make him feel worn down. He agreed that the imbalance in his life likely triggered the panic attacks. He thought about the answer carefully and said, "Working and playing this hard makes me feel tough and strong. I can't be a weakling." His father had always ridiculed him for taking breaks as a kid, for reading, for relaxing, and actually called him lazy when he wasn't doing physical labor, saying that, "Only lazy men need a break." When I asked him what the downside was of letting go of this self-sabotaging behavior of neglecting his self-care, he said, "If I start to relax, then my father would be right. I'd be weak and lazy." Derek had of course heard of the advice they give on airplanes to put the oxygen mask on yourself first before helping anyone else, but he had never considered that level of self-care a good practice for his own life.

He started to identify the vision he wanted for himself – it included peace and quiet, balance, time for deep reflection about his childhood challenges, and time to explore this new field of self-care that was foreign to him. He admitted that he didn't enjoy "playing hard" as much as he pretended to, and knew if he wanted to be successful long-term, he was going to need to stop "chasing a good time."

After using tapping to reduce this fear of being seen as weak, he immediately started his next yes steps of self-care practices, including meditation and daily tapping. Those next yes choices led to bigger yes steps, including going to bed much earlier, giving up some of his late nights out, and exploring the new field of energy medicine. The tapping exercises helped him feel an immediate improvement in his mental health around anxiety. He didn't have any more panic attacks, and this helped give him the incentive he needed to keep his commitment to going to bed earlier and staying out late less frequently. He enjoyed the new sense of calm and balance in his life.

Maggie

Ignoring our intuition is another casualty of neglecting our self-care. Without our intuition, we are only working with part of our brains, and not the smarter part.

When I asked Maggie why she was seeking counseling, she said, "I'm tired of shutting down and ignoring my intuition." I asked her if she could state her vision in a positive light. She said she wanted to be free of judgement from herself and others, and wanted to "feel relaxed with her authentic self." In her work as a Nurse Practitioner, Maggie received "answers" and "emotional hits" for her patients. She also received these "hits" about her friends and family, but didn't want to let them know this about her because she feared their ridicule. When I asked if she thought she was taking care of herself enough, she admitted that she had abandoned her self-care practices because when she did them, her intuition became even stronger and harder to ignore.

I asked her: "What is the upside of ignoring your intuition?" She said: "Well, then I can fit in. I don't have to seem weird." This was an important upside for Maggie since she never felt like she fit in during her school years either. When I asked her what the downside was of stopping this form of self-sabotaging behavior, she said, "Then I'd have to admit how strong my intuition is and admit that I want to build a part-time coaching practice that would include using my gifts." She worried becoming an *intuitive coach* might offend many people in her life.

After using tapping to own and acknowledge her intuition and the extra "guidance" she often received, Maggie released the pressure to ignore her needs and changed how she worked and how she related to her friends. As she was building her coaching practice, she started using her intuitive guidance in her nursing job when she felt it would be well-received. She also told her friends that she was embarrassed to tell them, but she was planning to open a new coaching practice. She said she felt much calmer, more centered, and trusted her gut when she got her intuitive guidance. Her next yes was to sign up for a certification course in coaching, which she felt excited to do.

The Yes Code for Self-Care Neglect

Step One: Clarify your vision by answering: What do I really want my life to look like as a result of taking good care of myself? Why is this important to me? Then ask yourself: What is the upside of neglecting my self-care? What is the downside of letting it go and reaching my vision? These questions will help you identify your fears and limiting beliefs that block your progress.

Step Two: Use the answers to the upside/downside questions and the tapping sequences below to clear your fears and limiting beliefs that cause you to neglect your self-care.

Step Three: Once you've cleared your blocks, identify your next yes by answering: What feels like the next best step to take now? If it's too big, what is a smaller step I could take instead?

I have grouped the tapping sequences below into the fears and beliefs most common for people who neglect their self-care. If you identify fears and beliefs that cause you to neglect your self-care that I haven't included, go ahead and create your own tapping scripts around those targets. For instance, if you think "self-care practices are a waste of time…" then your setup phrase would be: "Even though I'm convinced that self-care practices are a waste of time, I deeply and completely love and accept myself anyway." And your target phrase to repeat on the subsequent acupoints would be: "Self-care practices are a waste of time," or "I don't believe it's important to have self-care practices."

Fears:

1. **Fear of facing conflict**
2. **Fear of looking lazy**
3. **Fear of standing out/rocking the boat**

Beliefs:

1. **Taking care of yourself is selfish.**
2. **Life has to be hard.**
3. **I am supposed to struggle.**

TAPPING TARGET:
Fear of Facing Conflict

If you're afraid of facing old or current emotional conflicts in your life, one common pattern to keep you safe will be to ignore your self-care. If we take care of ourselves with enough quiet time, work-life balance, and introspection, it's likely we're going to remember old emotional conflicts. They will eventually surface and demand attention.

Measure your fear of facing old emotional conflicts in your life on the 0–10 point scale. Start tapping:

> **SIDE OF HAND:** Even though I don't want to be still and quiet because I'll have to face my old emotional conflicts, I deeply and completely love and accept myself anyway. Even though I'm avoiding self-care so I don't have to feel old emotional conflicts, I accept who I am and how I feel.
>
> **EYEBROW:** I'm afraid to face old conflicts.
>
> **SIDE OF EYE:** I'm afraid to feel these feelings.
>
> **UNDER EYE:** No wonder I'm so busy all the time.
>
> **UNDER NOSE:** I'm afraid of facing these conflicts.
>
> **CHIN:** I don't want to slow down.
>
> **COLLARBONE:** I don't want to be still and quiet.
>
> **UNDER ARM:** I don't want to face these conflicts.
>
> **HEAD:** I'm afraid to feel these emotions.

Take a deep breath, and measure your fear again on the 0–10 point scale. Continue tapping.

> **SIDE OF HAND:** Even though I'm still afraid of facing these old emotional conflicts, I choose to trust that I can handle my feelings. Even though I'm still afraid to face some of these old emotional conflicts, I accept who I am and how I feel.
>
> **EYEBROW:** I'm still afraid to face these emotions.
>
> **SIDE OF EYE:** I'm still avoiding facing these conflicts.
>
> **UNDER EYE:** I'm worried I'll have to deal with them.
>
> **UNDER NOSE:** No wonder I'm so busy all the time.
>
> **CHIN:** I'm trying to avoid facing these conflicts.
>
> **COLLARBONE:** No wonder I don't want to slow down.
>
> **UNDER ARM:** I know I'll have to address these feelings.
>
> **HEAD:** No wonder I won't take care of myself.

Take another deep breath, measure your fear on the 0–10 point scale, and proceed to the more positive statements below.

> **EYEBROW:** I want to feel inspired to take care of myself.
>
> **SIDE OF EYE:** I want to start handling these old feelings.
>
> **UNDER EYE:** I appreciate that I'm worried.
>
> **UNDER NOSE:** But I know I can handle these emotions.
>
> **CHIN:** I'm ready to face some of these old conflicts.
>
> **COLLARBONE:** I'm ready to face and address my feelings.
>
> **UNDER ARM:** It's time to start taking care of myself.
>
> **HEAD:** It feels so good to take care of myself.

Take a final deep breath, and measure your fear now on the 0–10 point scale. You may return and repeat any of these tapping scripts if your fear still feels too high. Take note of any memories or new fears or beliefs that pop up during these tapping sequences so you can use these as new targets in the future.

TAPPING TARGET:
Fear of Looking Weak and Lazy

If, like Derek, you got any messages that taking care of yourself or taking a break during the day was being "weak and lazy," this is a great tapping script for you. Your caretakers may have told you that taking time off was lazy, but that's simply not true.

Measure your fear of looking lazy on the 0–10 point scale. Start tapping.

> **SIDE OF HAND:** Even though I don't want to slow down because then I'll look lazy, I deeply and completely accept myself anyway. Even though I'm afraid to take care of myself because then they'll think I'm weak and lazy, I accept who I am and how I feel.
>
> **EYEBROW:** I'm afraid I'll be accused of being lazy.

SIDE OF EYE: I'm afraid they'll think I'm weak.

UNDER EYE: It doesn't feel safe to slow down.

UNDER NOSE: It doesn't feel safe to take care of myself.

CHIN: I'm afraid I might look weak and lazy.

COLLARBONE: What if they think I'm weak and lazy?

UNDER ARM: I'm afraid I'll look weak and lazy.

HEAD: No wonder I avoid taking care of myself.

Take a deep breath, and measure how high this fear is now on the 0–10 point scale. Does it still bother you as much? Or are you able to put it into perspective and realize that putting the oxygen mask on yourself first is the best practice for you?

SIDE OF HAND: Even though it feels foreign to me to take care of myself, I accept who I am and how I feel. Even though it feels scary to consider taking care of myself, I accept that I wasn't taught how to put myself first.

EYEBROW: I'm afraid to take care of myself.

SIDE OF EYE: What if I look lazy?

UNDER EYE: What if they think I'm weak?

UNDER NOSE: I'm afraid to take care of myself.

CHIN: No wonder I avoid self-care practices.

COLLARBONE: I'm afraid to take care of myself.

UNDER ARM: I don't want to look weak or lazy.

HEAD: No wonder I'm so exhausted all the time.

Take another deep breath, and measure this fear again on the 0–10 point scale. Are you still worried about other people's reactions to you relaxing, having downtime, or enjoying time to rejuvenate? Keep tapping with the scripts above if you would like to continue reducing this fear. Then proceed to the more positive tapping below:

EYEBROW: I know it's time to take care of myself.

SIDE OF EYE: I'm ready to take care of myself.

UNDER EYE: It feels strange but I'm ready.

UNDER NOSE: I appreciate myself and want to feel good.

CHIN: I appreciate my health and stamina.

COLLARBONE: I'm ready to feel good and take care of myself.

UNDER ARM: It feels good to feel good about myself.

HEAD: I appreciate taking care of myself.

Take a final deep breath and measure your fear on the 0–10 point scale. Hopefully, you feel inspired to add some self-care practices to your "to do" list.

TAPPING TARGET:
Fear of Rocking the Boat

Are you like Maggie – afraid to rock the boat or stand out because you are different or have different skills that don't fit neatly in an expected box?

Measure how high your fear is of rocking the boat on the 0–10 point scale. Start tapping:

SIDE OF HAND: Even though I'm afraid that if I own my authentic self it will rock the boat, I deeply and completely love and accept all of me. Even though I'm afraid embracing all of me will rock the boat, I accept who I am and how I feel.

EYEBROW: I don't want to stand out.

SIDE OF EYE: I don't want to rock the boat.

UNDER EYE: I'm afraid they'll see me as too different.

UNDER NOSE: I already rock the boat.

CHIN: I don't want to own this part of myself.

COLLARBONE: I'm afraid it will rock the boat.

UNDER ARM: I'm afraid to rock the boat.

HEAD: It's easier to just fit in.

Take a deep breath, and measure this fear again on the 0–10 point scale. If you are truly yourself, are you afraid others won't accept or like you? Notice any specific memories that arise as you tap and use them for future tapping targets. Continue tapping.

> **SIDE OF HAND:** Even though I'm still afraid being me will rock the boat, I accept who I am and how I feel. Even though I'm still afraid of owning all of me, I accept who I am and how I feel.
>
> **EYEBROW:** I'm afraid to admit my fears.
>
> **SIDE OF EYE:** I'm afraid to own my skills.
>
> **UNDER EYE:** I'm worried they won't accept me.
>
> **UNDER NOSE:** I'm afraid I'll rock the boat.
>
> **CHIN:** I don't want to be different.
>
> **COLLARBONE:** I don't want to stand out.
>
> **UNDER ARM:** I'm afraid of rocking the boat.
>
> **HEAD:** I'm afraid to rock the boat.

Take another deep breath, and measure your fear now on the 0–10 point scale. You may repeat the tapping sequences above for additional clearing or move forward to the more positive round below.

> **EYEBROW:** I need to be me.
>
> **SIDE OF EYE:** Even if they don't like it.
>
> **UNDER EYE:** I want to accept myself.
>
> **UNDER NOSE:** I deserve to accept myself.
>
> **CHIN:** I appreciate my differences.
>
> **COLLARBONE:** I appreciate all of me.
>
> **UNDER ARM:** I'm grateful I am who I am.
>
> **HEAD:** I'm ready to embrace all of me.

Take a final deep breath, and measure your fear again on the 0–10 point scale. Continue tapping on any fears you have about being your true authentic self.

TAPPING TARGET:
Self-Care Is Selfish

It's easy to see how society and families have pressured us into thinking taking care of ourselves is selfish. While it's not true that self-care is selfish, millions of people who try to take care of their needs have been told this. Remember, it's always about balance. I'm not advocating putting yourself first 24 hours a day. But the less you take care of yourself, the less you have to give others. So, in fact, neglecting your self-care is selfish. Please put that oxygen mask on yourself first.

Measure how true the belief that self-care is selfish feels to you on the 0–10 point scale. Start tapping:

SIDE OF HAND: Even though I'm convinced self-care is selfish, I deeply and completely love and accept myself. Even though I'm convinced taking care of myself is selfish, I choose to consider a new definition.
EYEBROW: It would be selfish to take care of myself.
SIDE OF EYE: I don't want to be selfish.
UNDER EYE: They told me not to be selfish.
UNDER NOSE: I have to take care of everyone else.
CHIN: I'm afraid they'll think I'm selfish.
COLLARBONE: I believe self-care is selfish.
UNDER ARM: I'm convinced I'm already selfish.
HEAD: Taking care of myself would be selfish.

Take a deep breath, and measure how true this belief seems to you now on the 0–10 point scale. Does it still seem selfish to take care of yourself? Continue tapping:

SIDE OF HAND: Even though I still think it would be selfish to take care of myself, I accept who I am and where I learned this. Even though I still think it would be selfish to take care of myself, I accept who I am and how I feel about this.
EYEBROW: I feel so selfish.

SIDE OF EYE: I learned to ignore my self-care.

UNDER EYE: I'm afraid to take care of myself.

UNDER NOSE: I would feel so selfish.

CHIN: I feel so selfish.

COLLARBONE: Aren't I supposed to ignore my own needs?

UNDER ARM: I was taught to feel selfish.

HEAD: I would feel so selfish if I took care of myself.

Take another deep breath, and measure how true this belief feels to you now on the 0–10 point scale. Then proceed to the positive round of tapping below:

EYEBROW: I want to take care of myself.

SIDE OF EYE: I don't want to feel selfish.

UNDER EYE: We all deserve to take care of ourselves.

UNDER NOSE: I appreciate myself.

CHIN: I deserve to take care of myself.

COLLARBONE: I appreciate taking care of myself.

UNDER ARM: It's time to take care of myself.

HEAD: I appreciate that I deserve to take care of myself.

Take a final deep breath, and measure this belief on the 0–10 point scale.

Scan this QR code or visit www.TheYesCode.com for a video demonstrating how to use EFT for the tapping target, Self-Care Feels Selfish.

TAPPING TARGET:
Life Has to Be Hard

Check this belief for yourself – how *true* does it feel to you? Where did you learn this? I can promise you that you didn't start out with this belief: you had to learn this lesson and turn it into a belief. Someone else who was important to you either believed this or thought it was a good idea to teach it to you. Measure the intensity of this belief, or how true it feels to you, on the 0–10 point scale. Try this tapping sequence:

> **SIDE OF HAND:** Even though I'm convinced that life has to be hard, I deeply and completely love and accept myself. Even though they taught me that life has to be hard, I accept who I am and how I feel about that.
>
> **EYEBROW:** I'm convinced life has to be hard.
>
> **SIDE OF EYE:** That's what they taught me.
>
> **UNDER EYE:** I'm convinced that it's true.
>
> **UNDER NOSE:** I really believe life has to be hard.
>
> **CHIN:** I'm convinced life has to be hard.
>
> **COLLARBONE:** I've never known any other way.
>
> **UNDER ARM:** I don't see how it could be easy.
>
> **HEAD:** I'm convinced life has to be hard.

Take a deep breath, and measure how true this belief feels to you now. Does it still feel like an ironclad truth? When this belief no longer has a grip on you, you will start to see your life through a different lens and it will be emotionally liberating.

Keep tapping.

> **SIDE OF HAND:** Even though I'm still convinced that life has to be hard, I accept where I learned this and I'm ready to let it go. Even though I'm still convinced that life has to be hard, I deeply and completely love and accept myself anyway.
>
> **EYEBROW:** I'm still convinced life has to be hard.
>
> **SIDE OF EYE:** My life has always been hard.
>
> **UNDER EYE:** Why would it change?
>
> **UNDER NOSE:** Life has to be hard.
>
> **CHIN:** That's what they taught me.
>
> **COLLARBONE:** I'm still convinced life has to be hard.

UNDER ARM: I don't believe it can be any other way.

HEAD: Life has to be hard.

Take a deep breath, measure your belief on the 0–10 point scale again, and then move right into the more positive phrases.

EYEBROW: What if my life could be different?

SIDE OF EYE: What if this belief is not true.

UNDER EYE: What if they believed it but I don't have to?

UNDER NOSE: What if I let this belief go?

CHIN: I'm almost ready to let it go.

COLLARBONE: I don't think this is true for me.

UNDER ARM: I'm ready to release this belief.

HEAD: I'm ready to let it go and move on.

Take a final deep breath, and measure how true this belief feels to you now on the 0–10 point scale. Continue tapping until this belief no longer drives your behavior.

TAPPING TARGET:
I'm Not Worthy Unless I Struggle

Do you believe in struggle as a way of life? If you grew up in a family where struggle was rewarded or seen as noble, you will have a challenging time relaxing and enjoying your life when it becomes calmer. While this is very similar to the "life has to be hard" belief, the language carries enough subtleties that it's worth a slightly revised script.

Measure this target – I'm supposed to struggle – on the 0–10 point scale. Proceed with the tapping below.

SIDE OF HAND: Even though I'm convinced that I'm supposed to struggle, I deeply and completely love and accept myself anyway. Even though I believe that I have to struggle, that's what they taught me, I deeply and completely love and accept myself now.

EYEBROW: I'm supposed to struggle.

SIDE OF EYE: That's just the way it is.

UNDER EYE: I'm supposed to struggle.

UNDER NOSE: That's what's right for me.

CHIN: That's what they taught me.

COLLARBONE: I'm supposed to struggle.

UNDER ARM: I'm used to it anyway.

HEAD: I'm just supposed to struggle.

Take a deep breath, and measure how true this belief feels to you now on the 0–10 point scale. Has there been any movement on the intensity or "truth" of it? Continue tapping.

SIDE OF HAND: Even though I'm convinced that I'm supposed to struggle, I accept who I am and how I feel. Even though I believe I'm supposed to struggle, I accept who I am and how I feel.

EYEBROW: I'm convinced I'm supposed to struggle.

SIDE OF EYE: Isn't everyone?

UNDER EYE: I'm convinced life will always be a struggle.

UNDER NOSE: That's what I believe.

CHIN: I have to struggle or I'm not worthy.

COLLARBONE: I don't know any other way.

UNDER ARM: I have to struggle.

HEAD: That's just how it is.

Take another deep breath, and measure how true this feels to you on the 0–10 point scale. If you've believed this for as long as you can remember, it might feel odd to let it go. If you struggle with letting go of this belief, you can tap on that as well. Your setup statement would be: "Even though I'm afraid to let go of this belief, I accept who I am and how I feel" and your target phrase for the additional acupoints would be: "I'm afraid to let go of this belief" or "It doesn't feel normal to believe in ease." Proceed with the more positive statements below.

EYEBROW: They taught me I was supposed to struggle.

SIDE OF EYE: I never questioned it.

UNDER EYE: It was their belief and it became mine.

UNDER NOSE: What if I don't have to struggle?

CHIN: What if my life could be easy and fun?

COLLARBONE: I appreciate so much about my life.

UNDER ARM: I'm ready to start expecting ease.

HEAD: I feel excited about moving forward.

Take a final deep breath, and measure how true this belief feels to you. Sometimes after enough rounds of tapping, the belief feels "silly" and you are ready to let it go. Other times, it will take several more rounds to loosen up the belief enough to notice a difference downstream in your self-sabotaging behavior.

In this chapter, I discussed several typical dilemmas for people who neglect their self-care, and then gave examples of common fears and beliefs for tapping sequences. You may revisit these sequences any time you need to in order to start making your self-care a sacred priority. Make sure to identify some next yes steps for you that feel inspiring and doable in the near future. Once you have chosen them, make a plan with an accountability partner to follow through. If any new fears surface, return to one of the tapping scripts provided or create your own.

CHAPTER 16

BONUS TAPPING SCRIPTS

Comfort Zones

When we stay within a personal or financial comfort zone, there's no anxiety, no worry, and no concerns about feeling challenged if we stretch beyond what we're used to. Comfort zones are familiar and feel safe to us. Whether we're trying to earn more money, lose weight, have a long-term relationship, or increase social activity, our comfort zones will keep up us where we're accustomed to being.

While profoundly familiar and useful, these comfort zones also keep us stuck. They keep a lid on our success, keep us playing small, and keep us confined to where we're emotionally safe.

If you want to improve your life, you're going to need to expand your comfort zones. Choose an area where you know you are playing safe by staying within your comfort zone. Focus there, and then try this tapping sequence. If you can measure your fear of moving beyond your current comfort zone, go ahead and measure on the 0–10 point scale.

SIDE OF HAND: Even though I'm afraid to stretch beyond my comfort zone in this part of my life, I deeply and completely love and accept myself anyway. Even though I'm afraid to get out of my comfort zone, I accept my fears and that I'm doing my best.

EYEBROW: I'm afraid to stretch beyond my comfort zone.

SIDE OF EYE: I'm afraid to expand my comfort zone.

UNDER EYE: It feels safer to stay where I am.

UNDER NOSE: I want to stay right where I am.

CHIN: This feels familiar and safe.

COLLARBONE: I like feeling safe.

UNDER ARM: I don't like the unknown.

HEAD: I'm afraid to stretch beyond my comfort zone.

Take a deep breath, and measure your fear on the 0–10 point scale again and keep tapping.

SIDE OF HAND: Even though I'm still afraid I won't like the new space if I stretch beyond my comfort zone, I accept who I am and how I feel. Even though I want to stay under the radar by fitting in my comfort zone, I accept who I am and how I feel.

EYEBROW: I'm still afraid of going beyond my comfort zone.

SIDE OF EYE: I'm still afraid of the unknown.

UNDER EYE: I'm still afraid of stretching beyond what I know.

UNDER NOSE: I want to stay under the radar.

CHIN: I'm fine where I am.

COLLARBONE: Why do I have to stretch?

UNDER ARM: Can't I stay where I'm comfortable?

HEAD: I'd prefer to stay where I am.

Take a deep breath, and measure this fear of stretching beyond your comfort zone on the 0–10 point scale again. Now proceed to the more positive round of tapping.

EYEBROW: I could stretch a little and still feel safe.

SIDE OF EYE: I could expand a little beyond and enjoy it.

UNDER EYE: I can handle a little stretch.

UNDER NOSE: I'm grateful for where I am and where I'm going.

CHIN: I appreciate all of me anyway.

COLLARBONE: I look forward to stretching myself.

UNDER ARM: I feel safe when I imagine that stretch now.

HEAD: I appreciate stretching beyond my former comfort zone.

Take a final deep breath, and measure this fear on the 0–10 point scale. If you were focused on expanding your comfort zone in your financial life, you could now focus on expanding your comfort zone in your romantic life. Go ahead and switch the focus, measure your fear on the 0–10 point scale, and use the same tapping sequences above.

Identity Issues

Surprisingly, even though we keep telling everyone we want to change, one of the big emotional threats to us is loss of our identity. Who will you be if you no longer procrastinate? Who will you be if you no longer try to be perfect? Who will you be without your clutter? A client said, "What if I make these changes and I don't recognize myself anymore?" She wanted to change but wasn't sure what the new version of her would feel like to her, her friends, or her family. If you've always been the failure in the family, and you clear your blocks, how would the new "successful you" be received by your family? This kind of change would likely rock the boat. If you've always been overweight and you finally lose the extra pounds and keep them off, what happens to your identity then?

Let's use the tapping target: "I'm afraid I won't recognize myself if I change." Measure this fear of losing your identity on the 0–10 point scale. Try this tapping sequence below:

SIDE OF HAND: Even though I'm afraid I'll lose my identity if I change too much, I deeply and completely love and accept myself anyway. Even though I'm afraid I might lose part of my identity if I make these changes, I accept all of me anyway.

EYEBROW: What if I lose my identity?

SIDE OF EYE: I'm afraid to change.

UNDER EYE: What if I change too much?

UNDER NOSE: I might lose my identity.

CHIN: Who will I be if I change?

COLLARBONE: I'm afraid to change too much.

UNDER ARM: What if I don't recognize myself.

HEAD: No wonder I keep sabotaging myself.

Take a deep breath, and measure your fear of losing your identity on the 0–10 point scale again. You may focus on a particular part of your identity you fear losing if you make the changes you intend to make. Keep tapping.

SIDE OF HAND: Even though I'm still afraid of losing my identity, I accept who I am and how I feel. Even though I'm resisting change because I'm worried I'll lose my identity, I accept who I am and how I feel.

EYEBROW: I'm still afraid of losing my identity.

SIDE OF EYE: What if I change too much?

UNDER EYE: I'm afraid I won't recognize myself.

UNDER NOSE: I don't want to change too much.

CHIN: I'm worried I might change my identity.

COLLARBONE: What if I change too much?

UNDER ARM: No wonder I've been resisting change.

HEAD: I've been resisting change because I'm afraid.

Take another deep breath, and measure this fear on the 0–10 point scale again. Proceed to the more positive tapping phrases below.

EYEBROW: I can make any changes I want to.
SIDE OF EYE: I will maintain my identity.
UNDER EYE: I appreciate all of me.
UNDER NOSE: I appreciate the parts I want to change.
CHIN: I appreciate all of me.
COLLARBONE: I'm ready to make the changes.
UNDER ARM: I can keep my identity.
HEAD: I look forward to the positive changes.

Take a final deep breath, and measure your fear on the 0–10 point scale and keep tapping on this topic if necessary.

Tapping for Your Nervous System

We know that old traumas and daily stress get trapped in our nervous system, especially when we don't have enough downtime in between each crisis to process and metabolize the stress. When I'm doing my daily tapping practice, if I don't feel drawn to tap on something specific, I will often tap to acknowledge the obvious: stress and old traumas are being held in my nervous system. I focus on this assumption and then gently guide my body and mind to release the built-up stress.

Your tapping target would be: "I have built-up stress and traumas stuck in my nervous system." You may focus on one particular trauma or stress from a part of your life, or an overall feeling of stress. How true does this target feel to you on the 0–10 point scale?

SIDE OF HAND: Even though I know that built-up stress and old traumas have been stuck in my nervous system, I deeply and completely love and accept myself anyway. Even though I know my nervous system has been weighed down by stress and old traumas, I choose to release all of it now.

EYEBROW: I have this built-up stress in my nervous system.

SIDE OF EYE: Old traumas have been stuck in my nervous system.

UNDER EYE: No wonder I'm so tired.

UNDER NOSE: Daily stress has been stored in my nervous system.

CHIN: Stress and trauma have been stored in my nervous system.

COLLARBONE: My poor nervous system is exhausted.

UNDER ARM: My nervous system has been storing old stress.

HEAD: My nervous system has been protecting me.

Take a deep breath, and measure how true this feels to you now on the 0–10 point scale. Keep tapping.

SIDE OF HAND: Even though I'm convinced that my old traumas have been stuck in my nervous system, I choose to heal and release them now. Even though I'm convinced that my old stress and traumas have been stuck in my nervous system, I accept who I am and how I feel.

EYEBROW: My old traumas have been stuck in my nervous system.

SIDE OF EYE: All my built-up stress has been stuck in my body.

UNDER EYE: No wonder I'm exhausted.

UNDER NOSE: No wonder I feel tired all the time.

CHIN: Old traumas have been stuck in my nervous system.

COLLARBONE: My poor body has been so stressed out.

UNDER ARM: All these old traumas need to be released.

HEAD: I'm tired of holding on to the old stress and trauma.

Take a deep breath, and measure how true this still feels to you on the 0–10 point scale. Also measure the stress level in your body when you think about this. Has it gone down? Then proceed to the positive tapping statements.

> **EYEBROW:** I choose to release the old stress now.
>
> **SIDE OF EYE:** I'm releasing the old traumas.
>
> **UNDER EYE:** My nervous system feels better already.
>
> **UNDER NOSE:** I'm releasing these stored traumas in my nervous system.
>
> **CHIN:** I feel better already.
>
> **COLLARBONE:** I appreciate my nervous system so much.
>
> **UNDER ARM:** I feel so much better already.
>
> **HEAD:** I'm releasing the stress and old traumas.

Take a final deep breath, and measure on the 0–10 point scale how true it still feels that you've been storing the old stress and traumas in your nervous system. You may keep tapping on any variations of this theme.

Scan this QR code or visit www.TheYesCode.com for a video of using EFT for the tapping target, Stress Relief and Your Nervous System.

Gratitude Tapping

I created a branch of tapping called **Gratitude Tapping** or **Thank You Tapping** in my practice years ago, and it caught on very quickly in the EFT community. Everyone adds their style and preferences, but the point is to express your gratitude out loud while you are accessing the acupoints on the face and the body. In general, people say that expressing gratitude makes them feel better, but if you have any resistance to it, adding the tapping sequence will help you reduce this resistance. You may start with a setup statement such as, "Even though I'm feeling low today, I still accept who I am and am grateful for my life." Or

"Even though I still feel stressed out about work, I realize I have a lot to be grateful for anyway."

> **SIDE OF HAND:** Even though I still feel so much stress in my life, I accept who I am and how I feel. Even though I am still struggling in many aspects of my life, I accept who I am and I'm ready to express my gratitude.
>
> **EYEBROW:** I do have stress in my life.
>
> **SIDE OF EYE:** But I'm so grateful anyway.
>
> **UNDER EYE:** I feel stress, but I love my life.
>
> **UNDER NOSE:** I appreciate my life.
>
> **CHIN:** I appreciate my health.
>
> **COLLARBONE:** I'm grateful for my family.
>
> **UNDER ARM:** I'm grateful for my friendships.
>
> **HEAD:** I appreciate so much about my life.

Take a deep breath, and enjoy the sensation of feeling grateful. Another way to use Gratitude Tapping is to identify a particular problem, and then act as if you've received the solution. You may use the phrase "I'm grateful for the solution" or "thank you, universe, for sending me the solution." Tap as follows.

> **SIDE OF HAND:** Even though I'm having trouble in this relationship (or with my health, or at work) I deeply and completely love and accept myself anyway. Even though I can't figure out how to move forward in this relationship, I accept who I am and how I feel.
>
> **EYEBROW:** Thank you, universe, for sending me the solution.
>
> **SIDE OF EYE:** I didn't even see it.
>
> **UNDER EYE:** I'm so grateful for the solution to this problem.
>
> **UNDER NOSE:** Thank you, universe, for the solution to this problem.
>
> **CHIN:** I'm grateful I figured this out.

COLLARBONE: I'm so grateful the universe sent me this solution.

UNDER ARM: I feel so grateful right now.

HEAD: I feel so much better already.

Take a deep breath, and consider what else you'd like to express gratitude for even before it shows up in your life.

EYEBROW: Thank you, universe, for my health solution.

SIDE OF EYE: I didn't even see it before.

UNDER EYE: Thank you, universe, for the solution you sent.

UNDER NOSE: Thank you, universe, for sending me this health solution.

CHIN: I appreciate my new health solution.

COLLARBONE: These solutions are so obvious now.

UNDER ARM: Thank you, universe, for these solutions.

HEAD: I feel relieved and grateful now that they're here.

Take a deep breath.

As you can see, the opportunities for expanding this Gratitude Tapping or Thank You Tapping are endless. Have fun with it.

Scan this QR code or visit www.TheYesCode.com for a video on how to use EFT for Gratitude Tapping.

CHAPTER 17

ADDITIONAL TOOLS FOR SUPPORT

The main way to change your patterns of self-sabotaging behavior is to identify the real problem (feeling unsafe with the changes you say you want to make) and then use tools to heal the underlying emotional conflicts and limiting beliefs that keep you stuck in these patterns. Tapping is my favorite tool, and if you tried even a few of the scripts in the EFT chapters, you will have already felt the power of this emotional technology to help you let go of the fears and beliefs that are fueling your self-sabotage.

In addition to EFT or tapping as a tool to get to the real feelings and beliefs underneath the sabotaging behaviors, I recommend some additional supportive self-care habits. Any time you are strengthening your ability to identify, feel, and release your emotions, you will be letting go of the need to sabotage yourself.

Stillness/Meditation

Some people refer to meditation as simply *being still*. Some people refer to stillness itself as a kind of meditation. Either way, stillness can be a powerful way to support you in reducing any self-sabotaging behavior. If you're never still or quiet, you won't know exactly what you are feeling, and you won't have the space to examine any current or past conflicts that might be contributing to your behavior.

Consider how much stillness you have in your life today. Do you want more? Are you afraid of it? What might come up as a result of being still?

> *When you lose touch with inner stillness, you lose touch with yourself.*
>
> *When you lose touch with yourself, you lose yourself in the world.*
>
> **Eckhart Tolle, *Stillness Speaks*[11]**

Meditation as a self-care modality has many versions and variations, so please choose a meditation style that you feel drawn to that suits your lifestyle and preferences. Choose the type of meditation you know you will actually do and what meshes well with your personality. The point is to calm your mind, stop making "to do lists" in your head and have some quiet time in your otherwise busy day. This will help you examine and release your emotional conflicts that have been contributing to your self-sabotaging behavior.

As you know about me, being quiet and still did not come naturally. In fact, stillness scared me. That's when all the emotions would surface and when I really felt anxious. Being busy and distracted and working too hard "worked" well to keep me in the fast lane and a few steps ahead of my feelings. Of course, over time this changed. I was continually working on myself and had started doing regular tapping, so I no longer needed to distract myself with the busyness. Working on myself and using tapping helped slow down my mind and worries, so I was able to actually start a meditation practice. Slowly but surely, I was able to sit still enough to feel all my feelings, including the anxiety and grief, without overreacting, eating, smoking, distracting myself, or feeling scared. Over the years I learned to feel, deal, and heal. I learned how to feel the emotions, deal with them as they came up, and heal the pain with the help of wise and thoughtful counselors, therapists, coaches, and colleagues. It's an ongoing process and will never end, as life keeps throwing curveballs, but not much throws me for a loop anymore.

So not only did I learn to be still, I grew to actually appreciate being still. Just getting through a meditation isn't what it's about. I wanted to be present and notice everything that I felt, and still be able to breathe and feel peaceful, even if what I was feeling was challenging. This kind of practice without a mantra or key word can be difficult. Some people prefer to add a mantra or a key word to help keep them focused and reduce the typical monkey mind that gets activated during their practice. If listening to chimes, someone's voice guiding you, or having a mantra works for you, please start there.

For me, having music, chants or a special word is too distracting to my already distractable mind. I really need the quiet to find a sense of peace, So I sit quietly. I breath. And I notice. I try not to fill out my to do list, but when I do, I just notice that's what I've done. And I try not to be too judgmental. I just say "…interesting…" Then I go back to being quiet, empty, and still. I try not to think of the conversation from last week that bothered me, but when I do, I go back to being quiet and still. I keep noticing what that feels like.

The only meditation practice that really works is the one you'll start and stick to. In addition to hundreds of "how to" books on a variety of meditation practices, there are multiple free apps and YouTube videos on how to meditate, in all shapes and sizes. Choose one way and get started. If it doesn't fit well, try another. Again, the key is to *practice* this self-care method, so keep the research to a minimum or you might get distracted. The important thing is to just get started.

Why meditate? What's the point?

If you want to continue to release your sabotaging behaviors, you'll need to give yourself, your thoughts, and your feelings more emotional space so you can make new choices and see more inspiring next yes steps. If you have some regular quiet time outside of the din of daily life, you will build your emotional resilience and be more mindful about your self-care, your intuition, your fears, and the beliefs that are getting in your way. If you're chronically stressed, your reactivity levels are heightened, you won't breathe calmly, and you have less ability to bounce back after the incident that made you feel stressed in the first place. Meditation and stillness can calm down your nervous system, so you don't overreact to the stressors that keep showing up in your life.

Some people think that handling a lot of stress makes them stronger and better able to handle even more, but the opposite is true. Research shows that we become less resilient when we're faced with chronic stress. Instead of building a muscle, we become weaker and stretched too thin. If your battery is constantly drained from everyday stress, you won't be or feel resilient in your life and you will be more susceptible to your old ways of sabotaging yourself. All your energy will go towards putting out the daily fires, and there will be nothing left for you at the end of the day. You'll be tempted to use your addictions or ignore your self-care when you get this exhausted.

Any time we are calmer in our minds and nervous systems, we are able to access more internal and external resources. And we all need more resources for our busy lives. When our nervous systems are hijacked by stress, we lose any ability to "pause" and control our emotional outbursts and reactivity. Any time we build in more time or space to breathe, reflect, pause, and be still, we'll choose a more productive and resourceful response.

In addition to reducing your tendency to regress towards self-sabotaging behaviors, the emotional benefits of meditating include reducing anxiety, improving concentration, developing a deeper focus, and improving compassion towards yourself and others. A regular practice can slow down your racing thoughts and help regulate your breathing, as well as help you become more present. Creating the space for calmer responses and more thoughtful interactions is liberating.

Physical benefits of meditation include a strengthened immune system, and most importantly, the practice can reduce your body's stress response and calm your nervous system. This will in turn lower the cortisol – the stress hormone – that is released in your bloodstream when you are under too much stress. Anything that calms your nervous system is a good practice, especially when you don't need to buy, watch, or ingest anything to feel calmer.

And of course, a wonderful benefit is that meditation practices are extremely affordable and convenient.

When I prescribe meditation to my clients, some of them say, "I don't have the time to meditate." I respond with the classic cliché – "You can't afford NOT to make time for meditation."

Here's what I do for my daily meditation practice:

1. I get physically comfortable with where I'm sitting, what I'm wearing, and what the temperature is. I do not use the floor and I don't lie down, because I'll fall asleep quickly, so I use a chair or my office couch.
2. I set my timer for 20 minutes.
3. I close my eyes, take a few deep breaths, notice any sounds inside and out, and keep breathing. When my mind wanders, I go back to noticing sounds inside and out, and focus on my breathing. I may get distracted many times, but I just go back to my focus on being still and quiet.

Sometimes when the alarm goes off, my 20 minutes has flown by. Sometimes it's been quite dreamy and pleasant. Other times, I have felt agitated or the practice has felt a bit tedious. Sometimes I can't concentrate. But it's never boring. A friend recently asked, "How was your meditation today?" I said I had a "terrible" meditation. His response:

"That's not possible. If you sat through your meditation, you did it, and if you did it, you're on the right path."

It's simple yet profound. Nothing fancy, nothing forced. But if you want the benefits, you'll need to make the commitment to do it regularly.

One particular challenge with meditation is that many people don't experience immediate effects – positive effects tend to build over time. And in our give-it-to-me-now culture, everyone wants the prize immediately. (Instant gratification works!) I am always happy and relieved I got my meditation done. I always feel calmer afterwards, but I don't always connect it to a deeper sense of resiliency. I appreciate the consistent research finding long-term benefits, and I know I like having this practice, so I won't give it up.

I highly recommend putting aside 15-20 minutes in your day where you sit quietly, don't let yourself get disturbed, turn your phone off, and set a timer for your private time to just be still. You'll start to cherish and protect this quiet time, and "forgetting" to meditate won't even occur to you.

Notice if you're having any blocks to getting started. What are your fears? What are your concerns? What might be preventing you from starting a meditation practice today? Why haven't you put aside just a few minutes a day to start to calm your mind and your stress response? "I'm too busy" is just not an answer I accept from clients or myself anymore. If after learning about all the benefits isn't enough, or meditation is not your cup of tea, that's ok. But make sure you aren't avoiding it for emotional reasons. If you are avoiding it because of your fears about what emotions might surface, continue to ask yourself the questions to identify what's blocking you. What is the upside of avoiding meditation? What is the downside of incorporating some quiet and stillness into your life?

Connection

One of my deepest values is *connection*. I love connecting with my friends and my family, even a stranger for a brief moment – you know what it feels like. But in order to connect to others, you'll need to be connected to yourself and your feelings first. You can't connect with others if you're not connected to your own interior world. You need to know how you feel, what you believe, and you need to be interested in how you "work." If you don't, you are in danger of sabotaging yourself.

If you do the emotional work outlined in The Yes Code™ process to get connected to yourself, you will increase your capacity to connect to others. When you are connected to others, you have more resources, more resilience, and fewer reasons to sabotage yourself. All the trauma experts say that to heal from trauma, you need to heal within a social context.

> *Being able to feel safe with other people is probably the single most important aspect of mental health; safe connections are fundamental to meaningful and satisfying lives.*
>
> **Bessel van der Kolk, *The Body Keeps the Score*[12]**

Build these necessary connections and you'll feel less isolated, more alive, and safer in the world.

Speed Walking/Movement

Someone asked me how many calories I burned on my morning walk. Since I don't care about burning calories anymore, I didn't know.

I use my morning walking routine as another way to express and release built-up stress, to move my energy through my body, and to genuinely enjoy the start of every day. A day I don't walk is a day I don't feel as resilient and happy. But I don't do it as a physical fitness routine so much as for the emotional fitness boost. Sometimes I incorporate my gratitude practice during my walk. I state what I appreciate and what I'm grateful for out loud as I walk around the park.

Moving your body is what's so important. We don't want anything to stagnate and get stiff – our emotions, our joints, and our world viewpoints all need to be flexible, or else we might resort to our unhealthy self-sabotaging behaviors like addictions, perfectionism, or creating relationship drama.

If yoga is your thing, great; or jogging, hiking, and dancing of course work too. Just choose your favorite way to move. Again, people are often invested in and appreciate the cardiovascular benefits, but don't dismiss the emotional benefits of getting your energy moving.

Music

All humans and even animals respond to sound. It is one of my favorite pastimes – to listen to music of all kinds. My father taught me to love classical music, but I love the soundtracks from the old musicals, reggae, and sappy love songs too. It's hard to be upset when you're listening to a beautiful song, bells chiming, singing, or drums. I spent years in choirs and musical groups, so music has been a faithful friend throughout my life. While it is totally enjoyable, it is also an instant "mood changer" if you have trouble shifting your state of mind. If you don't use natural ways to shift from troubling emotional conflicts, you may resort to your old self-sabotaging behaviors such as neglecting your self-care or triggering relationship drama.

Listen to what makes your heart sing. Listen to what moves you. Listen to what uplifts you. Listen to what makes you cry. I cry a lot when I listen to music; when the emotional response comes over me,

I can't control the tears. I'm not sure I can even explain it more succinctly than when I am moved to tears, I feel free, open, and happy. Looking at exquisite art or beauty in nature also moves me, but not like listening to music. Music helps me process my feelings and changes my state of mind.

Conclusion

All self-sabotaging behavior solves a problem for you. No matter which behavior you use, the root cause is the same – trying to stay safe and protect yourself from a consequence you fear if you succeed. The reasons you want to stay safe are often hidden from direct consciousness but will be revealed when you stop focusing on the behavior and start asking the right questions to uncover why you would rather play small and stay safe than shine and be visible, why you'd rather drink and use drugs than feel your grief, why you'd rather pick a fight than be close, collect clutter than be free.

Calming down your nervous system is an efficient and safe way to facilitate healing the old fears and traumas in your mind and body, and will allow you the space to examine what fears and limiting beliefs may have been fueling your self-sabotaging behavior. EFT is the best tool I have found for this, as it pairs a stressful memory or event with sending calming signals to the stress center of the brain, lowering the stress, including cortisol, rapidly and safely, thereby allowing you to relax, accept, forgive, and move forward.

No matter how much we hate our people pleasing, procrastination or our perfectionism, our addictions or our clutter, our relationship drama or self-care neglect, the faster we understand the purpose of these behaviors, the faster we can unpack the past and release the need for the emotional safety that limits our lives.

Taking myself through my own process of The Yes Code™ helped me clarify the vision I had for writing this book. I wanted to share my personal story for the first time so you might recognize common themes even if you came from a totally different background. More importantly, I wanted to communicate clearly to help you understand where your self-sabotaging behaviors came from, help you feel comforted by knowing that you are not alone, and help you feel inspired to know that there is a way out, the way I was inspired all those decades ago during my family week experience.

Continuing with Step One of The Yes Code meant I had to ask myself the upside/downside questions whenever I hesitated to move forward on this project. The upside of not writing the book was that I wouldn't have to spill my guts all over these pages and rock the boat in my family. The downside of writing this book was that people might be upset with me for telling the truth. But after taking myself through Step Two of The Yes Code and using my own detailed tapping sequences, I released these fears and beliefs and could move to Step Three. My next yes steps were obvious and inspiring – let go of my worry about what other people might think and write this book, one chapter at a time.

My hope for you is that the examples, exercises, and suggestions in this book give you a roadmap for deep and profound healing so that you can forgive yourself for any and all self-sabotaging behaviors you have been engaged in, no matter what the consequences have been, and move forward with ease and grace. I hope that you look forward to returning to these pages and the information on The Yes Code portal as many times as necessary to develop the daily habit of tapping to continue to release any blocks along your path and to enjoy the satisfying and fulfilling life that you deserve.

Carol Look, LCSW, DCH, Founding EFT Master

RESOURCES

Websites

For professional training in numerous Energy Medicine techniques, including EFT, visit the Association for Comprehensive Energy Psychology website: **www.energypsych.org**

For research and the most recent professional advancements in the field of EFT, visit: **www.evidencebasedeft.com/research**

For templates for your personal scripts, video demonstrations of EFT, testimonials, and additional EFT materials, visit: **www.TheYesCode.com** or **www.CarolLook.com**

END NOTES

1. Viktor E. Frankl, *Man's Search for Meaning: An Introduction to Logotherapy, (Boston, Beacon Press, 1992)*.

2. Jack Flynn, *20 Telling Procrastination Statistics: The Prevalence of Procrastination*, December 4, 2023, www.Zippia.com/advice/procrastination-statistics/.

3. Jack Flynn, *20 Telling Procrastination Statistics.*

4. Oprah Winfrey and Dr. Bruce Perry, *What Happened to You? Conversations on Trauma, Resilience and Healing* (Macmillan Publishers, 2021).

5. Donna Bach, Gary Groesbeck, Peta Stapleton, Rebecca Sims, Katharina Blickheuser, & Dawson Church, (2019). "Clinical EFT (Emotional Freedom Techniques) Improves Multiple Physiological Markers of Health," *Journal of Evidence-Based Integrative Medicine* 24, no 1-12 (2019), https://doi.org/10.1177/2515690X18823691.

6. David Feinstein and Donna Eden, *Tapping: Self-Healing with the Transformative Power of Energy Psychology* (Sounds True, 2024).

7. Peta Stapleton, Craig Buchan, Ian Mitchell, Yasmin McGrath, Paul Gorton, & Brett Carter, "An Initial Investigation of Neural Changes in Overweight Adults with Food Cravings after Emotional Freedom Techniques," *OBM Integrative and Complementary Medicine* 4, no 1 (2019), https://doi.org/10.21926/obm.icm.1901010.

8. Peta Stapleton, Oliver Baumann, "Neural Changes after Emotional Freedom Techniques treatment for chronic pain sufferers," *Complementary Therapies in Clinical Practice* 49, no 101653 (2022), https://doi.org/10.1016/j.ctcp.2022.101653.

9. Peta Stapleton, PhD, *The Science Behind Tapping: A Proven Stress Management Technique for the Mind and Body* (Carlsbad, CA, Hay House, Inc., 2022).

10. David Feinstein and Donna Eden, *Tapping.*

11. Eckhart Tolle, *Stillness Speaks*, (Yogi Impressions Books, Pvt, Ltd, 2003), 3.

12. Bessel van der Kolk, MD, *The Body Keeps the Score: Brain, Mind and Body in the Healing of Trauma* (Penguin Books, 2015), 128.

ACKNOWLEDGMENTS

I would like to express my appreciation for the following people who helped me during the process of writing *The Yes Code*™.

I would first like to acknowledge and thank all the clients I have had the privilege of working with over the past 30 years. I'm grateful for your trust, your openness, your brilliance, and your bravery.

I will always be grateful to EFT Creator, Gary Craig – first, for giving us this life-changing technique, and then, for trusting me to be an ambassador for EFT in the world.

To Sara Connell and your exceptional Thought Leader Academy team, thank you for your consistent presence, guidance, and support throughout the entire process of writing this book.

To Ed Bajeck and Jane Ubell-Meyer of the superb Thought Leader Academy Publishing Team, many thanks for making the publishing process as smooth as possible.

To my editor, Mary Nelligan, I don't know where you got the patience. Thank you for your intelligent, thoughtful, and loving support. Your depth and clarity around details as well as the big picture made all the difference in the world.

To my friends and colleagues who supported me during the ups and downs of this challenging process – Leslie Vellios, Heidi Garis, John Cisternino, Michele Stoudmann, Roos van der Blom, Alissa Smith, Yuberka Cabrera, and Carissa Brockman. Thank you for listening to me. And to my Diamonds – Paula, Miriam, Nancy, Rosie, Elsa, and Linde; I am deeply grateful for your vulnerability, connection, and insight.

To Peta Stapleton, thank you for your beautiful foreword, your friendship, and for your professional support. I look forward to our future projects together.

To Rick Wilkes, thank you for your wisdom, depth, friendship, and your impeccable technical support with all my projects. I couldn't do it without you.

To Dana Pemberton, words are not enough to express my gratitude for your profound and constant support. Thank you for reminding me that when you know better, you do better.

To Colleen Robinson, I'll never be able to thank you enough for making such incredible sacrifices of time and energy to get this book across the finish line.

To my parents, this book would not have been possible without you. You taught me to love deeply and forgive generously. You told me I could do anything I put my mind to, and I believed you.

And to my family, for weathering your own storms, and for sharing the incredible bonds our family has had the privilege to enjoy. I love you all.

And to my husband, John, your unwavering support for this project from the very first spark made it happen. You encouraged me to take the leap, and I did.

ABOUT THE AUTHOR

Carol Look is a Founding EFT Master, licensed psychotherapist, author, international speaker and creator of her signature coaching method, The Yes Code™. She combines her traditional training as a psychotherapist with clinical hypnosis and advanced applications of EFT for unprecedented results with her clients. Known for her laser-like focus and state-of-the-art approach, Carol has used EFT for over 25 years to help clients release their limiting beliefs and emotional conflicts, so they can experience transformational changes and enjoy lives of exceptional success and fulfillment.

Carol is a world-renowned EFT workshop presenter and has taught workshops in England, The Netherlands, Belgium, France, Canada, Australia, and all over the United States. She is a regularly featured energy medicine expert on leading global summits and is a featured expert in the field's documentaries: *The Tapping Solution*, *Leap*, and *Exploring Energy: The Ultimate Healer*. She has been invited to teach workshops for The Omega Institute, Kripalu, The Eden Energy Fest, and the energy field's primary teaching conference, ACEP.

Carol authored the original abundance book for the EFT field: *Attracting Abundance with EFT*, as well as *Improve Your Eyesight with EFT*, and *Overcoming Overwhelm*. She is also known for creating downloadable tapping programs of the highest quality for practitioners and clients on the topics of success and abundance, weight loss, grief relief, PTSD, clearing clutter and procrastination.

For more on Carol's programs and workshop schedule, visit www.CarolLook.com.

www.ingramcontent.com/pod-product-compliance
Lightning Source LLC
Chambersburg PA
CBHW071144130626
46553CB00004B/1521